GEOFFREY MACNAB is a journalist and critic. His previous books include *Ingmar Bergman: The Life and Films of the Last Great European Director* (I.B.Tauris); *The Making of Taxi Driver, Searching for Stars, Stardom and Screen Acting in British Cinema* and *J. Arthur Rank and the British Film Industry.*

LIVERPOOL JMU LIBRARY

3 1111 01496 5089

'Geoffrey Macnab's book provides an insight into how the real business of film has evolved and works today. It should be required reading for anyone with an interest in the world of film or working in the industry.'

NIK POWELL
Director of the National Film & Television School

DELIVERING DREAMS
A CENTURY OF BRITISH FILM DISTRIBUTION

GEOFFREY MACNAB

I.B. TAURIS
LONDON · NEW YORK

Published in 2016 by
I.B.Tauris & Co. Ltd
London • New York
www.ibtauris.com

Copyright © 2016 Film Distributors' Association Ltd

The right of Film Distributors' Association Ltd to be identified
as the copyright holder of this work has been asserted by them in
accordance with the Copyright, Designs and Patents Act 1988.

All rights reserved. Except for brief quotations in a review, this book, or any part
thereof, may not be reproduced, stored in or introduced into a retrieval system, or
transmitted, in any form or by any means, electronic, mechanical, photocopying,
recording or otherwise, without the prior written permission of the publisher.

Every attempt has been made to gain permission for the use of the images
in this book. Any omissions will be rectified in future editions.

References to websites were correct at the time of writing.

ISBN: 978 1 78453 489 9
eISBN: 978 0 85772 951 4

A full CIP record for this book is available from the British Library
A full CIP record is available from the Library of Congress

Library of Congress Catalog Card Number: available

Typeset by Tetragon
Printed and bound in Great Britain by T.J. International, Padstow, Cornwall

CONTENTS

LIST OF ILLUSTRATIONS

1. Film industry champion: Lord Puttnam has been president of Film Distributors' Association since 2008, adding to his roster of parliamentary, educational and media duties.

Photography by Ian Gavan (Getty Images/FDA)

Unsung heroes by David Puttnam

Amid the seemingly incessant media coverage that the film industry inspires, it's inevitable that actors and film-makers will occupy most of the limelight. Yet it's widely acknowledged that, behind the scenes, a film director is supported by a skilled crew of artists and technicians, sometimes running into hundreds on any given production.

Even this, however, is only part of the picture. During and after a film's production phase, another quite unheralded though utterly vital branch of the industry comes into focus. It is *distribution*, which, despite its name conjuring up images of lorries and warehouses, is in fact the highly risky and multi-faceted business of connecting films with audiences.

Human beings retain an unquenchable thirst for wonderful stories; and as a means of slaking that thirst, I believe movies are without equal. But self-evidently movies can *only* realise their extraordinary power to thrill, surprise, move and amuse when they are experienced and shared by us – the audience.

As a child in North London, I adored going to the cinema, as often as I could. It was only when working at an advertising agency in the 1960s that I began to appreciate just what was involved in motivating audiences – and how costly it was to cut through the blizzard of messages, let alone other entertainment options, competing constantly for attention. I became fascinated by the process; and later, during my career as a film producer, I was always keen to start work with each film's distributor as early as possible. I found that distributors could offer extremely valuable opinions on a variety of production choices, typically from the perspective of a potential paying audience, and help to identify some distinctive production elements as 'publicity hooks'.

Among the professional branches of the film industry, distribution is necessarily the one with the biggest impact on determining the breadth and depth of audiences' access to films. In today's digital world of super-abundant supply, around 700 feature films are released in UK cinemas and on other platforms every year. This means that the distribution machine is operating with tremendous vitality – creating posters, cutting trailers, arranging junkets or premieres, pitching titles to cinema bookers, confirming advertising plans, evaluating the potential of new scripts, and so on.

Predicting box-office receipts accurately has always been tough, the more so because what audiences want fluctuates perpetually and all too rapidly according to a host of market conditions and societal factors. While the channels that distributors deploy to engage audiences have multiplied greatly over the years, the underlying principle that distributors serve as the 'engine' of the film business, connecting each new title compellingly with filmgoers, remains utterly intact.

As UK film distribution reaches its centenary in 2015, I am proud to be the president of its trade body. Film Distributors' Association delivers a busy programme of generic services to its sector and the wider industry, from highly regarded training and internship schemes to well-researched audience development initiatives and more. At such a significant milestone, I am delighted that the story of film distribution is finally being told in *Delivering Dreams*. Geoffrey Macnab's captivating book reveals the multitude of challenges the sector has confronted, while casting a long overdue spotlight on some of the remarkable people who have shaped the ways films and their audiences find each other, and in doing so enrich all of our lives.

LORD PUTTNAM OF QUEENSGATE CBE
President, Film Distributors' Association
www.launchingfilms.com/100

Presidents of Film Distributors' Association, 1915–2015

The trade association was founded in December 1915 as the Kinematograph Renters' Society Ltd (KRS). Twenty-three presidents (chairs) have served the company and the sector it represents during the first hundred years, two of whom, Messrs Graham and Griffiths, each completed two stints. The president, whose term of office is not fixed but at the discretion of the member companies, is supported by a chief executive managing a small office staff. In 1979 the name KRS was updated to Society of Film Distributors (SFD); in 2001 it became Film Distributors' Association (FDA).

1915–17	A. C. Lovesy
1918–20	E. G. Turner
1920–1	F. W. Baker
1922	H. J. Boam
1923	R. C. Bromhead FCA
1924	J. C. Graham
1925	A. G. Smith
1926	S. Rowson MSc FSS
1927	T. C. Elder
1928	C. M. Woolf
1929	A. Clavering
1930	J. C. Graham
1931–3	S. Eckman Jr CBE
1934–5	J. Maxwell

1936–9	D. E. Griffiths
1940–2	S. W. Smith
1943–7	R. P. Baker FCA
1948–57	D. E. Griffiths OBE (knighted in 1953)
1957–8	Sir Arthur Jarratt KCVO
1959	A. Abeles
1959–78	M. C. Morton
1978–92	P. Livingstone CBE
1992–8	J. R. C. Higgins MBE
1999–2006	A. F. Pierce
2008–	Lord Puttnam of Queensgate CBE

(*The post of president was vacant in 2007.*)

INTRODUCTION

Distributors are the invisible force within the UK movie business. Most people outside the film industry have some sense of the role of directors, producers and even exhibitors in the film-making process but few understand the distribution business. 2015 marks the centenary of the UK distributors' trade body, Film Distributors' Association, and is a timely moment to celebrate their contribution to British cinema (which wouldn't exist in its current form without them).

The aim of this book is to prise the distributors out into the light; to explore what exactly they do and to chronicle their achievements over the last 100 years. Their work has always been about much more than delivering films into cinemas. The best distributors combine an extraordinary range of skills. They're artists and hustlers, curators, salesmen, accountants, detectives and sometimes gamblers. Their taste and instincts inform what we see on screen. They mount elaborate and imaginative campaigns to lure us to new films. They devise the posters and the tag lines. They choose when and how to launch a movie. At the same time, they pay painstaking attention to logistics: to transporting films to far-flung cinemas, collecting the prints and checking their box-office returns. From the days of silent cinema to the new digital era, they have played a crucial role in ensuring that film-makers find the audiences that they crave.

The history of film distribution in the UK has never been told properly. British cinema has been written about extensively in terms of its stars, its big-name directors, its producers and its big-name companies. There have been studies of British cinema's relationship with government, of 'British cinema and censorship' and of British 'B' film. Lavish books have been published about the cinemas themselves (the 'dream palaces') and about the studios where the most famous movies have been shot. The distributors, though, remain in the background in almost all accounts of British cinema. That is an injustice that this study aims to redress. 'It's a faceless profession, really. We do the donkey work,' states UK distributor Will Clarke, the founder of Optimum Releasing and then of Altitude Films. 'We are the people that do the nuts and bolts. It's a thankless task.'[1]

David Puttnam, the celebrated producer of *Chariots of Fire* and *The Mission*, and the widely respected FDA president at the time of writing, acknowledges that his initial understanding of distribution came from his partners at the 'old boys' badminton club' when Puttnam took up the sport to stay fit after leaving school. 'It so happened that two of the three people I played with each week were in film distribution. They were the guys in the shipping departments, responsible for shipping prints out, posters and the weekly ads,' Puttnam recalls. These badminton players were responsible for making sure that films reached cinemas all over Britain and that these cinemas were provided with the appropriate marketing materials.

The two men had their own private game during badminton. One would shout out the name of a newspaper – *The Advertiser* or *The Post* – and the other would respond by giving the name of the town where it was based.

> I got to know the fact that their job (as distributors) was weird. It was both getting physical prints out but also making sure that there was a poster and an ad in the paper. This was what both these guys had to do for different companies. If you asked me what distribution was, I thought of it as a physical process by which films, posters and ancillaries got delivered from somewhere, a warehouse if you like, to cinemas. I thought distribution was literally that, a physical thing – you sent stuff out.[2]

The youthful Puttnam's sense of the distribution business being about 'sending stuff out' was accurate but, in those early, badminton-playing days, he didn't even begin to think that there were so many other crucial aspects to the business.

Paul Brett, who has worked in distribution and marketing at many film companies including Pathé/Guild and CIC (a joint venture between Paramount and Universal), picked up more quickly on the 'selling' aspect of distribution. As a boy watching films at his local cinema, the ABC in Hammersmith, he was fascinated by the trailers for 'coming attractions' shown in advance of the main feature.

> I got this from a really early age – that if someone is in a cinema watching a film, you have a captive audience that will be inclined to return to the same venue to watch another film. That (the trailer) was a good way to tease them with it.[3]

On his way to school on the London Underground's District line, Brett could see the 'quad' posters on walls of the stations. (The 'quad' is the 30×40 inch poster size introduced in the UK in the silent era that soon became the industry standard and is still used today.) Brett worked out for himself what the distributors were doing – namely, trying to make the public aware of a film's release. Brett also realised that the distributors weren't above using hype and sleight of hand if it suited their purposes.

When Robert Wise's *The Andromeda Strain* (1971), a sci-fi movie adapted from a Michael Crichton novel about a deadly alien organism that causes fatal blood clotting, was released, the posters went up in the normal fashion. Then, a day or two later, big stickers were plastered over the posters announcing that 'due to the sensitive nature of current events', the film was now not going to be released. This, of course, was a marketing ruse. There was no explanation as to what these 'sensitive' current events were. The intention was simply to tantalise anyone looking at the posters. As Brett puts it, 'Something had been engineered to increase public awareness.'[4]

Half-brothers Philip and David Livingstone are the sons of Percy Livingstone, the Yorkshire-born distributor who worked his way up from branch office clerk in Leeds to become managing director of Twentieth Century Fox in London. Philip had little idea of what his father actually did but couldn't help noticing that whenever a big new film from Fox was released, his father would make a series of phone calls from home. 'Every evening, about 9pm, he would phone somebody up and find what the takings were.' Philip realised quickly that distribution was something to do with money.[5]

David Livingstone, meanwhile, was very struck by the number of West End premieres his father attended. When a prestigious new film was about to be released, Percy Livingstone (pictured right) would dress up in a black tuxedo and polish his shoes. David and his other siblings were occasionally brought along to these premieres. They have memories of being introduced to the Queen or Princess Margaret and the Queen Mother at such films as *The Prime of Miss Jean Brodie* or *Dr Doolittle*. They realised that distribution involved extravagance and showmanship. David was impressed by the 'four-wall' roadshow deal his father did for *The Sound of Music*, which played in the West End for month after month and became the highest-grossing film in Britain of its era. (It played at the Dominion, Tottenham Court Road, for an astonishing 170 weeks.)

2. After his stint as UK managing director of film distribution at Twentieth Century Fox, Percy Livingstone served as KRS president for 14 years.

Photograph courtesy of Variety, the Children's Charity

Four-walling is a practice whereby the distributor takes over the cinema, renting the building and paying for every seat – but then gets to keep all the receipts. The arrangement with *The Sound of Music* was that it had to stay on the screen until its box office fell below a certain level. 'It played forever,' David recalls.[6]

Philip was also startled by his father's accounts of his early days as a salesman, holding business meetings with the exhibitors who wanted to rent films from Fox: 'There was one particular cinema owner in Cleethorpes or wherever and he would only do business in the sea.'[7] Percy Livingstone would have to roll up his trousers and wade out to the little boat where his client was fishing.

IMPECUNIOUS MIDDLEMEN

'Impecunious middlemen' is how the French director François Truffaut once disparagingly described distributors, but even he was forced to acknowledge their importance.[8] Their contribution is still overlooked by the public at large and yet, without them, the business would shudder to a halt.

One leading independent distributor, Trevor Green, describes his craft in a typically blunt and prosaic way:

> Distribution involves marketing and sales. Like any product, once it has been manufactured, it doesn't automatically turn up in your local shop without a distribution network. The shelf life of a film is also much shorter than other products because how long the film will play is an unknown quantity, whereas the likes of a box of cereal will be on the shelf indefinitely until it is sold or goes out of date![9]

What such remarks understate is the sheer effort that goes into making a film a success with the public. Cinema remains the medium in which film-makers intend their works to be seen; the most immersive way to experience any film; a unique experience even now and a memorable way for people to see stories on screen about their lives or those of other people. The distributors are the ones who enable this to happen. It is never a case of just booking the film into cinemas and waiting for the public to turn up. In 2014, UK distributors invested an estimated £350 million or more in releasing films into British cinemas – and devised some very ingenious campaigns in the process. Unlike physical consumer goods, films are never alike. Each is a prototype. You're never quite sure whether it will catch people's imaginations or not.

French-born but UK-based distributor Xavier Marchand, who was behind the British release of Oscar winner *The King's Speech*, rejects the idea that film distribution is simply a matter of selling goods into shops. 'Selling a product into a shop, you have the ability to relaunch it if it doesn't work,' Marchand states. By contrast, he suggests, film distribution provides no such second chances. He sees it as a 'real art'.[10] 'You have a piece of entertainment – I hate to call it a product – that people have worked on for three, four or five years. You have that one weekend to make it work. If you fail that weekend, you can't relaunch the movie.'

A 'good distributor', Marchand suggests, is someone who knows how to convince 'tens of thousands of people to come and see your movie on one particular weekend. You have to do that against all the noise of all the other forms of entertainment.'

'It's not like a retail business,' Marchand continues. 'It is quite a crazy business if you think about it. You have all these investments going into production and launching a movie – and really you have that one weekend to make it work. So I call it [distribution] an art.'[11]

'In the right hands, distribution is an art form,' Lord Puttnam agrees. The best distributors, he contends, understand that each film is unique, 'with its own specific challenges and opportunities'.[12] You can't just feed it through a machine. The 'very fine' decisions as to when to release a film and on how many screens to show it will go a long way to determining its fate. (The biggest movies in the period 2010–15 – films from the *Harry Potter* series, or *Skyfall* or *The Hobbit* – were released at the same time in around 600 venues and on well over 1,000 screens in Britain.)

The business now is very different from what it was a hundred years ago when Film Distributors' Association was founded under its original name, the Kinematograph Renters' Society. Back then, there were no 15-screen multiplexes or digital platforms through which the latest movies could be streamed directly onto 'smart' (internet-enabled) TVs in people's homes. The cinemas themselves were vast.

Stan Fishman, later to be Odeon Cinemas' chief booker (and one of the most powerful figures in UK exhibition during the 1980s and 1990s) speaks with awe about some of the huge, single-screen cinemas he remembers from his youth. For example, the Gaumont State Cinema in Kilburn, North London, had seating for over 4,000 people. 'The average was 1,000 to 1,200 seats but many were 2,000 seats.'[13]

Fishman had come into the business in 1948 as a trainee projectionist, cleaning the fittings and sweeping the floor at the Astoria, Finsbury

Park, a huge cinema that had been built by Paramount. At that stage, there was still an emphasis on luxury. The cinema's foyer had a big fountain with goldfish. There was a restaurant upstairs and sales girls were always on hand during intermissions between features to walk the aisles, selling ice cream.

The cinemas were (in Fishman's words) 'large investments',[14] predominantly located in city centres. There were so many of them ('one in every block' as it used to be said) that their owners and investors were fiercely protective of their turf. That was why the practice of 'barring' emerged and why exhibitors negotiated with distributors for films on the basis of 'exclusivity'. When a cinema booked a movie, its manager wanted to make sure that the takings would not be diluted by a rival cinema playing exactly the same film next door.

Exclusivity was measured in miles and sometimes in yards as well. If there were many cinemas right next to each other, the one that booked the movie first would insist on the others within a certain radius being 'barred' from showing the same film. 'Therefore, the exhibitor actually would know what he was buying.' Fishman explains the practice: 'The takings in the cinema were shared between the distributor and the exhibitor. They were both sharing similar risks.'[15]

'Barring' was later seen as a restraint on trade and a very creaky and restrictive way of doing business. However, it was a long-established way in which both exhibitors and distributors could protect their businesses.

Similar, self-protective feelings drove the 'alignment' system that also quickly took hold. This was the practice whereby certain distributors would release their films through one exhibition chain (with which they were 'aligned') while their rivals' films would be shown in cinemas belonging to a different circuit. 'It suited both parties in as far as when a distributor was planning his release and marketing, he had a base from which he could work,' Fishman recalls.[16]

Predictably, smaller independent exhibitors, especially those with second- or third-run cinemas, who were 'barred' from showing certain films on their initial release or who weren't 'aligned' with the big distributors, complained vociferously and regularly to the Office of Fair Trading. (Second-run cinemas showed films that had finished playing in first-run cinemas. They charged lower admission prices but the films they booked would be likely to be several months old.)

'Barring' disappeared during the 1980s but the practice still continues under another name. There is nothing to stop distributors coming to an agreement with exhibitors to show films on an 'exclusive' basis.

'There was an unofficial agreement that the monopolies commission was always very interested in,' recalls former FDA [then SFD] president James Higgins. 'Certain companies would deal with one of the major exhibitors. There were three major exhibitors – ABC, Odeon and Gaumont. Then there were lesser ones like Star, Classic and Essoldo. It became pretty locked in that MGM dealt with ABC and United Artists dealt with Odeon.'[17] The big exhibitors and distributors liked to deal with each other and to exclude outsiders.

Arcane rules were put in place to protect a cinema's exclusive rights. For example, if a film was showing at the Curzon Mayfair, it couldn't screen anywhere else within a 50-mile radius.

Some of those rules may have vanished but distribution remains in some ways exactly the same business. Whether in the silent era or at the birth of TV or in the digital age, the technology has always been in flux. In an era of Instagram and Facebook, contemporary distributors are still doing what their forebears did – delivering movies to cinemas and trying to get the public to see them. The three key decisions haven't changed: when to release a film; how much to spend on it; and how to market it.

Film distributors can be compared to poker players. Their cards are their movies. The way they play their hands will often determine success at the box office. They can cajole and even hoodwink the public into buying tickets for films they themselves didn't realise they wanted to see.

The business works on a Micawber-like optimism. No one knows quite what will catch on. As Puttnam puts it,

Hope does spring eternal for them [distributors]. You can actually believe that you're going to walk into a screening room in Cannes, find a film, buy it and actually do very nicely thank you. Why do you believe that? It's because every year it happens to somebody.[18]

Such breakthroughs may be rare today, given the intensely crowded nature of the marketplace, but they still happen.

As this book will show, distributors have long had a fraught but mutually dependent relationship with exhibitors. They need access to the exhibitors' cinema screens – and the cinemas need the movies they provide. Nonetheless, the tensions between the different sides of the business are apparent. The complaints from distributors about the historically low level of 'rentals' (the money paid by the cinemas to the distributors for rights to show films) have remained constant throughout the last century. So, too, has the distributors' anxiety about cinema bookers, who can determine where and for how long a film will be shown and have the power to cut it off from its potential public.

Originally, distributors offered films to cinemas on 'flat' rentals. The cinema owner paid a single, upfront fee to secure rights to show the film and then held on to all the profits, if there were any, or swallowed the losses. Eventually, these arrangements were renegotiated and the distributors began to ask for a share in profits. This led to a complex formula whereby exhibitors calculated their operating costs (heating, staffing, insurance, repairs, etc.). The number they reached would be known as the 'break figure'. The initial takings would go to the exhibitor to pay for these expenses. The remainder would be divided between exhibitor and distributor. The system evolved and the distributors and exhibitors came up with the idea of the 'house nut'. This was the amount that the cinema owner would take for operating costs plus a fixed percentage of the profits. (Anything over and above the 'house nut' went to the distributor.)

There are many theories as to why 'rentals' are so low in the UK. On blockbuster movies, distributors can negotiate better terms with exhibitors, but for smaller films – those making less than $1.5 million (£1 million) at the box office – the distributors' rental rates can be as little as 25 per cent. (This compares with the 40 per cent or more in rentals that distributors in other territories might hope to receive from exhibitors.) Terms are also better with independent chains than they are with multiplexes. One theory is that in the 1930s and 1940s, film companies like Warner Bros. and Rank owned or were affiliated to their own cinemas. They didn't lose out regardless of how small a share went to their distribution arms.

Occasionally, when distributors were releasing a film that no cinema wanted or, conversely, were convinced that they had a hit on their hands, they would strike 'four-wall' deals. This meant renting the entire cinema for a set period of time, paying all of its expenses and taking all of its profits. As mentioned, Fox struck a four-wall deal for *The Sound of Music* at the Dominion, Tottenham Court Road, London (below), which played with enormous success from 19 March 1965 until 30 June 1968. Paramount followed suit with another musical, *Paint Your Wagon*, which opened at the Astoria, Charing Cross Road, also in London, on a 70mm print in January 1970 and played for more than a year.

The balance of power between distributors and exhibitors has continually shifted ever since the silent era. During the early 1930s, as exhibitors struggled to pay for the conversion of their cinemas to

3. The tills are alive: Having opened in 1929, the Dominion Theatre became a full-time cinema operated by Gaumont in 1933. It accommodated extended runs of *South Pacific* (1958) and *Cleopatra* (1963) before *The Sound of Music* set new all-time box-office records.

Photograph courtesy of Variety, the Children's Charity

sound, distributors were in the ascendant. More recently, the distributors have felt hard done by, not just over the rentals they are paid but over the costs they have incurred (rather than the exhibitors) in paying for new digital equipment. 'There is an unnatural antagonism between them. They are in the same business and very few decisions strike me as being made on an industry-wide basis,' says Puttnam. 'Each one seems to have their hand in the other one's pocket. You get the impression that anything which works for distribution will somehow disadvantage exhibition and vice versa.'[19]

Former Odeon booker Stan Fishman likens the relationship between distributor and exhibitor to a marriage. 'One day, you go out and you slam the front door but the next day, you ring the door bell,' Fishman says, recalling his own long experience of dealing with distributors. 'We relied on each other.'[20]

The industry certainly has an unconventional business model: while box-office revenue is shared, the copyright in the film remains the property of its 'authors'; exhibitors alone benefit from the further income from concessions, sales, advance booking fees and screen advertising.

The distributors know they need to placate their producers, who look to them to turn their movies into financial successes and then blame them when the box-office tills fail to ring. These producers sometimes think they can release their films themselves – but they very quickly discover they have neither the marketing skills nor the contacts to secure the bookings they need.

It is a battle to keep the censors onside too. The 'wrong' certificate can mean that a film has no chance of reaching its target audience. If you have what you think is a family movie and it is passed as a 12A or 15, your business plan will be in tatters.

It used to be that if a film had an X certificate, its poster would need to be approved by FDA's self-regulatory poster committee. This meant presenting the artwork to representatives from the British Board of Film Classification, the Advertising Standards Authority, the Cinema Exhibitors' Association (CEA) and London Transport. There were all sorts of arcane rules used to adjudicate on whether a poster was suitable for display in the London Underground or on a bus or

LIVERPOOL JOHN MOORES UNIVERSITY
LEARNING SERVICES

outside the cinema itself. For example, if the poster displayed a gun, the weapon was only allowed to be pointing sideways, not outwards. This Advertising Viewing Committee still exists today.

Then, there was the media. Distributors continue to fret about critics writing negative reviews and thereby sometimes suffocating movies at birth. 'The press often are intelligent individuals – not always! They review and appreciate film. If you are talking about Jack from the local wherever cinema, maybe he can't even read and write,' one leading UK distributor remarks, pointing to the fact that reviewers don't always reflect the public's tastes.

Distributors have to cook up the ruses to advertise their films and to persuade the press and TV companies to pay attention. They are the ones who, working with PR companies, bring in the big-name stars to meet the journalists.

At various times in the last 100 years, distributors have been attacked for their inflexible approaches to everything from programming to credit control.

The rigidity, though, was also often a sign of the strength of UK distribution, its organisation and unity of purpose. There is an irony in the sector being described as too regulated when you consider that the Kinematograph Renters' Society was founded in 1915 precisely to impose order on a sector that, at the time, seemed chaotic in the extreme.

For example, piracy has dogged the industry from the very beginning. Stealing movies, copying them, showing them or selling them illegally has been happening from the silent era onward.

At the very first meeting of the KRS in December 1915, when the new trade body identified its goals, 'the suppression of piracy or the duplication of films' was one key early target. In the early days of British cinema, the piracy tended to concern exhibitors copying prints and sometimes retitling (and rereleasing) old ones. In the video and internet age, piracy moved into the domestic sphere. Anyone can be a pirate now, either buying a bootleg movie at a car-boot sale or accessing a film on an illegal website, and often doing so without realising the damage they are doing to the producers and distributors who have made and are trying to release these films.

Traditionally, there was a two-tier system in British distribution. On the one hand, there were the UK distribution offices of the US majors, releasing big-budget Hollywood films. On the other, there were the many British indies, handling foreign-language, art-house and exploitation fare. These indie operators were expert at spotting and exploiting whatever gaps in the market might emerge. They knew they couldn't compete head-on with the Hollywood studios and so used guile instead.

These distributors regularly provided the cinemas with 'marketing manuals' which guided them on how best to promote any given film. They would make sure the posters for their movies were in the most prominent positions (even if it meant fly-posting over their rivals' advertisements).

Trevor Green cites the cautionary tale of the distributor who declared he only wanted to release films he was proud of – but soon went out of business. 'Unfortunately, distribution is about distributing what the public wants, not what you want.'[21]

How do you know what the public wants? Most distributors will acknowledge that nobody can ever really know what will work and what won't. If you have experience and can see a hook for a film, you'll have a chance of reaching an audience. But what the public wants changes all the time, sometimes all too rapidly, according to a host of factors.

Martin Myers of distributor Miracle Communications is the fourth generation of his family to enter the cinema business. His grandparents and great-grandparents owned cinemas in South London and on the south coast. In the 1970s, as cinemas closed down to make way for bingo halls and the British film industry fell into the doldrums, Myers's father, Michael, the boss of Miracle Films, had moved into distribution.

One of Michael Myers's canniest decisions was to release John Carpenter's seminal 1970s horror movie *Halloween*. Myers had seen Carpenter's previous film, *Assault on Precinct 13*, and was keen to release it in the UK. That meant haggling for the rights. Generally, when independent distributors licensed new movies from sales agents and producers' reps, the asking price was calculated as a percentage of the budget. A British distributor would expect to pay roughly 7.5

per cent of the production cost of the movie to acquire it for the UK market.

Assault had already opened in the US. In Myers's son's words, it had 'died on its arse'.[22] Myers was able to persuade producer Irwin Yablans to sell him the movie for the UK and then to find a slot for it at the London Film Festival. After its sold-out LFF screenings, the film turned into a full-blown phenomenon. Miracle Films booked it into the Odeon circuit of cinemas, where it played to packed houses. It was reassessed by US critics and Carpenter's reputation was made.

A year later, Yablans called Myers to tell him he had another film with Carpenter and to ask: would Miracle take the UK rights? 'My dad said of course I will. At that moment in time, my dad didn't realise – and Irwin didn't tell him – that they didn't have all the money [to make the film].'[23]

Michael Myers and his wife visited the *Halloween* set in LA. The budget for the movie was $300,000, of which $30,000 went to the one recognised star, Donald Pleasence, who confided to Myers that he was making the film because his daughter had liked *Assault on Precinct 13* but he couldn't see any point in it. (If he had asked for a share of the box-office receipts, he would have made a fortune.) He (Myers) backed the movie at a very early stage, thereby enabling the cash-strapped producers to complete it.

Eventually, *Halloween* became a huge success and spawned many imitators. Carpenter was so grateful for the British distributor's support that he named the fictional killer in the movie 'Michael Myers'. When Myers finally saw the completed film, he realised he and the killer shared the same name. 'My dad phoned John at the end. He [Carpenter] said it was his way of thanking my father.'[24]

Fortunately, Myers saw the funny side.

This may seem like a colourful yarn but it is also very telling. It underlines the fact that distributors aren't just there to deliver movies. They help coax them into being and frequently finance them too. Another intriguing aspect of the story, as true now as it was at the beginning of distribution in the UK, is what it reveals about the relationship between distributor and producer. You don't just buy films from a mail-order catalogue. A key part of distribution is the personal connection between distributor and producer. 'It's all networking,' as Martin Myers points out. 'My father always said to me, out of sight is out of mind.'[25]

Michael Myers also showed foresight in realising that a 'slasher movie' in an era of so-called 'video nasties' had the potential to reach a mainstream audience.

In the digital era, films can be distributed everywhere at once. Instead of having to transport hefty tins of 35mm or 16mm film from cinema to cinema, film files are delivered electronically (although computer drives are still sent by transit vans up the motorway). There are fewer transport costs. If the train breaks down or the motorway is blocked, the movie will still be shown – as long as the technology is working.

The distribution landscape was very different when *Halloween* was being released. Myers remembers that his father released the film on around 40 prints – but then made those prints 'work'. Those 40 copies were shown at cinemas all over Britain.

'In those days, it was different. You would do North London and South London and vice versa. You'd move the prints.'

After the London screenings, the prints would move out to the regions. 'We did it by TV regions,' Myers recalls. 'We'd open the film in Scotland and if it was successful, you'd move it down to Granada [the Manchester region] and Yorkshire.'[26]

Movies that were successful were allowed to sit in cinemas and keep on showing week after week.

In a pre-digital era, film distribution was a far more labour-intensive business. Each major company had dozens of clerks, salesmen and branch managers.

There was a haphazard quality to a career in distribution. It was relatively easy to find an entry-level job as a clerk or a messenger, a secretary or a typist, and to work your way up into sales or accounts. In 1946, for example, 17-year-old John Hogarth started in film distribution almost on a whim. He had been to the local polytechnic for a commercial course of shorthand, typing, book-keeping and commerce, and had the vague thought that he might become an estate agent. A friend of his mother's suggested film distribution instead and that there might be an opening at the British Lion Film Corporation. Hogarth had read that Louis B. Mayer at MGM was, in this period, the highest-paid man in the world.

Hogarth later recalled in a 1994 interview:

> I thought, 'Well then this film lark probably has got something going for it.' And it sounded a bit more interesting than estate agents. So I joined British Lion, as I say, in September of 1946 as what was then described as an office junior, which was rather a grand title for office boy and general factotum.[27]

The point at which Hogarth entered the industry was a golden period for British cinemagoing, a time when attendances were at 1.6 billion a year.

The paperwork was mind-boggling, as Hogarth recalled:

> Every cinema that booked a film from a company had a con-tract, and so there were thousands of these contracts floating through in the course of a week, let alone a year. And each one had to be recorded in three or four places. Quite why it was necessary to have that amount of documentation I never did find out, but it was absolutely essential and so for many, many years I recorded all this stuff.

Geraldine Moloney, a veteran distribution publicist, talks of the 'Dickensian' quality of distribution offices, even as late as the 1970s.[28] In this period, box-office analysis was also a less exact science. Cinema owners didn't always share the most accurate details about their takings. Records were handwritten, not computerised. Distribution companies didn't have an exact knowledge of how their rivals had performed.

Some people express nostalgia for this period. In today's more brutishly direct digital age, everyone knows everything about everyone else. The business still works on trust when it comes to the number of 'comps' or free promotional tickets that appear on a box-office return. Relationships are as important as ever. However, the box-office figures are instantly available through services like Rentrak (a global media research company), and if a film is perceived to be underperforming, it will be taken off screen within days. In the past, bookers might do independents favours on the sly, keeping their films on screen, even when the figures didn't justify it, on the grounds that they needed the revenue more than the big US studios. Today, such special treatment would be unthinkable, if only because the studios would see the figures and cry foul.

When British cinemagoing was in its pomp in the mid-1940s, 'holdovers' (films that stayed on the same screens for weeks at a time) were also rare, but for very different reasons. In many small-town cinemas, everyone would have seen the film during its first three days of release and would be hungry for the next programme.

Prior to the video boom, distributors simply bought the theatrical rights to films. There was little thought of exploiting them outside the cinemas.

One of the paradoxes of the British film industry is that it has always thrived on innovation at the same time as it has resisted change. Distributors have continually been called on to embrace new business models at exactly the same time they are busy consolidating old ones.

TV was treated as an upstart rival. An organisation called FIDO – the Film Industry Defence Organisation – had been set up to protect cinema from its new small-screen rival in 1958. It used to take a small eternity, several years, for films to wend their way from the big screen to television.

Video was likewise regarded with extreme suspicion, at least initially. Jack Valenti, president of the Motion Picture Association of America, predicted in the early 1980s that home video would destroy the film business. 'VCR is to the American film producer and the American public as the Boston strangler is to the woman home alone,' he told Congress in 1982.

British distributors were likewise wary about what they saw as 'a smash and grab' operation.

In the event, by the end of the 1980s, video was worth more to the Hollywood studios than theatrical and was also driving the British film business.

As the video market grew and grew, so did the debate about 'windows'. Distributors began to question how long cinemas should have an exclusive 'window' on a film and how quickly it should be made available for 'home entertainment' rental or sale. The 1980s saw a rapid growth in straight-to-video fare, especially action and horror movies.

For distributors in the video, DVD and VOD era, an old truism applied. The theatrical release was the 'engine that drove ancillary sales'. In effect, the cinema screenings were serving as a 'loss leader' and the profits came later, through sales to TV or to airlines or, most importantly, through VHS and DVD. The distributors' business model evolved, and remained broadly profitable overall, thanks to these new revenue streams. It is a paradox of the movie business today that the high cost/low return cinema release on its own is very rarely profitable for the distributor.

The first goal, though, is always to get access to the screens. That itself is a challenge, often dependent on the whims and tastes of the bookers at the big movie chains. George Pinches, Rank's booking director in the 1970s, was an immensely powerful figure, known to pursue vendettas against various producers and also to be strangely reluctant sometimes to book hit movies that didn't appeal to him. He was unimpressed by Woody Allen's 1977 Oscar winner, *Annie Hall*. Although the film had opened to considerable acclaim in the US, he didn't want it screening in Odeon cinemas. There was a prolonged campaign to 'butter him up' and persuade him to change his mind but he wasn't to be swayed. In the end, he only booked Allen's film into Odeon's smaller, less prestigious sites.

Pinches was similarly unimpressed with Martin Scorsese's *Raging Bull* (1980), which he eventually booked into the Odeon Swiss Cottage, provoking the fury of distributors United Artists in the process.

There are many tales about Pinches, few of them sympathetic. He was married for a time to actress Ingrid Pitt (best known for her roles as voluptuous vampires in Hammer horror movies). It was claimed that, on Monday mornings, depending on how harmonious a weekend he had spent with her, he would either book her latest film onto more screens or, if he was angry, pull it altogether from cinemas.

The best that could be said for Pinches was that he protected other people's money as if it was his own.

'If I was an investor, not knowing anything whatsoever about the film industry and I was just lending George a pound, I know he would do everything he could to give me £1.25 back. Who he upset was another matter,' reflects Stan Fishman, who took over from Pinches as Odeon's chief booker in 1981.[29]

This is a business that relies on timing. Distributors are very careful at picking the best moment at which to release their films. Historically, June was considered a month to avoid and the summer in general was slow. That has changed in the era of so-called 'summer tentpoles', the huge-budget films that land in British cinemas throughout the summer.

'January is quite a good time to open a big action film or even a horror film because you have come out of the Christmas period when you've had all the slush and gush over on TV,' Myers suggests. 'They've played *White Christmas* for the sixtieth time and all the kids have been coming to the cinema. There has been nothing really for the adult market. They [the adults] want to go and see something strong.'[30]

The appeal of cinema for British audiences has always lain partly in an idea of comfort: of old-fashioned opulence and escapism. It wasn't just the movies themselves that attracted audiences but the conditions in which they were shown. In the days before homes had central heating, people used to admit freely that they came to the cinema because they wanted 'a pennyworth of warmth'. In times of depression and austerity, British cinemagoers were looking for an escape from a world that seemed determined to grind them down. The unwritten contract between cinemas and audiences may have been broken for a period in the 1970s, when British cinemas became run down and their owners stopped investing in their upkeep, but the medium has always retained its mystique. It is still a means of escape from the everyday.

The purpose of this book is to look at the attempts of British distributors over the last 100 years to provide this means of escape. The sector has been in a well-nigh permanent state of upheaval. It has attracted its share of hustlers and con artists alongside the many visionaries. There have been bankruptcies, disputes with cinema owners and censors, and some occasionally very misguided, restrictive and outlandish trade practices. Nonetheless, the industry's unsung and often invisible messengers have continued to play an absolutely fundamental part in British cinema, delivering 'dreams'.

CHAPTER 1
The Tramp

1915 was the year that British cinema (in its own eyes at least) came of age. By its own calculations, it had reached 21 – and had 'attained its majority'.[1] (The Lumière brothers' 'first' film of workers leaving a factory had been made in 1895 but, in the trade press at least, the British industry dated its own origins back to 1894.) Now, those working within the industry reasoned, the cinema had grown up and deserved to be taken more seriously by politicians, the press and the public alike.

In its own pronouncements about itself, as articulated through the trade press, the British film business was in both a boastful and an anxious mood.

The reasons for crowing were obvious. Millions were being invested in cinemas. As the *Cinema Year Book* of 1915 noted, films had moved 'from the ephemeral stage into a practical possibility and a paying commercial proposition'.[2] The idea that the pictures were just a passing fad was beginning to dissipate.

Early concerns about the safety of the 'cinematograph' (as it had been called since the Cinematograph Act of 1909) had faded. Nitrate film was known to be highly flammable but venue operators had been able to reassure the politicians and the public alike that their premises were safe.

The make-up of the cinemagoing audience was changing, too. Early concerns that film was a depraved form of entertainment, and damaging to children in particular, had been addressed.

The Cinematograph Act came into force at the start of 1910. As a result of the new legislation, a licence, to cost not more than £1 a year, was now needed to show a film. Steps had been taken to stop films being shown on Sundays or on Good Friday or Christmas Day.

In the wake of the new act, trade body the Kinematograph Manufacturers' Association (KMA), which represented the makers and suppliers of film equipment, lobbied the Home Office for a self-regulatory body to be set up to deal with censorship. This was regarded by the industry as a better option than opening itself up to external regulation from local authorities or even the courts. The British Board of Film Censors (BBFC) was therefore established in 1912.

The industry was being policed and fussed over by Parliament and local councils, and was busy regulating itself. It was also showing signs of civic-mindedness. For example, when disabled soldiers returned from the Great War, some were trained as projectionists. (It was a job they could do behind the scenes, away from prying eyes, in darkened projection booths.)

All this activity helped convince the public that film was above board. 'Two or three years ago, the cinema was mainly the entertainment of the lower classes. Today, it has won the patronage and complete enthusiasm of at least two thirds of the entire population,' noted a correspondent for trade paper the *Bioscope.*[3]

Royalty had attended cinema screenings, which were being held in increasingly luxurious surroundings with ticket prices as high as a guinea a seat.

'Twenty-one years have witnessed the development from the converted shop theatre to luxuriously appointed cinemas capable of holding as many as five thousand people,' enthused a journalist writing in the *Cinema Year Book* 1915. 'The penny show has given place to the theatre with boxes, orchestra stalls, dress circle, and grand circle.'

1909 marked the opening of the first purpose-built cinema in Britain (previously films had been shown in music halls and makeshift venues) and a construction boom quickly followed.

Even the Church had 'realised cinema's power for the good and its elevating possibilities'.[4]

It wasn't just the make-up of cinema audiences that was changing – so was the film-making personnel. Major figures from the theatre, like Sir Johnston Forbes-Robertson, Sir Herbert Tree and Sir Charles

Wyndham, were condescending to appear in front of the film cameras. So were leading music-hall artists. No longer were British films dominated by the relatives and friends of the manufacturers who made them. There were the flickerings of a star system.

This was the Klondike era for British cinema. Vast fortunes were there to be made – or so many assumed. If it took a little skullduggery and trickery, that was only to be expected.

Then, as now, distributors were crucial in ensuring that films were seen and paid for. Then, as now, they were an invisible and unacknowledged force within the industry. Their basic job, then as now, wasn't just to buy films from producers and to hire them out to exhibitors. They were in the marketing and publicity game. Delivering the movies themselves was all very well but, unless they could find ways to attract audiences to see them, their businesses would very quickly stall.

For the first time, films were being sold to exhibitors and audiences on the basis of the well-known performers who appeared in them. 'You should have a Turner Film in Every Programme,' proclaims a full-page ad trumpeting the appeal of actress Miss Florence Turner in the *Kinematograph Year Book* for 1914. Turner was a highly popular American actress who had been nicknamed the 'Vitagraph Girl' earlier in her career and had subsequently become one of the first screen actors whose names were known to a general cinemagoing public. She had come to Britain to make shorts through her own company Turner Films just before World War I.

An astonishing 6,700 films had been released in 1914 at the rate of about 19 a day. Admissions already ran at an estimated 8 million weekly in 1914 and had more than doubled by the end of World War I.

London was still known as the 'clearing house of the world's film industry'. Many films were imported to the UK in negative form and then printed in London for foreign buyers. 'London was a distributor of whole foreign outputs, imported for a round sum and sold over a period of months,' historian Rachael Low noted.[5]

Hollywood hegemony over the global film business was not yet fully established. France, then the dominant force, had 36 per cent of the British market, the US 28 per cent and the British 15 per cent. New cinemas were being opened across the country on a daily basis and many new film companies, some with substantial capital behind them, were being registered.

World War I was underway, but sections of the British film business regarded this as an opportunity rather than a hindrance, 'the production and importation of foreign films from all the belligerent nations having been practically stopped'.[6]

'In sustaining and strengthening the national spirit, in keeping confidence alive, the picture theatres in Great Britain [...] are performing a patriotic duty,' the *Bioscope* pronounced. According to the trade paper:

> By far the most important result of the war has been the consolidation of all branches of the trade upon one common platform – the maintenance of prosperity and the convincement of the public – especially those who in recent years have had so much to say upon the question of the 'pictures' being but a fleeting craze – that the cinematograph industry, with its millions of invested capital, has come to stay.[7]

Audiences were keen to see the latest war films. The ban on the sale of alcohol after 10pm was considered to be of benefit to the film business. Punters forced to forfeit the pub were coming to cinemas instead.

Constant technical improvements were being made. Already, in 1915, industry analysts were predicting that films with sound were inevitable. 'The day cannot be far distant when the drama now contained on five thousand feet of silent film will give place to the picture that talks,' predicted the author of the end-of-year editorial in the *Cinema Year Book*. That author also confidently foresaw the arrival of colour photography:

> It is not too much to hope that with the new patents which are almost daily being applied, we shall soon have solved the question of holding nature's mirror up to the public gaze, and of flashing upon the screen the exact counterpart of that which our eyes behold, whether in the glorious tropics or in this more sombre-clad country of our birth.

Even 3D – the 'stereoscopic picture' that would remove the flatness of film and enable it to become the cinematic equivalent of the 'drama that lives and moves and has its being upon the boards' – was seen as an inevitable new development in the medium.[8]

For all the signs of growth in the industry, a mood of fretful uncertainty also lingered. It wasn't even yet entirely decided what the cinema experience should entail. A typical cinema programme consisted of a mixture of a dozen or more adventure films, comedy, animation, travelogues and newsreels. It was still a matter of anguished debate as to whether the public wanted to see feature films. 1915 was the year of D. W. Griffith's spectacular and controversial American Civil War epic, *Birth of a Nation*, which clocked in at three hours. Nonetheless, some industry observers were already sounding the death knell for 'longer films'. There was evidence that audiences were fiercely resistant to the very idea of the feature-length movie: 'The abnormally long film has seen its day, and there is a reversion to popular favour of the one thousand footer,' pronounced the *Cinema Year Book*.[9]

Cinema may have been growing more respectable and reaching a more affluent, middle-class audience than before but it was still considered tawdry and immoral by some, the offspring of an 'unholy liaison between the magic lantern and the novelette', as it was later styled by film-maker Anthony Asquith. Distributors and exhibitors in London grumbled that they were being picked on by the London County Council and City Corporation, whose methods of persecution they likened to 'cinema-baiting'.[10]

Exhibitors were regularly sued for hiring a film for one cinema and then showing it surreptitiously at another. There were instances of distributors changing the names of movies so that they could resell them as if they were new, or of shortening them or combining them with other films. Some cinemas were brought up before the magistrates for opening illegally on Sundays. Others got into trouble for their marketing gimmicks. There were reports of wily showmen setting up small laboratories to make their own dupes – an early form of piracy. Local authorities took exception to many of the marketing ruses used to hype new movies.

For several years, in the face of fierce opposition from the industry itself, the London County Council had been trying to secure 'Parliamentary powers for the control of premises in which celluloid was stored or sold'. (This was interpreted by the industry as an over-reaching power grab – a shameless attempt by politicians to exercise control over an industry already facing tight censorship.)

Writing in 1915 in the *Cinema Year Book*, columnist Mr Bannister Merwin, scenario editor of the London Film Company, claimed that the industry had for too long been taking advantage of an undiscrimi-nating public drawn to the cinema regardless of what was being shown.

'It has, until recently, been too easy to make money by producing films. As bad films naturally entail less trouble and skill than good ones, the bad ones were in a majority [...] with various, fine exceptions, pic-ture plays are cheap, bad and vulgar.'[11] It was obvious, too, that the film industry attracted its share of hucksters and petty crooks. The trade papers of the day are crammed with endless stories about legal cases involving sharp practice.

'Mr F. Peters of Haggerston was summoned for driving a four-horse van by way of advertisement in a manner not approved by the Commissioner of Police,' reads one 1915 entry in the trade press.

> On the van were a man and woman in fancy costume, represent-ing the two films *Excelsior* and *The Triumph of Progress* which were shown at a local picture theatre. The magistrate (Mr Hedderwick) stating that the intention of the Act was that traffic should not be impeded by moving advertisements, fined defendant 10s and costs.[12]

'The distributor is the one who creates the revenue for the film. The distributor is the vital link between the producing of the film and the generating of income,' veteran British distributor James Higgins (pic-tured on facing page) noted in an interview in 2014. 'No one ever hears of the distributor and no one has any idea of what the distributor does. The distributor is a very underrated character in the development, success or failure of a film.'[13]

It was understandable that distributors wanted to organise and protect themselves. In the 1890s, hardware suppliers had sold the films alongside the projectors – and had often made and starred in these films

4. Distinguished service: Having retired as managing director of the major film distributor United International Pictures (UK), James Higgins served as SFD president for most of the 1990s. At the Screen trade awards in 2012, he was feted for his Outstanding Contribution to the industry.

Photograph courtesy of Variety, the Children's Charity

too. Such ramshackle arrangements no longer satisfied an industry that, by 1915, was desperate to run itself along more professional lines. There were estimated to be around 300 'renters' (as distributors were styled) operating in Britain. Disputes were already simmering about what kind of business practices they should be pursuing. There were the beginnings of block booking – this was the practice of compelling cinemas to take a number of other films in order to be able to show the one they really wanted.

The most sought-after films were being auctioned off as 'exclusives'. Distributors would pay very high prices to ensure that they had the most coveted movies all to themselves. Prestige productions like the Italian-made epics *Quo Vadis* (1913) and *Antony and Cleopatra* (1913) were sold for vast sums. (These films had fetched £6,700 and £8,100 respectively – a huge increase in the '£12 or £13 [that] had been the previous price of a best seller' only a few years before.)

There was an obvious market logic to 'exclusives'. As the *Kinematograph Year Book* for 1914 had noted, when films were simply sold on the open market, there was little differentiation between them. 'No matter what were the extra merits or sums of money which had been spent on its production, the film was open for purchase by anyone and everyone at the ordinary rates.'[14] Films were quite literally being sold by the yard with no differentiation as to their quality. Nor were distributors keeping track of box-office receipts. They sold their films outright to exhibitors and saw no advantage if those films turned out to be huge successes.

'Exclusives' enabled distributors to charge a premium for films with obvious box-office potential. The badge of exclusivity was also a marketing hook and a way of eclipsing rivals who didn't have the means to pay the premium required for 'exclusivity'. Unfortunately, the value of exclusives was debased by unscrupulous distributors who passed off cheap, mediocre fare as 'exclusive'. Exhibitors and cinemagoers alike quickly realised that they were being gulled.

That wasn't the only problem with 'exclusives'. This was the period in which Charlie Chaplin films were emerging as box-office gold. 1915 saw the production of *The Tramp*, Chaplin's sixth film for the American company Essanay Studios. That little man with the bowler hat and stick seen walking down a dusty road, avoiding cars and turning somersaults, was becoming the biggest phenomenon in cinema. 'Made in only ten days, this remarkable film shows a staggering leap forward in its sense of structure, narrative skills, use of location and emotional range,' Chaplin's biographer David Robinson noted of *The Tramp*.[15]

It is impossible to imagine early cinema without Chaplin. It is no exaggeration to claim that the comedian, who had grown up in poverty in South London, had caught the imagination of the entire cinemagoing world. Laughter plus pathos was the magic formula for Chaplin. There were other screen comics who could match his flair for slapstick and one or two who could pull on the heartstrings just as effectively – but none could do both. He was able to make knockabout shorts but was also a pioneer in feature-length comedy. Somehow, for reasons that a century later are still not entirely straightforward to pinpoint, he mesmerised cinemagoers.

As Robinson points out, neither Chaplin nor his producers and distributors anticipated the effect his films had on the public. 'To the audiences of the time they [Chaplin's films] were new and astonishing. From the very start, Chaplin had created a new relationship with the audience, provoking a response that no one had elicited before in films or in any other medium.'[16]

1915 was the year of the Chaplin 'explosion'. Long before the mass merchandising that accompanied the releases of Hollywood blockbusters, Chaplin was everywhere. 'Every newspaper carried cartoons and poems about him,' Robinson wrote. 'He became a character in comic strips and in a new Pat Sullivan animated cartoon series. There were Chaplin dolls, Chaplin toys, Chaplin books.'[17] He inspired songs and dances. Without much aid from publicists or distributors, who in future years would go to extreme lengths to boost the profile of stars in the public eye, he became a phenomenon: the first movie actor who was instantly recognisable even to those who hadn't seen his films.

Chaplin movies reached everywhere. There is an intriguing letter in the *Bioscope* in October 1915 in which one of its correspondents, Corporal W. Hardman, then serving with the British army on the front line, noted that a cinema had opened 'not far from the trenches in an old livery stable'. Beside this makeshift movie theatre were posters and a cut-out of 'the most popular man in the world – Charlie Chaplin'.

From the distributors' point of view, Chaplin was a dream. His name was instantly recognisable and his films (in modern marketing parlance) could therefore be 'branded'. His bandy-legged walk was imitated by fans. The bowler hat and the walking stick were instantly identifiable as his hallmark, his props. He was prolific. His ruthlessness helped too. He was as interested as his distributors were in making money and furthering his career. He had the force of personality to stand up to producers. Many other early screen stars had had messy private lives or had been pawns in their managers' hands. As important to Chaplin's success as his genius was his reliability. He may have been demanding and difficult (and he would later get into trouble for his relationships with younger women), but he had a ferocious work ethic. He was able to supply the huge and ever-growing demand for his films.

Essanay was determined to get the most out of Chaplin in Britain (which was, after all, the comedian's home market). The company's London office resolved to supply packages of films (including the latest Chaplin comedies) directly to exhibitors, cutting out the distributors. The exhibitors were desperate to have the Chaplin comedies. Essanay saw a way of using Chaplin to help it secure favourable terms for its other, less desirable films. In November 1915, the company announced that all of its films (shorts, features, Chaplin comedies and everything else) would henceforth be issued as 'exclusives'. The company realised that it could make more money by selling fewer prints of the Chaplin

LIVERPOOL JOHN MOORES UNIVERSITY
LEARNING SERVICES

movies at a higher price and on an exclusive basis than by saturating the open market with them.[18] The exhibitors cried foul when Essanay added that it would only deal with cinemas that took a regular supply of 'three reels a week' from the firm.

In effect, this was an early example of block booking – a practice that has continued in one form or another for many years. The exhibitors ended up blaming Chaplin for the mess in which they found themselves. The comedian was portrayed as unpatriotic and disloyal and there was a short-lived backlash against his movies. Maybe, the exhibitors tried to convince themselves, Chaplin wasn't that funny after all.

What was most alarming for the distributors about the ongoing controversy was the idea that they were redundant. They were 'middlemen' and Essanay, an American production company, was endeavouring to do without them, dealing directly with the cinemas.

This sentiment is a familiar one. There has long been a tendency to see distributors as parasitical. They don't produce the films. They don't show them. They're providing a glorified delivery service. Producers resent the expense of their services and have continually looked at ways of releasing their films themselves. Invariably, they quickly begin to shudder at the daunting logistical complexities of film distribution and accept that this is a crucial and highly specialised craft in its own right. Distributors are the facilitators without which the entire business would grind to a halt. They are also a sector of the British film business that appears to operate under a permanent state of siege.

Buffeted by politicians, often at loggerheads with exhibitors, and wary about the dubious methods of some of their own brethren, Britain's leading 'renters' came together at the end of 1915 to form their own trade body, the Kinematograph Renters' Society, declaring:

It has been felt for some time that an organisation conducted on new lines was imperatively necessary to cope with the increasing difficulties and problems that are facing film renters throughout the country, and there can be no doubt that these developments can only be satisfactorily watched and met by concerted action.[19]

The new organisation held its first committee meeting at the Connaught Rooms, Great Queen Street, London, on 14 December. Practical matters were quickly addressed. The annual subscription for members was set at ten guineas. A bank account was opened at the London City and Midland Bank Ltd at its Cambridge Circus branch. £12.10 was set aside to pay for equipment, a typewriter and furniture at the new KRS offices at 2 Gerrards Place. A letter was swiftly dispatched to the trade press, announcing that the society had been 'formed and incorporated with a view to watching and safeguarding the interests of film renters throughout the country'.

The first president of the KRS was A. C. Lovesy of Ruffell's Imperial Bioscope Syndicate Ltd (whose releases included such titles as *Dealers in Human Lives*, *The Kiss of Hate* and George D. Baker's *The Wager*). Lovesy had to resign in 1917 because of military duties. Another prominent member, vice chairman and treasurer, was F. W. Baker of Butcher's Film Service, a company set up in 1898 that went on to produce and distribute quota quickies and *Old Mother Riley* comedies. The secretary was H. Cluett Lock.

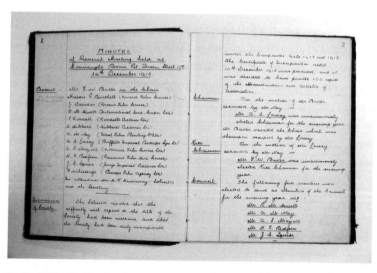

5. By the book: The handwritten minutes of the inaugural KRS Council (board) meeting record that the dozen distributors present unanimously elected Mr A. C. Lovesy as their first president.

Photography by Tim Whitby (Getty Images/FDA)

Membership of the new society was initially to be confined to renters 'purchasing or leasing at least 20,000 feet every calendar month of first release, open-market films' although plans were put in place to invite 'exclusive renters' to become members as well. (It was soon decided that these renters could join but that they would not be allowed to vote 'on any question arising under the issue of open market films'.) The founding companies were all London-based but the society made it clear that 'bona fide renters throughout the country' would also soon be allowed to join.

It is intriguing to read the 12 objectives that the society set itself. Alongside the predictable resolutions to 'centralise information' about defaulters, to 'obtain railway concessions' and to 'protect members from any unfair or illegitimate methods of business', the new distributors' body was determined to suppress 'piracy or duplication of films'.[20]

Every subsequent generation of British film-makers has felt that it has faced uniquely challenging market conditions. That is why these objectives make such salutary reading. Long before camcorders, car-boot sales of knock-off videos, illegal downloads and online piracy, distributors were already confronting the same problems that would dog their successors a full century later.

At one of its earliest meetings, the KRS called for the creation of an 'information bureau' to collect details of the status of exhibitors throughout Britain. The real intention here was to share information about cinemas that didn't pay or reneged on contracts. This was to be one of the new organisation's main preoccupations. The distributors were meticulous in working out who couldn't or wouldn't pay them what they felt that they were owed.

Battle lines were also already being drawn with the London County Council over the vexed issue of Sunday opening.

The KRS wasn't the first trade body to have tried to represent distributors' interests. A 'Film Renters' Association' had previously been in existence and had entered into an agreement in December 1911 with the Manufacturers' Association to regulate the conditions of the sales of films. A Scottish Film Renters' Association, also formed in 1915, was already in existence – although it was soon agreed that the two organisations should amalgamate.

Not all the leading companies signed up at first to join the new trade body. Historian Rachael Low is withering in her assessment of the KRS in its early years. She describes it as 'an organisation that looked backward rather than forward' (because of its initial exclusion of distributors handling 'exclusives') and suggests that its 'uselessness' contributed to the feelings of self-pity and oppression that distributors were feeling.

Low states that the KRS was weakened at its inception by the fact that it lacked the support of the major companies, Pathé and Gaumont.[21] In fact, a Gaumont Film Hire representative, Mr H. T. Redfern, was on the council of the society at its very first meeting. Vitagraph was also represented.

'Determined men intent on bringing some kind of order in a film industry situation bordering on chaos', is how the newly formed society was later characterised by A. Roland Thornton of the MPEA (the American Motion Picture Export Association).[22]

Early on, the distributors clearly couldn't agree among themselves as to what goals the new society should be pursuing. There were obvious divisions between renters, and the KRS was struggling to work out whose interests it should be representing. Some major firms, among them Famous Players, declined to join the society.

There was a major shake-up of the society three years after its original creation. Restrictions were waived so that smaller firms and those based in the provinces could have full membership.

'The great point is that there has been found in the industry a sufficient number of far-sighted men of business who realise that self-preservation demands organisation, and who have been ready to back their belief by forming the nucleus around which their colleagues can group themselves,' the trade press reported as the KRS was reorganised in October 1918 amid bickering between its members. 'To be really effective it is necessary that every renter should join and to bring this about there must be no question of discriminating between the "big" and the "little" man […] it is most urgent that the Society should get into its stride with as little delay as possible.'[23]

It didn't help that, as the KRS struggled to establish an identity and a policy framework, the CEA (the Cinema Exhibitors' Association, today named the UK Cinema Association) was perceived (by the trade press at least) to be representing its members' interests robustly and effectively. Founded in 1912, the CEA had set itself three simple goals, all of which it pursued with exemplary zeal: 1) To maintain the rights and further the interests of its members across the British Isles. 2) To protect exhibitors in 'their general relations with Parliamentary and Local Authorities'. 3) To promote the interests of the whole cinematograph industry.

By comparison, the KRS seemed unfocused and ineffective. Its preoccupation early on was with the bigger members' interests. The others, the 'lesser' renters, were left to fend for themselves. They formed their own local bodies but these were too small to have much impact.

The handwritten minutes of early committee meetings hint at the unrest. There are frequent references to the gripes of smaller renters who wanted modifications to the terms under which they could join the new society. They were asking for full representation on the council and were chafing against the deposit of £100 (a significant sum) that the KRS demanded from them along with their subscription fees. It didn't seem that the society was being efficiently run either.

The secretary, H. Cluett Lock, resigned abruptly in early 1917. The members made it very clear 'that the efficiency of the Society could not be promoted without the provision of sufficient funds to pay a capable and reliable secretary well used to propaganda work and who would be prepared to give his whole time to the Society'.

In spite of the protests of the chairman that KRS had been formed 'solely in the interests of the trade as a whole and not in that of any section of the trade', it was clear that KRS was flailing and that reorganisation was necessary.[24]

There was an Extraordinary General Meeting on 16 July 1918 at which many of the grievances and concerns were aired.

By the late autumn, a new council had been elected. A split was still evident between 'larger' and 'lesser' firms (the former were now defined as those that released at least 26 'exclusive subjects' every year) and between London-based and regional renters, but KRS resolved to represent all members equally, regardless of size or location.

Members looked to the KRS for practical support in coping with the everyday problems that they all faced. Transport issues were high on their agenda. In May 1916, the minutes of the council meeting report the chairman's concern at delays being 'experienced at Euston in the collection of films mid-week from the provinces owing to trucks not being unloaded for some hours after the arrival of trains'.[25]

There was sometimes a Pooterish quality to the council meetings. Like film-industry equivalents to the famous fictional London clerk written about in the 1892 comic novel *Diary of a Nobody* by George and Weedon Grossmith, the film distributors were forever fretting about such matters as the weather, the railway timetables, the cost of paper for posters and whether membership subscriptions would count as authorised expenditure that could be written off against tax. Nonetheless, for KRS members, these concerns were all very pressing. The distributors were in the delivery business and anything that stopped them getting prints of films to the cinemas where they were booked in to be shown was regarded with horror.

The KRS was lobbying for the creation of a new umbrella organisation, the Kinematograph Board of Trade, that would bring together representatives from the three main trade organisations: the KRS itself, the CEA and the Manufacturers' Association. They may have been in competition with each other but they also had common enemies ranging from the press to the censors to the municipal authorities. It would be to all of their advantages to place the film industry 'on a higher plane in the public mind'.[26]

The teething pains at the KRS mirrored those in the industry as a whole. What was evident, though, was the absence of strong, flamboyant figures in UK distribution who matched their counterparts in the US. There was a conspicuous lack of figures with the flamboyance and huckterism of Hollywood pioneers like Carl Laemmle, later to found Universal, and Adolph Zukor, the founder of Paramount, who came into the business as distributors.

The British distributors seemed just a little bit timid and reticent. They weren't empire builders. The image that British distribution presents at the end of World War I is of a market full of small- and medium-sized players whose default position was defensive. In its early

6. Hire, hire: The Walturdaw company, formed by John Walker, Edward Turner and George Dawson, was well known in the early British film industry. The basement of its London head office (seen here) was devoted to hiring films to cinema operators. The films available were arranged on hardwood racks around the walls in numbered, iron fire-proof boxes, with the clerks working at desks down the centre of the room. Incidental repairs to returned reels were carried out at benches in the corner. Edward Turner died aged 90 in 1962.

Source: *Walturdaw Knowledge: The House of Cinema*, a trade catalogue, reproduced by kind permission of Ivan Sharpe, Edward Turner's great-grandson. Photography by Tim Whitby (Getty Images/FDA)

years, the KRS was always reacting to crises. These ranged from the problem of duplication of negatives to exhibitors asking for 'concessions on account of the closing of cinemas in consequence of the influenza epidemic'. (The 'Spanish flu' pandemic of 1918 was estimated to have killed over 50 million people worldwide and well over 200,000 people in Britain.)

By the end of 1918, there was a sense that the KRS was becoming better attuned to the concerns of its members and was beginning to represent these members' interests in a more forceful fashion.

It helped that the society's second president, E. G. Turner, was a colourful figure with nearly 20 years of experience in the industry and a fair claim as one of British cinema's very first distributors.

Turner and his business partner J. D. Walker had toured the country from the mid-1890s onwards, first with kinetoscopes and phonographs and then with projectors. Turner was credited with inventing one of the earliest synchronised sound systems, the Cinematophone, founded his own studio, Walturdaw, in 1904, and began renting out films early in his career.

As early as 1912, the trade paper the *Kinematograph Weekly* was pointing out that the Walturdaw company 'have always had claim to being the originators of the renting business'.[27]

Other firms 'condemned' the hiring of films but very quickly adopted the practice themselves. Walturdaw was more than just a distribution company. It supplied every last item that cinemas might need, from buckets for sand and water (to put out fires) to projectors, screens, seating, clocks, box-office tills, ticket rolls and everything else imaginable.

In the early days of British film, most companies were based in Cecil Court, a pedestrian street behind Leicester Square tube station, linking Charing Cross Road with St Martin's Lane. The old film companies' premises are occupied today by antiquarian booksellers. Their shops all have big basements which, at the turn of the century, had been used for early trade shows at which showmen would come and pick up the films they would project in tents and halls. Cecil Hepworth and James Williamson had offices there as did companies like Gaumont and Nordisk, still trading more than 100 years later.

'The great bar to progress was the difficulty of getting new subjects except by buying them outright,' Turner, writing in the *Kinematograph Weekly* in 1926, reminisced of the late 1890s, when anyone who wanted to show a film had to purchase it from a manufacturer. 'I think my partner and myself solved the problem for the world by instituting the renting system. Little did we think that that system would spread all over the wide world, and grow to the great business it is today.'[28]

The KRS thus had as its second chair/president the figure who claimed to have invented the very business of film distribution. There is something wonderfully parochial about the first distribution deals that Turner struck:

> In those first days we only did it spasmodically, because we had very few customers, but later on when the pictures had caught on, and village halls, churches, and chapels were taking up the

pictures and giving regular weekly displays, our hire system grew rapidly. We would buy as many as ten and twelve prints of a film, which was entitled *Landing an Old Lady from a Small Boat*. Our first regular hirer was Ted Lacey, of Barnards M. H. Chatham. My first customer to buy films was Mr Henderson, of Newcastle.[29]

7. Flicker Alley: The buildings in Cecil Court in 2015 look very similar to the way they appeared a century ago when the street was a hub for the burgeoning businesses dealing in cinema equipment and the hire of film prints. 'Between 1897–1915 Cecil Court became the heart of the early British film industry and was known as Flicker Alley,' reads the green plaque on the street today (bottom right).

Photography by Tim Whitby (Getty Images/FDA)

Later, Turner reminisced, he and Walker went on to sell films to such firms as 'Whiteley's, Keith Prowse, Harrods, Gamages, Webster and Girling, H. L. Toms, Woods of Cheapside, Ashton and Mitchell, Army and Navy Stores, the Church Mission Halls, Salvation Army, the Leysian Mission, City Road, and many more whose names at the moment I cannot remember.'[30]

The two young British tradesmen, dealing with churches and chapels, were laying the basis for what would turn into one of the biggest, most flamboyant businesses in the world. Those summer blockbusters released on thousands of prints and earning billions at the global box office were following the pattern of business first established by Mr Turner and Mr Walker with Mr Henderson of Newcastle as client.

There was an obvious logic to the 'rental' business that Turner and Walker developed in the late 1890s. It was common sense for these distributors to provide a bridgehead between the producer/manufacturers and the exhibitors. Without their emergence, a crazy scenario in which exhibitors bought films outright would have endured. It was already obvious that the appeal of the new medium lay in its novelty and in its universality. Without distributors to spread films, that appeal would have been very much diminished.

As the trade press noted, there were plenty of problems for the newly reorganised body to tackle: 'It is most urgent that the Society should get into its stride with as little delay as possible. Many questions are calling out for solution. Railway carriage, the damage to films, the disputed points in hiring contracts.'[31]

CHAPTER 2

Blackmail

The 1920s was a decade of consolidation for the Kinematograph Renters' Society but one of flux and upheaval for the British film industry as a whole.

Look at the distribution arrangements in the period and what is striking is how similar it is to the model that still applied close to a century later. The market was lopsided. There were many companies releasing films but a few major companies dominated the market.

The KRS membership consisted of both 'larger' and 'lesser' renters. 'Lesser' was defined in the early years of the society as a company whose 'yearly output of exclusive subjects did not exceed 26'.

From a later vantage point, 26 seems a huge number – the equivalent of a new film every fortnight. In the era of silent shorts when thousands of films were being released every year, such high rates may have been viable but the logistics must still have been daunting in the extreme. That would have meant huge amounts of prints to transport and collect and a small mountain of paperwork dealing with contracts and delivery.

Given the moves toward consolidation across the industry, it was little wonder that the 'existence of the small man' in distribution and exhibition was becoming ever more precarious. These independents were competing against vertically integrated US companies which produced their own films in the US, distributed them, and often owned or at least had a stake in the British cinemas in which they were shown, too.

The 'lesser' distributors and exhibitors were perturbed by the emergence of British outfits as vast as their American counterparts.

In 1927, the Gaumont-British Picture Corporation was registered as a public company.

Gaumont-British had production interests through its studios at Shepherd's Bush and, a little later, through its acquisition of Gainsborough Pictures, based in Islington. The new outfit also pooled the resources of three leading distribution companies: Gaumont itself, Ideal Film and W & F Film Service. Combined, this made the company the biggest, most prolific distributor in the country by a distance. There was also access to cinemas through the company's acquisition of the Provincial Cinematograph Theatres Company. The new combined company owned around 300 cinemas and was estimated to have capital at its disposal of close to £14 million.

Another, almost equally strong new British outfit was British International Pictures (BIP), which had production facilities at Elstree and access to screens through ABC Cinemas. It also had its own distribution arm, Wardour Films, a company run by Scottish lawyer John Maxwell.

This was the beginning of a long-lasting duopoly. Over time, as there were changes in ownership and shareholding and new acquisitions, Gaumont-British (G-B) and BIP would mutate into, respectively, the Rank Organisation and ABC/EMI.

Maxwell was an example of a 'lesser' distributor who eventually became a very major figure indeed. He had entered the film business in Glasgow in 1912 as an exhibitor, buying an interest in a small cinema in the city. By the end of World War I, he had control of more than 20 cinemas. In 1918, he formed a Scottish distribution company, Waverley Films. A year later, he became chairman of Wardour Films, an increasingly powerful force in UK distribution in the 1920s, and that was the springboard for his later setting up of British National with US businessman J. D. Williams in 1926 and the subsequent launch of BIP.

There were obvious reasons for G-B and BIP to muscle up. A brutal economic logic gave their American competitors an advantage in the UK marketplace. US films that were released in the UK had already recouped their costs in their own cinemas and were made available to British exhibitors at 'prices, and with a publicity, which local producers could not match'.[1]

In 1920, 65 per cent of the total number of films released was handled by 'no more than nine major firms'.[2] A similar imbalance has persisted throughout the history of British film distribution.

US movies dominated the British marketplace and the number of British films being released was dwindling. In 1925, only 34 'British' films were made. In 1926, the number dropped yet further to 23. These were record lows. As the *Kinematograph Year Book* acknowledged, only a handful of these films could be defined as 'first class attractions' (among them Alfred Hitchcock's *The Lodger*).[3]

One set of statistics revealed that from 1 August 1925 until 31 July 1926, 761 movies were screened in Britain; '664 were US-made and 24 were British.'[4]

It was therefore apparent that no British distribution company could sustain itself by releasing only home-grown films. There simply weren't enough of them and those that were made weren't always of a high enough quality.

American movies were anyway much more popular with audiences. The six dominant distribution companies were Goldwyn, Vitagraph, Famous–Lasky, Fox, Film Booking Offices and Western Import. They were responsible for close to 40 per cent of the total number of films being rented to British cinemas in the early 1920s. All these companies were or had been members of the KRS, which was becoming an increasingly influential body in the UK.

As the trade press noted, independent exhibitors and distributors alike were 'anxious' about the 'enormous bargaining power' of the big new companies and fretted as to whether 'non-combine' films would be able to secure screen space.

The British film industry couldn't help but be alarmed by the glaring mismatch in its trade relations with the US. At one 1919 meeting of the Cinematograph Exhibitors' Association, it was noted that Britain, with just under 4,000 cinemas, remitted from £3,000 to £15,000 back to the US for each American film that was screened. Meanwhile, British films that showed in the US (which had 20,000 cinemas) generated an average return of only £800. According to a *New York Times* editorial, 90 per cent of films screened in Britain were American but only around 1 per cent of films screened in the US were British.[5]

British producers called for a 'reciprocal' arrangement with American partners. One idea was for American firms to be asked to 'undertake the distribution of British pictures in the United States on a proportional ratio to the pictures they imported', but this was a forlorn hope.

As an editorial in the *Kinematograph Year Book* for 1926 pointed out, the British-based representatives of American firms were in no position to make decisions on behalf of their bosses on the other side of the Atlantic. Another problem was that there wasn't yet much appetite in the US market for British films. Whether this was because American audiences simply didn't want to see such films or because of protectionist policies which kept foreign fare out of US cinemas is still a matter for debate.

What was also apparent was that the interests of British producers and those of British distributors and exhibitors did not always tally. The latter wanted films which would appeal to their audiences – and the US movies were generally far more popular than their British counterparts. British production may have been in decline but the distribution and exhibition sectors, which were closely intertwined with the American industry, were far more buoyant.

Nevertheless, there was widespread concern about the way that British films were being squeezed out of British cinemas and an acknowledgement that 'no voluntary scheme would clear up the problem'. The British industry was looking to the government to intervene. There was also a strong sentimental interest in the welfare of British cinema. Journalists wrote tub-thumping articles calling for the country to 'resume its former proud position among the world's biggest film producing countries'.

This led to the passing of the Cinematograph Films Act 1927, which introduced quota legislation requiring cinemas to show a certain number of 'British' films. The notion of what constituted a 'British' film was itself vexed. The Act defined 'Britishness' in terms of the nationality of a production company behind a film, its creative team and the locations in which it was made. The quota was originally set at 7.5 per cent British films but was to be raised in 1935 to 20 per cent.

The big new British combines, Gaumont-British and British International Pictures, were poised to benefit from the quota legislation. It was no accident that both had such patriotic-sounding names.

A British production boom soon followed, albeit one with unforeseen consequences. British films were being made by American companies (Fox at Wembley, Warner–First National at Teddington Studios) while other big US outfits were working closely with local producers to ensure they would have access to enough British films to fulfil their quota obligations. The downside was the rise of the so-called 'quota quickie', the cheap film made quickly, without any commercial ambition whatsoever, simply to meet quota requirements. One of the ironies was that the production boom was being financed by distributors, who needed, but didn't always especially want, British films. They supported them (and invested in them) because that was what the new law demanded. However, they also realised that US films almost always did better business at the box office.

This is one of the enduring paradoxes of British distribution. Then, as now, the most successful British distributors were often the ones who had the easiest access to American movies.

The US studios were largely run by immigrants from Europe who from the very outset had an eye on international audiences, not just American ones. Chaplin himself was British, of course. International audiences craved filmed entertainment, wherever it came from, and Hollywood was often better able to feed their appetites than their own domestic industries.

In 2015, without inward investment from the US, it could be argued there wouldn't be much of a British film industry. From a distribution/exhibition point of view, that was also already true in the 1920s. However, if you substitute the word 'international' for 'American', it gives a different perspective. The US studio films were targeted deliberately at global audiences, not just domestic ones. Hollywood drew both its creative personnel and its subject matter from all over the world.

British producers felt, somewhat fancifully, that there was untapped demand for their films in 'every part of the Empire', but there is little evidence that distribution companies were looking to meet that demand. Their focus was on the British marketplace.

Trade journalists spoke of 'ploughing' and 'seed time'. There was a sense of an industry that was continuing to grow. Distributors were also becoming far more aggressive about protecting their interests, even when it meant going against the spirit of the quota legislation. 'Barring', 'block booking' and 'alignment' were three practices that they embraced.

'Barring' was about providing cinemas with exclusivity. When a prominent cinema in a prosperous area booked a film, it was not shown anywhere else nearby until the cinema had had the chance to maximise box-office revenues.

'Block booking' was the familiar practice (mentioned in the previous chapter) of requiring cinemas to take a large number of films from a distributor in order to be able to show the one they really wanted. Often, these films, invariably American, would be taken 'blind', months or even years in advance, before the films had actually even been produced. These 'blocks' could amount to over 100 films a year. One report prepared by the CEA in the early 1920s discovered that '100 per cent of British exhibitors booked ahead for six months, 50 per cent for at least one year and 25 per cent for at least 18 months'.[6]

The practice would eventually fall foul of monopoly legislation as it evolved. Nonetheless, today, as in the 1920s, UK distributors often look to strike long-term deals with US partners. The talk is of 'output' deals or 'first look' deals but the effect is roughly the same. British distributors are prepared to take US movies in bulk, even if it means accepting the occasional dud, in order to acquire and represent the titles with box-office potential.

'Alignment' was about distributors striking relationships with specific cinema chains or theatres. They would offer their films exclusively to those chains.

An early concern, mentioned frequently in the minutes of meetings in the early 1920s, was the practice of exhibitors 'combining to keep down the hiring price of films'. If cinema owners shared information about their trading terms with distributors and then bargained collectively, they hoped to force prices down.

The KRS reacted to this by calling for a minimum price for film rentals. This, in turn, provoked debate as films were of different lengths.

Would the same minimum price apply to short subjects as to lengthy features?

There was the vexed but utterly fundamental question of how the pricing should be set in the first place. Should it be a flat fee? Should the renter receive a percentage of profits? If so, what percentage? From this early period, exhibitors were very wary indeed about revealing just how much money they were making.

As early as 1918, the KRS and the CEA were negotiating over the idea of 'model forms of contract'.

As we have seen, the issue of piracy was also already on distributors' and exhibitors' minds. The KRS committee held extensive conversations on the subject of 'duping'. Renters agreed that if they had to provide a cinema with 'a positive from a secondary negative', the exhibitor would be informed as soon as possible and would be given the opportunity to cancel the booking.

'In disclosing to the renter the money-earning propensities of one's hall, one is making a rod for one's own back,' an exhibitor was quoted as telling trade paper the *Bioscope*.[7] It is a wonderfully ironic remark and one which makes it very clear why distributors were so wary about the business practices of the cinemas with which they were dealing. The idea that cinema owners could somehow prevent distributors from finding out how much money their movies were making was fanciful in the extreme.

A document kept in the KRS archives, 'Notes on Checking Exhibitors' Returns on Sharing Term Contracts', points out the dilemma distributors faced. 'In approaching this matter one has first to consider whether or not exhibitors in the main are likely to render accurate accounts of their receipts,' the document begins. In other words, distributors still couldn't work out whether their exhibitor partners could be relied on to be truthful.[8]

There were tricky questions of good manners and trust to be broached here. If the distributors set up a system of 'general control', the very obvious implication would be that they simply didn't trust the honesty of the cinema owners who were, after all, their most vital trading partners. This was a time for discretion, not open conflict. Perhaps, the KRS notes suggested, the proper course would be for 'renters individually to appoint their own representatives to be present at those cinemas where they had reason to think inaccurate figures might be given by the exhibitor'.[9]

During the 1920s, films were becoming longer (features were taking over from shorts) and more sophisticated – and therefore more expensive to make. The added cost had to be recouped somehow – and putting up the price of tickets was an obvious first step.

At the same time, then as now, distributors were often made to feel beleaguered.

At a 1923 meeting of the KRS, a letter was submitted by distributor Ideal Films 'intimating that criticism of renters' methods was constantly appearing in the trade journals and that exhibitors through the medium of their branch meetings were led to believe that all the trade misfortunes were due to renters'.[10]

What made the criticism in the trade press all the more galling was the fact that (the distributors calculated) the trade papers were dependent on their advertisements for 95 per cent of their revenue. These papers took the distributors' money – and then proceeded to criticise them.

Confidential memoranda were circulated between KRS members on how best to bring the trade papers into line – and on whether intimidation or flattery was the best strategy. 'The complaint of the renters is that at present independence and impartiality are wholly absent from the trade papers, which on every important matter voice the exhibitors' view,' reads one briefing.[11]

The KRS recommended that 'an earnest attempt should be made to found an independent organ, which would be strictly impartial in all its editorial pages'. There is a measure of paranoia here. The existing trade press was already independent. The very fact that the trade papers were critical of the renters in spite of being dependent on them for advertising revenue was a sign of this independence. There was no guarantee that a new paper would be any more favourably disposed toward the interests of distribution.

What was really galling to the UK's independent exhibitors was the increasing strength of big US-owned 'producer–renter–exhibitor houses' which had the strength in the market to determine how trading should be conducted. An editorial in the *Kinematograph Year Book* 1928 (looking back on the events of 1927) complained:

> The most obvious injury inflicted by these chains was the 'outrageous' system of bars, both in time and distance, which they were able to enforce, and in addition there was a very strong feeling that the producing and renting interests, which represented only 10 per cent of the total capital involved in the industry (as compared with 90 per cent, in theatres), should not be allowed to dominate the situation.[12]

Exhibitors were lobbying for film hire to be set at 25 per cent of the takings and there were calls for the establishment of a national 'booking circuit' along co-operative lines. (A national 'booking circuit' would have been negotiating from a position of strength with distributors and would have been able to insist on fixed nationwide hire costs for film.) Such proposals were fiercely resisted by the distributors, who were determined to continue negotiating directly with individual cinemas rather than agreeing to collective bargaining.

The KRS issued a statement that it viewed any proposed national circuit with utter hostility. The distributors vowed that they would not rent movies to any such circuit.

Exhibitors also grumbled over such matters as who was liable if a lorry caught fire and the films it was carrying were destroyed or what should happen if screenings had to be cancelled because of smallpox or even 'the serious effects of the summer weather' on box-office takings. The distributors argued that they should not be held responsible but these were precisely the issues that caused such strained feeling between different sectors of the trade.

It may be overstating it to describe the relationship between distributors and exhibitors as one of bad-tempered anarchy but the latter found plenty to complain about. One issue highlighted in the trade paper *Cinema News and Property Gazette* was the lack of consistency in the prices exhibitors were charged by distributors for publicity material. Some distributors provided stills and trailers relatively inexpensively while others charged a very big markup. According to the exhibitors, there was no correlation between quality and cost. What it came down to was the mindset of the distributors:

> Some regard publicity supply as a service as advantageous to themselves as to the exhibitor, and are prepared to supply at cost [...] while others quite openly claim that they are entitled to get back from the exhibitor by way of charge for such service the whole cost of their publicity departments.[13]

As these remarks suggest, distributors and exhibitors were still trying to work out whether they were allies or antagonists. What right, the trade paper asked, have the renters/distributors 'to ask the exhibitor to pay through his advertising matter for propaganda calculated and intended primarily to benefit the renter?' It was further claimed that certain films had failed to 'get a second and third run in an area because the first run had not been sufficiently "boomed" to make the subsequent bookings worthwhile'. ('Boomed' was another way of saying 'hyped up'.) This, the article implied, was purely because the exhibitors couldn't afford to buy more than a bare minimum of publicity material.

Disputes over how basic costs should be divided between distribution and exhibition continue to the present day, notably in the debates over the so-called Virtual Print Fee (VPF) and who should pay for the digitisation of cinemas (a subject for a later chapter). As film disappeared and movies began to be projected digitally, distributors no longer had to pay the cost of striking prints – but the exhibitors still made them pay a 'virtual' fee to underwrite the cost of digital projectors and screening facilities.

Another annoyance for the exhibitors was the increasing involvement of the US majors in British distribution and exhibition companies. Famous Players–Lasky (which later morphed into Paramount) announced plans in 1919 to open its own chain of British cinemas – something which appalled local exhibitors.

There were calls for the KRS to organise conferences at which 'important trade problems' could be discussed from 'the renters' angle'. The distributors wanted the chance to tell their colleagues from other parts of the industry that they had plenty of problems of their own.

The infighting didn't help. On 1 November 1923, Lewis S. Levin, the European manager of the Fox Film Company Ltd wrote a mournful letter to the KRS, informing its chairman that Fox wished to disassociate itself from the society 'because we cannot appear to reconcile our views with regard to freedom of action in running our business with the views that seem to prevail amongst the members of the Society as at present constituted'.[14] The restraints imposed by KRS membership were, Levin complained, 'irksome' and 'harmful' to Fox's business interests. The society, he suggested, was stuck in the past. The real problem was that Fox didn't like the restrictions placed on it by the KRS.

Such departures weren't rare. As the chair of the KRS noted at the 1930 AGM, the society had never managed to achieve 100 per cent membership and there are always 'individuals' who 'for a time feel that they can carry on their business successfully without the aid or co-operation of their fellow businessmen'.[15]

What was clear was that the KRS was efficient and resourceful. By 1928, the organisation had 34 London members, including 'every important renter handling 18 or more films'[16] with the exception of a company called European.

Largely thanks to the KRS, British distributors were an increasingly powerful force in the UK industry of the 1920s. Low suggests they had 'secured virtual control of it'[17] by the end of the decade, an observation that suggests the trade body had come a very long way since its sometimes chaotic early years.

One of the obvious reasons for the growing influence of distributors was the number of astute, hard-headed and sometimes flamboyant figures working in the sector. As in Hollywood in the same period, many of the most prominent figures were Jewish.

One was Charles Moss Woolf, better known as C. M. Woolf. A former fur merchant in the City, he came aboard distribution company W & F in 1919. Alan Wood, biographer of British film magnate J. Arthur Rank, described him as 'dynamic, highly temperamental and often quarrelsome'.

Wood also quoted Woolf's lawyer testifying to Woolf's 'endearing quality of explosive excitability, tremendous if merciless fairness, surprising reasonableness when one put up with his irascibility, and immense popularity with the exhibitors with whom he had to deal'.[18]

In short, Woolf had the perfect temperament for working in the UK distribution arena. His critics claimed he had little instinct for film 'art' and that he had wilfully misunderstood and underestimated some of the early films from British wunderkind Alfred Hitchcock in which he had been involved. Nonetheless, however reluctantly, he did invest in and distribute such Hitchcock films as *The Lodger* (1927) and *Easy Virtue* (1928). (He allegedly told the young Hitchcock, 'your picture [*The Lodger*] is so dreadful, that we're just going to put it on the shelf and forget about it,' but was talked into releasing it by its producer, Michael Balcon, with whose company, Gainsborough Pictures, Woolf had very close ties.)

Another very prominent figure in UK distribution of the 1920s (also Jewish and briefly president of the KRS) was Simon Rowson. Together with his brother Harry, Simon had formed his own distribution outfit, the Ideal Film Company, in 1911.

Born in Manchester, the Rowsons were the sons of a butcher and meat keeper from Suwalki in north-eastern Poland. They had come into film in an unlikely and roundabout way. As historian Sarah Street notes, Harry had started off dealing in films for scrap while working in the US on a chess magazine in the early 1900s with German chess champion Emanuel Lasker. He had realised there was money to be made by exhibiting and distributing new films as well as selling old ones for scrap.[19]

The Ideal Film Company was based in Wardour Street, as were many other film companies. As Harry explained in his memoirs, there were practical reasons why these companies converged on Soho. As they stored highly flammable celluloid film, they were charged very high insurance rates – and it appears that Soho was an affordable and central location.[20]

Ideal had diversified into production, making a rousing, propagandist biopic about the British wartime prime minister David Lloyd George. As the silent-cinema blog the Bioscope points out, *The Story of Lloyd George* was the subject of outrageous anti-Semitic attacks by populist British nationalist politician (and later convicted fraudster)

Horatio Bottomley, who used his magazine *John Bull* to wage a campaign against the film. The Rowsons sued him for libel and won their case, but the film was suppressed and only emerged into the public eye many years later.

Simon Rowson was a brilliant lobbyist with a flair for statistics. In the early 1930s, he wrote a groundbreaking study of the British film industry (*A Statistical Survey of the Cinema Industry in Great Britain in 1934*) that revealed there was one cinema for every 10,600 people in Britain in 1934. That computed to one seat for every 15 people, a figure which, he justly claimed, emphasised the hold that the movies had on the British public.[21]

To some of the film-makers he worked with, Rowson seemed an overly cautious, even a pedantic figure. In his biography of the flamboyant producer Alexander Korda, Charles Drazin writes of Rowson's tortoise-like pace when it came to approving funding for new films and calls him 'a man who took pains to dot every I'.[22] Verbal communication and handshakes were no good for Simon Rowson. He wanted everything in writing. Nonetheless, the distributor was one of the towering figures in the British film industry in the 1920s and 1930s – and he was passionately committed to the KRS.

Other powerful players were A. C. Bromhead and his brother R. C. Bromhead, respectively managing director and general manager of the powerful Gaumont company. As early as 1898, they had opened offices to distribute films from the company in France. They also expanded into production and later, in 1922, with support from powerful financiers the Ostrer family, bought out their French parent company and began to operate as Gaumont-British.

A. C. (Claude) Bromhead had attained the rank of lieutenant colonel during World War I and had led a film propaganda mission to Russia in 1916–17. Sounding a little like Colonel Blimp, he liked to tell his trade peers in later years that he had come into the industry at a time before typewriters or cars were commonplace and when even the telephone was considered 'a rarity by no means in general use'. Given the times, he observed, it was no wonder that the cinematograph, when it first emerged, was regarded as little more than a novelty – 'at best a nine days' scientific wonder'.

KRS members managed to keep on delivering films to cinemas even in the most adverse circumstances. Neither war nor industrial strife hampered their activities. During the 1926 General Strike, for example, business carried on much as normal. As an admiring editorial in the *Kinematograph Year Book* enthused, the strike

> was met with a courage and resourcefulness which were wholly admirable. Normal transport being entirely held up, the trade organised its own dumps, and by a complicated but highly efficient series of motor connections, the supply of pictures to kinemas [*sic*] throughout the country was carried out with hardly a let-down from start to finish.[23]

TRANSITION TO SOUND

A new 'talking picture' device, by which 'sub-titles are spoken', had just been introduced by Paramount in America, the *Kinematograph Weekly* noted, as if in passing, in its look back on 'talking points' of December 1926.

In these early days, there was suspicion and puzzlement in Britain at the way the Americans had gone 'talkie mad'. The Brits were sceptical about the new technology, just as many of the Americans themselves once had been.

Talking pictures weren't just the novelty that the UK trade press seemed to think. They were going to have an utterly transformative effect on the industry. It wasn't just Paramount which was experimenting with talkies. So were the other studios. Warner Bros. won the race to make a full-length feature with synchronised sound when the studio released *The Jazz Singer* in 1927, using a Vitaphone sound-on-disc system, and followed it up with a crime drama, *The Lights of New York*, the first 'all talking picture', as it was billed, in 1928.

By 1928, the British film industry could no longer ignore the clamour and din about sound movies. Even so, the trade press had remained resistant to the lure of talkies. 'Every now and then, the human voice helps the pictorial action; for the most part it is merely a delaying, harsh, unmusical and often ridiculous force' was the verdict from one

8. Hitchcock thriller: *Blackmail* features a trademark cameo appearance by the director as a passenger on the London Underground. These images are from a set of publicity stills supplied by the distributor for front-of-house display in cinemas playing the film.

Source: Getty Images/Movie Poster Image Art

journalist who felt the new technology would clog up the fluency and visual grace of silent cinema.

The 'first' British talkie was Alfred Hitchcock's *Blackmail* (1929). *Blackmail* was made for British International Pictures at Elstree on the studios' new sound stages.

The original intention had been to shoot it as a silent film. As Hitchcock later told French director François Truffaut, 'after a good deal of hesitation the producers decided it would be silent except for the last reel.'[24]

Hitchcock claimed that he wasn't prepared to put up with such a tentative, half-hearted approach and therefore secretly reshot the entire film with sound.

This was a crime thriller featuring sex, murder and, naturally, blackmail. Hitchcock made wonderfully inventive use of his London locations and of everyday London life: the crowds, the policemen, the cabs. He also used sound in an expressionistic way that matched his own visual ingenuity. In one famous scene, we hear the constant repetition of the word 'knife' at the breakfast table as the heroine (played by the beautiful Anny Ondra), who has just stabbed to death a man who tried to rape her, begins to hallucinate.

The film may be celebrated for its use of sound but it also established the idea of the 'Hitchcock thriller'. In the years to come, the director was to make many other movies which used suspense, eroticism, bawdy humour and violence in a similar way. There was the sense of an artist finding his voice (a neat metaphor for his first sound film) and his register.

Distributors Wardour Films marketed the film on the basis of the patriotic British flavour that Hitchcock had so accentuated. This was not just another American talkie. This was home-grown fare with British characters speaking in British accents. The marketing campaign did not draw attention to the fact that the star, Anny Ondra, was in fact, a Czech/German actress who could speak hardly a word of English. (There were no facilities for dubbing so Hitchcock recruited a well-spoken English actress, Joan Barry, to stand just outside the frame and speak Ondra's dialogue. Ondra herself would then mimic the words she had just heard.)

'English as it should be spoken', trumpeted the headline in the Dundee *Evening Telegraph*.[25] 'The simple fact that we hear the Mother Tongue as it should be spoken is sufficient to recommend it to all patriotic Britons,' the journalist gushed, puffing up the film. 'Everything has been done to obtain realism, and the characters on the screen seem to be made of flesh and blood and not mere puppets, so deftly has the producer handled the material at his command.'

The Brits were looking for a film to champion – and *Blackmail* fitted the bill. 'England is undoubtedly in the mood to take English pictures,' wrote the prominent trade journalist Peter Burnup shortly after the release of Hitchcock's film.[26] Burnup had recently attended a conference of provincial salesmen called by British International Pictures. It was these salesmen's job to rent movies to cinemas and they all claimed that British films were now in demand. 'Salesmen are notoriously optimistic about the goods they have to sell, but here man after man had facts to report,' Burnup claimed. 'They all told me that they were selling at least twice as many pictures as they had disposed of last year.'[27]

The best British films weren't simply being seen in cinemas in the UK. Films like *Blackmail* and *Atlantic* were also finding audiences in Europe and even in the US.

In the late 1920s, as the industry prepared for the transition to sound, the challenge was not just to re-equip cinemas with sound projectors. Another problem was copyright law. Rights holders were asking for royalties for the use of copyrighted music in sound films. The KRS was calling for a 'comprehensive arrangement' for films to be granted world copyright to the music they used. (The alternative would be mind-boggling – a case of negotiating deals on every film with many different rights holders.) There was the question of who would pay for the cinemas to be equipped with the new sound projectors. Was this a cost that the distributors should pick up or was it the responsibility of the cinema owners themselves? As trade representatives fought among themselves to resolve such problems, what was clear was the central role that the KRS now played in a fast-changing British film industry.

CHAPTER 3

The Private Life of Henry VIII

The 1930s mark a typically paradoxical era in British film history. On the one hand, these were boom years. On the other, a lingering wariness about the future of the business persisted.

Filmgoing had taken root as the most popular pastime of its era. Attendances weren't unduly affected by the Depression. Cinemas were seen by the British public as both homely and exotic. The medium's appeal was universal, cutting across age and class lines. There was no TV, DVD or VOD to compete for the public's attention. Few people owned cars, music hall was in decline and there wasn't a widespread appetite for 'serious' theatre. By the middle of the decade, annual British cinema admissions were at well over 900 million and were continuing to rise.

'The country was in depression but business was quite good because at that time people with time on their hands and out of jobs used to go to the cinemas and they used to fill the afternoons,' the young Leeds bookings clerk Percy Livingstone, who would eventually work his way up to become managing director of Twentieth Century Fox, recalled of the early 1930s. Movies were regarded as an affordable entertainment.[1] The experience – the cinema and the films that were screened there – was an antidote to the strife of everyday life.

'The standard of living in people's homes was not very high and they loved to be transported to an unreal world and they could participate in this unreal world,' Livingstone remembered. 'The cinema provided them with a higher standard of living than they were able to get at home. Warmth and comfort, absolutely, although on matinees the heating was turned down a bit to save fuel.'[2]

Even so, British distributors sounded a wary note when contemplating their prospects. The trade press of the early 1930s was full of comment about the 'severe tests' which the industry had faced in converting to sound and to dealing with what *Kinematograph Weekly* editor S. G. Rayment called 'the novelty of the talkie appeal'.[3]

Rayment's editorial for the 1931 *Kinematograph Year Book* makes surprisingly downbeat reading. It suggests that, after the heady exhilaration of the early talkie era, a disillusionment among audiences was already creeping in. 'The peak attendances of the days when talkies were in their first flush could not be held,' the editorial laments.[4] His observations were underlined by the very long lists of bankruptcies and liquidations included in the trade papers.

Cinemas were still selling tickets in huge numbers but the exhibitors were complaining that outgoings were rising faster than revenues. It wasn't cheap to equip cinemas for sound and they had to bear the cost.

An inevitable consequence was the ratcheting up in tension between exhibitors and distributors. The former were paying for the conversion to 'talkies' and wanted their terms of trade changed to compensate for their added outgoings. The anger came to a head during 1930. The system under which cinema owners made a minimum guaranteed payment to distributors and then also shared the box-office receipts with them no longer seemed appealing. Rayment noted:

> The growing dissatisfaction felt by exhibitors with the system under which films were booked on sharing terms with a guaranteed minimum payment culminated in a definite and unanimous resolution, taken at the summer conference of the CEA, to refuse business with firms making this demand.[5]

At the same time, the distributors were complaining that the exhibitors were falsifying their returns or holding back payments.

It is a long-term characteristic of the relationship between distributors and exhibitors that each side feels hard done by and exploited by the other. In this period, in the aftermath of the conversion to sound, the distributors were in the ascendant. As historian Rachael Low notes, 'The Kinematograph Renters' Society, dominated by the American majors, was a small, united and aggressive body with a couple of dozen members, who held all the cards and kept the exhibitors in line with very real threats of boycott.'[6]

The KRS had been born out of 'confusion and convulsion' (in the words of MPEA director A. Ronald Thornton on the occasion of its fiftieth anniversary),[7] but the organisation had now become streamlined and ruthlessly efficient. From its offices in Old Compton Street in the heart of Soho, the KRS was able to dictate policy. Its 16-strong council then included such heavy hitters as Fox, MGM, Paramount, United Artists, Universal and Warner Bros.

By contrast, the CEA was a vast, unwieldy organisation with thousands of members, including both the major circuits and individual cinema owners who had very different interests.

At least there was consensus on one issue. The exhibitors, big and small, were in no doubt about what they wanted most of all – namely movies from Metro–Goldwyn–Mayer. Their first priority was always to 'do their Metro'. MGM was the studio with 'more stars than there are in heaven'. Its movies were easily the most bankable – something it trumpeted in ads in the trade press.

'Follow the Leader!' reads an ad in a 1931 trade publication which shows a cartoon of MGM's lion waving a placard promising 'Week to week hits!' Theatres were playing more MGM product than that of any other company, the ads proclaimed.[8] This was so obviously true that the US studio hardly needed to advertise. Exhibitors were clamouring for MGM movies.

MGM's salesmen represented dozens of new titles each year throughout the 1930s, including the Hal Roach and Marx Brothers comedies, and numerous Greta Garbo, John Barrymore and W. C. Fields films. MGM's *Anna Christie* was advertised with the slogan 'Garbo Talks!'

In *Anna Christie*, Garbo plays a barfly. Early on, we see her lurch into a waterfront bar, sit herself down, and order the barman to give 'give me a viskey, ginger ale on the side. Don't be stingy.' Her voice is husky and European-sounding but very powerful. 'Shall I put it in a pail?' the barman responds. The idea of the most glamorous actress of her era cast as a drunk on skid row is absurd, but Garbo somehow makes us buy it.

The studio did extraordinary business throughout the 1930s with Garbo films like *Ninotchka, Queen Christina* and *Camille*. She turned out 24 films for MGM over a 15-year period. They were almost all massive hits. Only with *Two-Faced Woman* (1941) did she have a failure. Garbo epitomised the classiness and upscale sophistication of MGM movies, qualities that had huge appeal in British cinemas as elsewhere.

In 1939, MGM distributed both *The Wizard of Oz* and the super-long *Gone with the Wind* (a Selznick production, adapted from the novel published three years earlier – and an amazing achievement coming just a dozen years after sound was first added to films). Both films used the three-strip Technicolor process developed in the early 1930s by Dr Herbert Kalmus. This didn't just offer ordinary, everyday colour. Through some strange alchemy, Technicolor films seemed preter-naturally rich and bright. In the Depression-era US of the 1930s or the austerity Britain of the postwar years, Technicolor offered a gateway to another world.

Robert Edmond Jones, the art director on Rouben Mamoulian's *Becky Sharp* (1935), one of the first films to use the new three-strip Technicolor process, wrote in the *New York Times*, shortly after work-ing on the film, that colour offered the prospect for motion pictures to become 'incomparably more powerful than ever before'.[9]

MGM didn't just have the biggest stars. As the studio's embrace of Technicolor suggested, it made the biggest-budget, most technically advanced films.

Salesmen from other companies would be told: 'I can't see you now because I am still waiting for the MGM man.' Only when the Metro titles were safely booked, often months in advance, would the exhibitor deign to look at 'product' from other distributors, big or small.

'MGM had the product that everybody wanted and no exhibitor would deal with any other company until he had got his Metro product in his book first. They were quite dominant in the industry. MGM had all the stars that mattered,' Percy Livingstone, selling films for Fox to Yorkshire cinema owners, recalled as what became conventional indus-try wisdom in the 1930s. This was the period when, as well as Greta Garbo, Clark Gable, Joan Crawford, Jean Harlow, Jeanette Macdonald, Charles Farrell, Janet Gaynor, Nelson Eddy, Norma Shearer and many others were under contract to MGM. Films were now being sold on the basis of their stars. The 1930s saw Hollywood 'icons' make lasting (even immortal) impressions on the growing audiences around the world: Errol Flynn as pirate *Captain Blood* and *Robin Hood*; Johnny Weissmuller as *Tarzan*; Jimmy Cagney as *Public Enemy*, ushering in an early 'crime wave' at the movies (for Warner Bros.); Fred Astaire and Ginger Rogers in their musicals together; and *King Kong*.

Other studios had stars too but none could match the box-office lustre of those on the Metro roster. British exhibitors knew that if they had regular access to MGM fare, they were almost certainly guaranteed to make money.

The strength of MGM meant that its chief executive in London, Sam Eckman, was an immensely powerful figure in UK distribution. His salary, a reported £46,000 a year, provoked awe. That was far more than those of the entire British Cabinet combined.[10] Percy Livingstone remembered that Eckman was the only KRS board member who had his own seat permanently reserved for him at meetings: 'None dared sit on Sam's chair. He always came in a little late but none would venture.'[11]

Eckman had entered the industry in 1910 as an exhibitor. Ironically, given his later battles with exhibitors, he had been president of the New York Exhibitors' Leagues. In 1914, he became New York manager of the Mutual Film Corp. In 1917, he took charge of the New York office of the newly formed Goldwyn Pictures Corporation. In 1922, he was elected vice president of the Goldwyn Distributing Corp. Following the amalgamation of MGM in 1924, he took over the management of the entire Eastern Division. In September 1927, he was appointed vice president and managing director of MGM Ltd, London. It was a very swift rise and he headed the company's British operations for many years.

The American was president of the KRS from 1931 until 1934. In later years, he wasn't especially modest about his own achievements on behalf of Britain's distributors. In a short essay he wrote to mark the society's fiftieth anniversary, Eckman recalled:

When in 1931, with three million unemployed and the people more concerned with bread and rent rather than cake and

pictures, and the small exhibitor falling before economic conditions as rapidly as later he fell before the onslaught of TV, I
hope I gave the KRS an authority it had never enjoyed before
and one which I would hate to see it ever abrogate.[12]

The MGM boss even credited himself with bringing about a rap-
prochement of sorts between the distributors and the exhibitors in
1931. With his persuasion, the exhibitors and distributors formed a
Joint Investigation Committee. Its intention was to investigate ticket
irregularities while also providing a forum for the much beleaguered
'smaller exhibitor'. This figure (always a 'he') had been 'hit hardest' by
the 'talking equipment costs' and the rise in film hire. 'He [the smaller
exhibitor] has, as a rule, less room for expansion, and therefore finds it
more difficult to make increased returns to balance increased expenses,'
the *Kinematograph Year Book* noted.

The idea was that the exhibitors could use the committee as a court
of appeal – they could test their case with 'a reasonable expectation of
receiving sympathy and justice'. 'Offenders against ordinary business
ethics will never be shielded,' the trade press warned, 'but here are
certainly hard cases, and these will be given consideration.'[13]

Eckman commanded respect among both his own kindred in the
distribution sector and among the exhibitors. He was an immensely
wealthy American who smoked fat cigars, as all moguls should, and
had the ear of Louis B. Mayer. His films were the ones the cinemas
wanted most of all. He was accommodating to exhibitors but made
sure that he was not regarded as a soft touch.

When a group of 200 small exhibitors secretly clubbed together
in the early 1930s to try to start a system of cheap collective booking,
Eckman headed them off at the pass. In his capacity as KRS president,
Eckman had just addressed the CEA General Council on 'the need
for frankness and unity', and took it very badly that a group of CEA
members were going behind his back. Eckman insisted that no KRS-
affiliated distributors would deal with the new 'booking combine'.
He was threatened with legal action but, as he later boasted, 'we
stood firm.'[14] In a bid to stop future attempts by exhibitors to group
together to drive down prices, the KRS passed a resolution 'that no

management' could 'book for a cinema unless it had a 50 per cent interest in the cinema'.

Eckman also claimed responsibility for the introduction of percentage bookings – the practice referred to earlier whereby cinema owners shared some of the box-office profits with the distributors. Historically, films had been booked by cinemas on a flat rate. Regardless of how well they performed, distributors were still paid at the same rate. Eckman lobbied for a system that would allow the distributors a share of any profits on successful films. He advocated increased prices and longer runs. In late 1933, he launched a campaign to limit film programmes to three hours to stop exhibitors securing too many films for too little money.

Inevitably, the British cinema business became increasingly polarised. The 'small men' were more and more marginalised while the big companies became yet more dominant. The big cinema circuits didn't need the help of their trade body the CEA anyway. Their 'bargaining power was so great' that they could secure bookings paying only 20 to 25 per cent of their takings to the distributors.[15] The small men, meanwhile, had to pay 40 to 50 per cent for big, prestigious movies and 33.5 per cent for run of the mill features.

Grumblings and recriminations between distributors and exhibitors continued throughout the 1930s. The cinema owners complained about the ever-decreasing profit margins. Distributors reacted to exhibitor customers who paid late by establishing a 'restricted credit' system and refusing to rent them movies. They accused the exhibitors of using the money that should have been used to settle their debts for 'various enterprises and developments of their businesses'.[16] This only served to exacerbate the bad feeling between them. By the mid-1930s, the trade press estimated that one third of the cinemas in the country were 'in Poverty Row, and the way out cannot be seen.' The distributors countered that exhibition was a cash business. The moment the cinemas showed their films, they received their money through the tills. The distributors, though, faced a very long wait for any returns to trickle back to them.

The opposition wasn't just between exhibition and distribution: it was between the majors and the independents. MGM didn't have its own cinemas but never faced problems in securing favourable terms. Smaller distributors and cinema owners were in a far weaker negotiating position. They, though, were in the majority. The KRS and the CEA eventually came to an agreement for new terms for 'small exhibitors'. Those whose takings did not exceed £125 a week were still able to rent films on a 'flat-booking' basis.

During the early 1930s, the big 'circuits' hadn't yet consolidated fully and exhibition was still crowded with smaller players. This led to intense competition even in the smallest towns. Eventually, this would change. By the end of the 1930s, the three main circuits, Odeon, ABC and Gaumont-British, would own 1,011 cinemas between them, 21 per cent of the total number of well over 5,000 cinemas in the UK as a whole.[17] Smaller circuits would account for another 15 per cent of cinema ownership, leaving a still sizeable 64 per cent of cinemas in the hands of 'independents'. In the postwar years, however, the circuits would grow and grow – and the independents' share of the market would shrink.

The trade press used very emotive language in its arguments, as if the 'small man' cinema owners were 1930s equivalents to small French peasant farmers, the 'backbone' of the rural community, pitted against big, bad industrialised business interests. The *Kinematograph Year Book* wrote of the small, salt-of-the-earth exhibitor:

> He is naturally not a prominent personality; his kinema [*sic*] is, as a rule, rather out of the way; he himself can hardly be expected to make systematic journeys to participate in general exhibitor activities, social or business; the value of his account is trivial compared with the cost of getting his order and supplying his films. No wonder, then, that he is only too frequently overlooked.[18]

And, pointing out that he and his kind still represented at least a third of cinema owners overall, the trade paper suggested:

> Providence once more shows itself on the side of the big battalions. However, the last has by no means been heard of this battle; it will certainly be waged with great earnestness, for it is one

more thrust at the small men who have, in spite of their numerical strength, had the worst of the deal in so many ways of late.

Read between the lines and it is easy to understand why the 'small men' were doomed. They ran their businesses in often chronically inefficient fashion. Their turnover was tiny. A KRS report in 1934 revealed that there were 1,200 exhibitors in Britain whose takings averaged between £1 and £8 a day – that's to say, peanuts. Their theatres hadn't been modernised. The trade press wrote of the strong bonds they had with their local customers but sentimental loyalty was never going to be enough to sustain their businesses. Their gripes weren't just with distributors but with fellow exhibitors. There were constant complaints about the 'over-building' of cinemas and the small men were often worried to see spanking new theatres springing up in their own neighbourhoods.

'Imagine the shock of a man who has spent years in building up a comfortable little clientele for his modest hall when he sees a big, smart, up-to-date house in course of erection,' the trade press in the late 1930s noted of the reaction of smaller exhibitors in outlying areas to being suddenly confronted with bigger, better-resourced competitors.[19]

With thousands of individual cinemas operating in the 1930s, the burden on the distributors who rented them films was immense. These films had to be booked, transported vast distances to out-of-the-way places and advertised. The KRS had refused exhibitors' appeals for standard contacts. This meant that almost every deal had to be hammered out individually.

It is intriguing to hear accounts of the lives of distributors' salesmen on the road, covering hundreds of miles every week as they dealt with the small cinema owners. The pace at which films were released was very different to what it became in the era of TV and home video. Cinema was the only outlet for a film. This meant that the same movies kept on playing for months. The cinema programme itself would change regularly – every week or twice or occasionally three times a week – but the films themselves would be made to work very hard. Roll-out was slow to save on the cost of prints, and some movies would have cinema lives that would last for up to two years.

Distribution companies were very big enterprises. Those based in London would have branch offices in the major regional centres. There were secretaries, clerks, office managers and sales staff. There were no training programmes as such. Instead, junior staff would work their way up the ranks. Sales jobs were highly prized not least because they would come with the use of a car.

The life of the salesmen was akin to that of the travelling sheet-music salesmen played by Bob Hoskins in the Dennis Potter-scripted drama *Pennies from Heaven*. They were continually on the road. They were called 'film travellers'.

John Hogarth recounted his early experiences after the war selling British Lion's films:

> I would leave home on a Monday morning and spend the whole week going from town to town, hotel to hotel, seeing independent cinemas because in those days of the 4,000-odd cinemas which were open by then, three-quarters were owned by individuals [...] We small independents had to have the crumbs from the rich man's table, so though we were selling in those days what I considered to be very important films, mostly made by the Boulting brothers or Frank Launder and Sidney Gilliat, you had to check into the hotel, let the secretary know that you were in Ipswich and available and then they would send a message. So you couldn't go very far and eventually when they had an hour or half an hour to spare they'd send for you and then you'd give them the spiel and show them what product you had.[20]

As a young salesman for Fox in Yorkshire in the 1930s, Percy Livingstone covered such towns as Huddersfield and Halifax. The trickiest cinemas to deal with were the small-town operators who had no opposition and therefore could pick and choose which films they wanted to book. Every week, across the country, thousands of deals were negotiated between distributors and cinema owners, each one recorded individually. Much of the work was done at night, when the cinema managers had time to meet the sales reps. The meetings seldom took place in offices. The sales reps were just as likely to meet their clients in fish-and-chip shops or pubs. They would be expected to make around 25 calls a week. They would license films to cinemas up to a year in advance. A law was eventually passed saying that bookings couldn't be made more than six months in advance.

The salesmen worked hard to keep their clients happy. They didn't carry much to help them beyond their contract forms and some basic publicity material. Often, the films they were selling weren't even completed yet. 'You had to alter your personality depending on the person you were going to see,' Livingstone recalled of his days on the road, selling films for Fox.

> In Huddersfield, which was my key territory, there was a man called Mr Hurst at the Premiere, Huddersfield, a little district cinema. He was a very dignified gentleman and the mode of address was very deferential. You'd move over to another place where there was a man called Jackson and unless you matched him with his swearing, you didn't stand a chance to get into it at all. You had to really subdue your own personality and take on the personality that would get the maximum reaction from the person you were trying to sell to.[21]

If a film had been doing bad business elsewhere, the salesmen would offer to switch it for one that had been received with more enthusiasm. They might also reduce terms on future bookings. (It was in neither of their interests for the exhibitors to lose money.)

Sometimes, the salesmen would use their own home-made ruses to try to tantalise their clients. For example, when Percy Livingstone was representing *The Riverside Murder* (1935), he sent out postcards to the exhibitors, asking them 'Who Committed the Riverside Murder?' This was an unprepossessing British murder mystery produced by Fox UK at Wembley Studios for quota purposes and mainly notable for the first screen performance of Alastair Sim, one of British cinema's greatest character actors.

To some, the life of the 'film traveller' seemed enviable. Salesman John Hogarth later remembered his astonishment at the vast salary and perks he was offered in the early 1950s: 'Twenty-five pounds a week and a car! Talk about being knocked over with a feather! I just really was so staggered by this. Amazing – I mean more than doubling your salary and getting a company car into the bargain.'[22]

The salesmen's work was relatively straightforward and they tended not to be paid on commission. Success was judged on the box-office performance of the films they were representing – and that was something over which they had little or no influence. Livingstone later recalled:

> You may have a year when you had a very dull patch and a year when you had an extraordinarily good patch. That was not within the control or due to the efforts of the salesman. You couldn't penalise a salesman if the product they were getting was not commercial.

By Livingstone's calculations, there was a margin of about 30 per cent dependent on good and bad selling. 'Good selling would make a difference of 10 to 15 per cent. Bad selling would make a reduction of 10 to 15 per cent.'[23]

Even so, it wasn't always a cushy life. Livingstone remembered a grim story, hopefully apocryphal, that did the rounds, about one company whose sales manager treated his 'film travellers' in utterly ruthless fashion:

> The story went a salesman visited a certain cinema and he was under pressure to get his quota by the end of the week. The result was that he had a heart attack and died whilst on the toilet. The exhibitor rang up the sales manager and said Mr So and So has passed away. He is on our toilet. The cynical response was, take the contracts out of his pocket and post them.[24]

Only once the contracts were safely dealt with did the sales manager worry about such matters as removing the body or informing the next of kin.

Neither side of the industry hid its exasperation at the quota legislation that forced them both to distribute and show a number of British films. As mentioned, the Cinematograph Films Act 1927 required British films to be shown in British cinema by law.

In their later comments, distributors were openly disdainful of the so-called 'quota quickies'. According to Livingstone:

> They were rubbish with an odd exception. Certain exhibitors used to play them before the audience was let in so they could enter it into their quota book. I also remember certain exhibitors would say 'you play the opening reel and the last reel, nothing happens in between.' They used to cut out the middle altogether. They [quickies] were not respected. They were programme fillers and they didn't do anyone any good at all.[25]

This was a familiar sentiment, echoed throughout the industry. Quota quickies were made to fulfil legal obligations and the fact that there were some decent films among them – including some of the brilliant British director Michael Powell's early directorial efforts – was regarded as no more than coincidence.

In his autobiography, *A Life in Movies*, Powell was very frank about the way the quota system worked in practice:

> In 1931, the only people interested in backing quota films were the big American companies who had hundreds of films to unload and couldn't, unless they shared the bill with a British film. To achieve this they were prepared to finance second features made in England. They drove a hard bargain, and the going rate for the intrepid producers and financiers of these quota-quickies was one pound sterling per foot of film, cash on the table.[26]

His first film as a director, *Two Crowded Hours* (1931), financed by Fox, was intended as a 40-minute film, to be made at the rate of four minutes of finished film a day. Powell finished the film in a fortnight and was shooting his next feature, *Rynox*, a week later. Powell recalled that *Two Crowded Hours* had its trade screening at the Palace Theatre in Cambridge Circus, London. It was customary to show quota quickies before the big Hollywood attractions and Powell was disconcerted that the audience, here for professional reasons, didn't turn up until halfway through the screening. Even so, the film was received with a fair amount of enthusiasm.

Powell's memories don't entirely support the idea that quota films were either ignored altogether or treated with contempt. Some, at least, appear to have been received respectfully.

The quota legislation prompted US distributors based in the UK either to commission low-budget British films from UK companies or to produce them themselves. These distributors were at the heart of a revival in British film-making that would win the Brits their first Oscars and transform international attitudes toward British cinema. It is a little-noted irony that the same legislation which led to all the supposedly 'unwatchable' quickies indirectly sparked a gold rush in British cinema.

As one quota quickie director, Adrian Brunel, noted, quota quickies gave technicians and artists 'continuity of employment' and enabled them to become 'expert performers in their fields'.

It was no coincidence that the 1930s saw major investment in new British studios, among them Denham, Pinewood and Elstree.

A pivotal figure in British distribution, whose contribution is still little acknowledged, was a monocle-wearing, public-school- and Oxbridge-educated British aristocrat nicknamed 'the Wicked Uncle'. Richard Norton (later Lord Grantley) was a World War I veteran and former banker who became a noted man about town in high-society London in the 1920s. One of Norton's bosses at bankers Kuhn Loeb was a director at Paramount. When Norton became 'obsessed' (as he wrote in his autobiography, *Silver Spoon*) with the idea 'of going into films', the contact offered to sort him out a job at Paramount to 'learn distribution'. In the event, on the advice of his old friend Sam Goldwyn, he decided to work for the London branch of United Artists instead. By his own admission, as a 'society figure' and retired Guards officer, he cut an incongruous figure in the world of British film distribution. He was starting at the bottom rung of the movie business, although, in his private life, he was close personal friends with Charlie Chaplin and Mary Pickford, the founders of United Artists (UA). Murray Silverstone, head of United Artists in the UK, was initially suspicious of him in the extreme – until he realised that Norton really was serious about his new profession.

Working 'extremely hard' as a film apprentice, Norton learned about printing and editing as well as about 'the technical details of distribution'. His hankering was to move into production. He later recalled:

> United Artists, like other distributors, were compelled by the Quota Act to include a certain proportion of British films among those they handled [...] Previously they simply met their legal obligation by buying ready-made British films as cheaply as possible. Somehow I bamboozled Murray Silverstone into agreeing that we should try something more ambitious, directly sponsoring British production by commissioning different people to make films for us; and I got him to agree that the man to do the commissioning was me.[27]

Thus it was, in the summer of 1931, that Norton, as an extension of his work in distribution, was put in charge of the production of a slate of six films. One of these was *His Lordship*, the debut feature by Michael Powell (soon to blossom forth as one of British cinema's most important directors). The relative success of Norton's upmarket version of quota quickies enabled him to work on more ambitious projects. He brought United Artists aboard *Perfect Understanding* (1933), a British-made vehicle for Hollywood silent star Gloria Swanson, who was then trying to revive her career in 'talkies'. The film, which co-starred Laurence Olivier, wasn't a success but, unabashed, Norton persuaded Silverstone to allow him to give the flamboyant Hungarian film-maker Alexander Korda a six-film contract. At the time, Korda had been making quota films for Paramount with mixed success.

The first of the titles that Korda made for United Artists was *The Private Life of Henry VIII* (1933) – and this turned out to be one of the most significant films in British production history. Scripted by Korda's fellow Hungarian Lajos Bíró, it was a determinedly bawdy and knockabout foray into Tudor times. Korda's starting point, according to Norton, was that his Yorkshire-born lead actor, Charles Laughton, looked like Henry VIII.

'Henry VIII had six wives. Catherine of Aragon was the first: but her story is of no particular interest – she was a respectable woman and so Henry divorced her,' reads the opening intertitle, signalling the film's debunking, tongue-in-cheek and often saucy approach to history at the very outset. Korda's interest is in sex, death and slapstick. 'I wonder what he looks like in bed,' is one of the first lines of dialogue as various pretty women clamour around his bed chamber. Next, we're straight on to an execution scene.

At the same time as it pokes fun at Tudor misbehaviour, the film foregrounds the trappings of heritage and royalty – magnificent palaces, crests of arms, lavish costumes.

Laughton ended up giving a very rambunctious performance as the English king with the gargantuan appetites and the morbid habit of executing his wives (played by Merle Oberon, Wendy Barrie and Elsa Lanchester, among others). We see him bellowing, laughing, chewing chicken legs and strutting out his chest. It's a magnificently hammy performance, albeit one touched with pathos. Laughton ended up winning Best Actor Oscar, the first British performer to do so, and the film was a runaway critical and box-office hit in the US and the UK.

'*The Private Life of Henry VIII* is the best picture made in this country, the finest film we have so far turned out in our studios,' enthused the trade press. '[It] will do more for the prestige of British pictures than all the "windy" writing and talk imaginable.'[28]

If anything, *Henry VIII* was more appreciated in the US than it had been back in Britain. As the *New York Times* wrote in an admiring review, the film 'was not always received with unstinted praise on the other side of the Atlantic, because, although it was admittedly a clever production, some of the critics resented the buffooning of the fiery and amorous monarch.'[29]

The film premiered at the Radio City Music Hall in October 1933. The advertising campaign emphasised the risqué elements in the story. The film was marketed as 'a super-colossal portrait of a forgiving soul, always ready to bury the hatchet – in his wife's neck'.

Korda's movie had a transformative effect on the British film industry. Its success suggested that British movies could work in the American market – something that had previously been only a pipe

9. Majestic: *The Private Life of Henry VIII* played for two months in autumn 1933 at London's showcase Leicester Square Theatre (building demolished in 2015). The distributor's publicity materials for cinemas included posters and front-of-house stills.

Film still (above) and poster (top left) – source: Getty Images/Archive Photos; poster (top right) – source: BFI Stills © ITV Global Entertainment dream. Back in Britain, financiers who had until then been wary about investing in British production began to regard the sector in an altogether more favourable light. Korda was offered a long-term contract by United Artists and eventually became a shareholder in the corporation.

There was yet more evidence that cinema was crossing class boundaries. The 1930s marked a golden age in cinema building in the UK. As the *Kinematograph Year Book* noted in its 1931 edition, there was 'an unparalleled expansion' going on. Small and large towns alike were 'erecting well designed and equipped' cinemas. In 1930 alone, 200 new cinemas were built.

What wasn't acknowledged (and never really has been) was the crucial role of the distribution company – United Artists' British branch – in financing and marketing the film. This was a project which might never have been made had it not been for the much-resented quota legislation of 1927 and the obligations it placed upon British distributors and exhibitors to showcase local movies. Korda's flair was as much for marketing and distribution – for old-fashioned showmanship – as it was for production.

The Private Life of Henry VIII was a quintessentially British film but one with an international feel and appeal. At the same time, the 1930s saw British producers making comedies and musicals with local stars – films that could recoup their costs in the domestic market alone. The attitude toward British film among distributors was clearly changing. No longer was there the habit of 'obliterating' from posters any hint that a film was British in case that put the spectators off. Distributors could now sell movies on the back of British stars like 'Lancashire lass' Gracie Fields, dancing divinity Jessie Matthews and gap-toothed, ukulele-playing comedian George Formby.

Formby's success was revealing. It was achieved without his ever becoming especially popular in London, let alone abroad. As *Picturegoer* noted, his popularity owed 'nothing to the shrill applause of the West End crowd'. Formby was born in Wigan in 1904. The cheery comedian and singer was the son of a music-hall artist. Formby was a regional star who became a national phenomenon. His film career was kick-started by distributors in the low-budget world of quota quickies. His debut feature, *Boots! Boots!* (1934), budgeted at £3,000, was shot in a one-room studio over a garage in Albany Street, London. His biographer John Fisher reveals that before shooting could even begin, the film-makers had to ring a bell 'to stop the clatter of engines down below'.[30] The 78-minute film, in which Formby starred as a boot boy in the upmarket hotel, was made by Blakeley's Film Company (Manchester-based and also known as Manchurian Films) and distributed on behalf of Blakeley's by KRS stalwarts Butcher's Film Service (one of the founding members of the society). George's wife – and de facto manager – Beryl co-starred as a maid. Watch it today and you can see just what Formby was going on about when he joked: 'it was so dark in places you had to strike matches to see it.' Nonetheless, the film and its successor, *Off the Dole*, were highly effective star vehicles in which, as the trade press noted, the humour was 'breezily dispensed by a star who knows his public'. The films were profitable enough to persuade Basil Dean, the producer then in charge of Associated Talking Pictures at Ealing, to sign up Formby. The comedian went on to make eleven films at Ealing, most of them distributed by United Artists.

By 1937, Formby was second only to Gracie Fields as a British box-office attraction.

Much of our knowledge of the specific detail of the British film industry in the early 1930s comes from the groundbreaking *Statistical Survey of the Cinema Industry in Great Britain in 1934* by Simon Rowson (see *Blackmail* chapter), who was a distributor and former president of the KRS as well as an academic. His research revealed that around 80 per cent of cinemagoers sat in the cheap seats. This suggested that, although cinema reached into every part of British society, it was still primarily a working-class form of entertainment. Formby and Fields inhabited a world a long way removed from that of Alexander Korda or the smart Mayfair comedies of their era, but their extraordinary popularity chimes with Rowson's research.

One of the eternal truisms of British film history is that success often seems the quickest path to failure. In the wake of *The Private Life of Henry VIII*, there was reckless expansion of the production sector. Local production became so over-extended that there was a mini crash toward the end of the decade, and even US production money retrenched from the UK as World War II broke out.

CHAPTER 4

The Third Man

There are some telling notes in the records of the KRS committee meetings held late during World War II. Throughout the war, distributors were confronted with daunting and unlikely new challenges which, eventually, they began to see as a normal part of their business. In March 1944, when the KRS came together for an emergency session, there was a sense of resignation about their deliberations. They were there to discuss 'what steps should be taken to provide exhibitors with stand-by programmes to cover the period during which troop movements in connection with the invasion of the Continent might cause dislocation of traffic'.[1]

D-Day was then less than three months away. The problem confronting British film distributors was how to get their movies to cinemas when the country's roads and railways were clogged up by hundreds of thousands of Allied soldiers, off to fight the Nazis. This was just another new challenge to be overcome. There was an air of stoicism about the way the distribution sector confronted it.

Almost five years before, it had looked briefly as if the film business was going to be mothballed for the entire war. In early September 1939, the government temporarily closed all places of entertainment. This provoked frantic lobbying from leading industry figures desperate to encourage the politicians to change their minds. The exhibitors and distributors had been wrong-footed by the decision, having been informed by the Ministry of Information before war was declared that the government 'recognised the importance of the film industry and the valuable assistance which it could render to the Government and country generally'.[2]

A deputation from the industry was dispatched to the Home Office for a meeting on the afternoon of 14 September.

The War Cabinet relented, accepting that 'closing theatres and cinemas, if continued indefinitely, would have a bad effect on public morale'.[3]

At a secret War Cabinet meeting, again on 14 September 1939, the government also acknowledged that unless it quickly provided detailed information about its future plans for cinema, the distributors and exhibitors would be forced into the 'disbandment of their organisation, the closing of the premises, the dismissal of the staff etc.'[4] There was some rapid backtracking. The Home Secretary proposed that 'cinemas and other places of entertainment in evacuation areas should, for the present, be allowed to remain open until 10pm, except in the case of a small area in central London where the closing hour should be 6pm'.[5]

In the short term, the distributors rushed into place special measures for 'substitute' and 'stand-by' programmes and for transferring bookings to later dates. They also moved quickly to stop exhibitors from using the chaos caused by the closing of the cinemas as an excuse to 'cancel any engagement for the hire of films already entered into'.[6] Their patriotic desire to support the war effort was counterbalanced by their continuing determination to run their businesses along sound economic lines.

'The immediate evacuation of millions of people from town to country, the temporary closing of every theatre in the land; the stringent ARP [Air Raid Precaution] regulations; the absorption of man power by the services; the restriction of transport facilities; the black-out' – the *Kinematograph Year Book* of 1940 listed the problems which had threatened to deliver the movie business 'a knockout blow'.[7] It was an obvious source of pride that the film industry, like the country as a whole, was managing to soldier on in such adverse circumstances.

The cinemas being allowed to stay open was a first step. Equally important was ensuring that new movies would be available to show in them. It was clear that fewer Hollywood movies would be in circulation while British production, in the short term at least, had all but stopped.

Alexander Korda sprang into action, making patriotic potboiler *The Lion Has Wings* in double-quick time to remind everyone of cinema's power as a rousing propaganda tool. The film (production of which, Korda's biographer Charles Drazin points out, had 'actually begun some days before war was even declared')[8] was co-directed by Korda, Adrian Brunel, Brian Desmond Hurst and Michael Powell. Korda combined newsreel, historical material and sentimental pleas for the Brits to fight for what they believed in, namely truth, beauty, fair play and kindness. *The Lion Has Wings* was shown for the first time in October 1939, and travelling cinema vans were set to work to take it to parts of the country which weren't served by cinemas. Its main distribution was undertaken by United Artists. This, Drazin notes, was a source of great annoyance to the film's backers at the Ministry of Information, who had felt that the first important British propaganda film of World War II should be distributed by a *British* company. The government hadn't quite realised the UK distribution market was so dominated by Hollywood companies.

Even when Korda, producer Michael Balcon and others lobbied for film-making to continue, production rates remained very low. Nonetheless, the appetite for cinemagoing had never been higher. West End cinemas stayed open (under licence) after 6pm and still did roaring business. By late 1939, Balcon was making films at Ealing. There was also activity at Gainsborough Studios under Maurice Ostrer, and at British National under John Corfield.

Michael Powell's *The Spy in Black*, distributed by Columbia, came out a fortnight before war was declared. The film hit a nerve. It may have been set during World War I with a German hero but, as Powell noted in his autobiography, England was all but at war and 'the public wanted to see war movies' regardless.[9]

Gone with the Wind, the David O. Selznick-produced American epic, combined lush romanticism with war and destruction – a very potent mix at the British box office. The film, distributed by MGM, played in UK cinemas for almost the entire duration of the war, from the Blitz to D-Day. Not even the premium ticket prices put off spectators, who turned up in vast numbers.

Although ticket prices were increased in general thanks to the government's hiking up of entertainment tax, and there was the obvious danger of bombing of cinemas, spectator numbers continued to rise. By 1940, annual British cinema admissions exceeded a billion and by the end of the war, they were at over 1.5 billion. There were over 30 million attendances every week at British cinemas, an astonishing figure given the country's population was then around 50 million.

Home Secretary and Minister of Home Security Herbert Morrison later wrote a memorandum (27 June 1941) circulated to the War Cabinet, which laid out government thinking on wartime leisure activities. The government wanted to provide 'reasonable facilities' for public recreation but did not want to divert 'man power' and resources that could be devoted to the war effort. Cinema's attraction was that it worked both as recreation and as propaganda.

Cinema, though, wasn't the only leisure form that the government allowed to continue.

The pros and cons of allowing horse racing in wartime were assessed in detail – and the sport was compared favourably, in safety terms at least, to filmgoing. 'The degree of dispersion over a racecourse is considerable,' Morrison mused. 'The risk to racegoers of attack is not thought to be greater than, for example, to cinema goers.'[10] This was a very obvious point. When a cinema was hit, given the concentration of people in one place, the death toll could be enormous. 'British cinemas had their full share of casualties. Out of 4,000 cinemas, 160 were totally destroyed, 60 of those in London,' Guy Morgan wrote in his 1948 book *Red Roses Every Night: An Account of London Cinemas Under Fire.*

Wartime Cabinet papers carry distressing reports of direct hits on a cinema in Brighton on 14 September 1940, with 'severe casualties', and one in East Grinstead in Sussex on a late afternoon in July 1943, also with heavy casualties.

The cinema in Brighton was the Odeon, Kemp Town. Four children and two adults were killed inside the cinema and 48 people in the surrounding area also died. The bombing happened during a Saturday matinee screening of a film called *The Ghost Comes Home* starring Billie Burke and distributed by MGM.

The cinema in East Grinstead was the Whitehall. At the time, according to author John Simkin, there were 184 people in the cinema, many of them children, watching a Hopalong Cassidy western. A warning had appeared on screen that an air raid was underway but most of the spectators ignored it. Other bombs landed in shops in the High Street. In all, 108 people were killed.

Some evidence suggests that the risks actually heightened the attraction of cinemagoing. In his study *The People's War: Britain 1939–1945*, historian Angus Calder writes that, during the Blitz, the Granada theatre chain 'offered shelter and entertainment throughout the night for their clients, and those who stayed might enjoy five feature films in succession, together with impromptu sing-a-longs and amateur variety'.[11] People took their blankets with them to screenings late at night. The cinemas were no longer just places of entertainment. It should also be added that, notwithstanding the dreadful dangers of going to the cinema during the Blitz, basement cinemas were relatively safe and popular.

Cinemas were 'new centres of communal life'. The distributors' task was to keep these cinemas stocked with the one commodity they needed more than anything else, namely new films.

Ironically, wartime upheaval which had initially threatened cinemas with closure ended up extending cinema opening hours. As Minister of Labour Ernest Bevin noted in a secret memorandum in February 1941, the 'necessities of production' required 'an ever increasing number of men and women to go and work far from their homes'. They had to live in lodgings and billets 'far away from home comforts and friends' and craved entertainment on their rest day. Bevin therefore lobbied successfully for cinemas to be allowed to open on Sundays, whatever the qualms of local authorities and churches. This was an issue which had long vexed distributors and exhibitors. (Bevin accepted, however, that in Scotland, there was such 'strong feeling' regarding 'Sunday observance' that the government would have to make an exception.)[12]

Bevin also argued that 'co-operative' Italian and German POWs should be allowed some access to British cinemas. In return for working in agriculture, forestry or quarrying, they would be allowed to go to the movies and would also be granted several other privileges. 'It will be necessary to take the press into confidence in order to guard against any misunderstanding of these changes on the part of the general public,' Bevin cautioned, realising that many British cinemagoers would be startled to learn that enemy soldiers were sharing in their recreation.[13]

There was, though, evidence of a new tolerance as well a change in appetite in British cinemagoers. They were open to argument and weren't just looking for easy escapism. As the bombs fell around them, their tastes seemed to become more discerning and more serious. These cinemagoers also showed a new-found pride in British films, which, all of a sudden, seemed to them more grown-up and more relevant to their everyday lives than the star-driven fantasies imported from Hollywood. 'Many of us believe that the war has raised the age level of mass intelligence in this country,' reads a memo from the technicians' union, the ACT, to the President of the Board of Trade on the Third Cinematographic Act. The memo continued:

> The music in *The Seventh Veil* would have been considered highbrow by the masses in 1939. In 1945, they sat through slabs of it. The argument about fascism in *Men of Two Worlds* would have bored audiences six years earlier; in 1946 they laughed with or resented our ridicule of the fascist woman according to their political viewpoint.[14]

These sentiments were widely shared. Young film-maker Roy Boulting wrote in *Picturegoer* in May 1946 about the way that British films had 'grown up' in the war. Even the names of some of the British wartime films hint at their concerns. These were films like *In Which We Serve* (1942), Noël Coward and David Lean's wartime flag-waver inspired by the experiences at sea of Captain Lord Louis Mountbatten; the same team's *This Happy Breed* (1944), a family saga stretching from 1919 to the start of World War II; and Frank Launder and Sidney Gilliat's *Millions Like Us* (1943), a home front drama set in a wartime aircraft factory. They all celebrated consensus, stoicism, and doughty British virtues of courage and fair play.

Countering these were the turbulent, seamy melodramas made at Gainsborough Studios during the war years – films like *The Man in Gray* (1943), *Madonna of the Seven Moons* (1944) and, released just after the war had ended, *The Wicked Lady* (1945). The Gainsborough stars – especially James Mason and Margaret Lockwood – were cherished by British cinemagoers.

The US studios were grumbling at not being able to take all the money their movies made at British cinemas out of the country. 'We are charged with draining the British Treasury although the earnings of American films in Britain are but small change compared with the millions that England receives from America for broadcloth, woollens, whisky and many other exports,' Paramount boss Adolph Zukor complained. Hollywood, he insisted, made the 'best pictures in the world', which was why cinemas everywhere wanted them. Britain, by contrast, 'makes them without even having America in mind'.[15]

Producer Sam Goldwyn expressed misgivings about Britain's attempts to compete with Hollywood:

> Hollywood has no monopoly on bad pictures. I find that as Britain attempts to imitate Hollywood in mass production, it is also permitting its standards of picture-making to drop distressingly. That can spell tragedy for British pictures. You do not have, any more than we do, enough great producers, writers, directors or actors to turn this medium of ours into mass production. When you attempt it, you will find British films in a rut that will take years to get out of.[16]

Leading Labour politician Herbert Morrison must have had these sentiments in mind when he responded at an exhibitors' dinner just after the war: 'I think that many good Americans will agree with me that by giving the world over-sentimentalised, over-glamorous and a quite false picture of American life, Hollywood has brought in money to the United States at the expense of American prestige and reputation.'[17]

It was clear that cinema in Britain was still a populist, working-class medium and that Hollywood films had invariably been more popular than locally produced fare. Research undertaken as part of a wartime social survey by the Ministry of Information and published in 1943 revealed that one third of the adult population went to the cinema at least once a week and that the highest proportion of cinemagoers belonged 'to the lower group of wage earners earning £5 a week or less'.[18]

Nonetheless, by 1946, the 'annus mirabilis' for British cinema, British movies were outperforming those from the US studios. Audiences who had just come through a war clearly warmed to films that reflected their experiences.

The morale of the film industry began to rise during the war years. It had certainly fallen to a low ebb in 1939, just as war was about to be declared. It wasn't so much Hitler who was upsetting the exhibitors and distributors as what they felt to be an ill-advised new Cinematograph Act of 1938, under which exhibitors' quotas had gone up.

According to the *Film Daily Yearbook*, there were 5,300 cinemas in the UK in 1938 attracting weekly admissions of 23 million and gross annual receipts of £50 million. Disney's *Snow White and the Seven Dwarfs* (1937), the first big animated feature from the 'mouse house', had done spectacular business.

The despondency came because British production had fallen into one of its familiar slumps and activity at British studios was close to grinding to a halt. There was a shortage of films and the exhibitors, as usual, were grumbling at the rental prices they were being charged by distributors. The exhibitors didn't like the barring system either. This gave certain cinemas the exclusive rights to films and stopped others from being allowed to show them. Those guilty of quota offences – and who didn't play the required number of British films – were subject to hefty fines.

According to research undertaken by *The Economist* in 1937,[19] the split in revenues was tilted toward the cinema owners. Of the approximately £40 million that the magazine calculated as being spent on cinema tickets in the mid-1930s (a figure that was continuing to rise), the government took an estimated £5 million in entertainment tax and, of the remaining £35 million, £22 million went to the exhibitors and only £13 million to the distributors. From the exhibitors' point of view, this was clearly still not enough. Their complaint was that rental costs were high even for second- and third-run films. With the shortage of product, movies were staying in circulation for even longer than they had earlier in the decade. This meant that prints were often in a poor state – which, in turn, made the cinema owners even more unhappy. Yet another grievance was the continuing cost of sound equipment.

Ten years after the talkies were introduced, the original licences the exhibitors had negotiated with manufacturers were lapsing and they were having to strike new deals.

Of course, all the squabbling and infighting began to seem petty once war was declared. Horse-trading over terms and looking for marginal commercial gains wasn't appropriate when the country was fighting for its existence.

The KRS had begun preparing for war early. Distributors were looking at how to keep their businesses running and to protect themselves against 'loss and damages resulting from air raids' should war break out from mid-1939 onwards. They were very conscious that Soho and the West End weren't likely to be the safest places for them. Beaconsfield, Pinewood, Denham, Teddington, Wembley and Elstree were all suggested as potential bases. The talk was all of streamlining and centralising. A move was made to set up a 'central dump' with its own petrol supply from which all film prints would be dispatched. It was also recommended that exhibitors place their bookings through a single address. It was debated whether extra insurance was needed for companies transporting the prints.

On 31 August 1939, the day before Hitler invaded Poland and three days before Britain and France declared war on Germany, the distributors held an emergency council meeting at the Old Compton Street offices they were shortly to vacate.

The KRS found wartime premises at Langley Park in Langley, Buckinghamshire, which it leased together with the British Board of Film Censors. The advantage of this country house was its relatively easy proximity to London, and its secluded setting. Langley wasn't too far, either, from the base on the North Circular Road that Film Transport Services was planning to use 'for film deliveries and clearance on behalf of distributors'. Their concern was to ensure that members had access to cars and petrol and that negotiations should be entered into with exhibitors as to what might happen if cinemas were closed.

Not that Langley Park was in especially good condition. The surveyors' report provided a grim list of plumbing problems. Flush tanks were out of order. Manhole covers were broken. There were leaks. The drains needed cleaning. Stoppers were missing and not all the WCs were in working order.[20] It was certainly a far cry from Hollywood.

To vex the distributors further, as soon as war started, the price of film stock (on which movies were shot and printed) shot up. As the war progressed and the shortage of stock became more chronic, various solutions were floated. One was to limit the length of credit titles. The KRS accepted this but only if safeguards were put in place against 'any breach of contractual obligation relating to credit titles'.[21]

The Board of Trade told the distributors that only 50 per cent of the revenue from Hollywood films booked into British cinemas before the war started would be allowed to leave the country and the figure would be reduced to nearer 20 per cent for contracts struck after war had begun. The KRS was also asked to combine with The Navy, Army and Air Force Institutes (NAAFI) to supply films to the troops – but it wasn't at all clear who was supposed to pay for this service.

Meanwhile, Sir Kenneth Clark, the highly distinguished art historian who had become advisor to the Ministry of Information, told the distributors about the ministry's new scheme to produce propaganda films for the war effort. Michael Balcon was producing three short films dealing with the 'possible harmful effects of gossip during wartime'. It was expected that the KRS and the CEA would make sure these films were shown at cinemas across the land. Again, the ministry didn't specify who was expected to pick up the bill.

Producer Basil Dean, who during the war ran the Entertainments National Service Association (ENSA), was lobbying for 'people in uniform being admitted to cinemas at a cheap rate', something which went against the grain for distributors and exhibitors alike. At the same time, there were calls for the trade as a whole to organise special shows outside normal times for munitions workers, who often worked nights. One proposal the distributors and exhibitors came up with (after the Blitz and when curfew wasn't enforced) was for midnight matinees of big new films just prior to their releases. The idea was that the proceeds from such screenings would go toward paying for new Spitfires to be built.

The minutes of KRS meetings from the early years of the war reveal increasing difficulties for distributors in getting movies to their destinations. The railways weren't always reliable. There are reports of films being left in Birmingham station and never reaching their destination. Potentially, an even greater problem was that the Ministry of Labour was refusing to exempt film salesmen from conscription.

Poster prices shot up as a result of the shortage in paper and some members discussed discouraging exhibitors from using posters at all. That, though, would have meant going against all the trade's instincts for marketing and publicity.

In the end, the committee reached compromise on the poster problem. It was determined that distributors should put out only two sizes of poster: 80 × 30 and 60 × 40 (inches). 'As regards synopses, trade show cards and press sheets, all of these should be reduced in size, the synopses consisting of one sheet,' the board recommended. Only one mailing card or advertising piece was to be allowed per film and all contract forms were henceforth to be reduced to foolscap size.

The agonising over poster size may have sounded banal and Pooterish given that Britain was in the midst of war but the distributors were being deprived of the tools they needed to run their businesses successfully. There was the very real danger that the entire distribution machine would grind to a halt.

The trade was told that 'there was a real desire on the part of the War Office to discharge its responsibility without interference with or harm' to the film industry's 'legitimate commercial interests', but this was not how it always appeared to renters and exhibitors confronted with an ever-increasing number of new challenges and obstacles. Their role, it sometimes seemed, was not so much to run a commercial business as to help provide the armed forces with free entertainment. The distributors were even asked to provide feature films for the offices of the War Cabinet at the cut-price rate of £2.10 per feature, 'the films being for exhibition to the staff of the War Cabinet who were not actually on duty'.[22]

One of the strangest items in the KRS minutes from wartime meetings is a request from the War Office for a 'proposed reciprocal arrangement' through the Red Cross for 'showing films to British Prisoners of War in Germany and German films to German Prisoners of War in this country'. The KRS board agreed to the proposal in principle, 'subject to all the necessary safeguards and provisions being made'.[23]

From a vantage point of many years later, the idea of shipping out British and American films to Nazi-controlled POW camps seems very strange. The sheer logistics of transporting prints behind enemy lines was daunting – but this was typical of the type of problems that confronted distributors throughout the war years.

Scrimping and saving, making do and mending became the everyday way of doing business. A special meeting was held by the KRS to discuss whether they could do more to conserve tin. This meant cutting back on the storage of negatives and dupes and making sure that when films were destroyed, the tins in which they were contained were not.

Distributors were told they would be the ones collecting purchase tax on behalf of the government.

They also faced huge difficulties in holding on to their staff, many of whom were commandeered by the Ministry of Labour for vital war work. A memo after a meeting with the Ministry of Labour made it clear that women in their twenties were now off limit. 'The industry must seek to obtain substitutes of girls under 17 or women over 30, principally married women over the latter age.'

This, of course, meant that the film business, previously dominated by men, was now accessible to female workers, many of whom had been trained as projectionists.

During the war, in spite of all the privations and harassments that distributors and exhibitors faced, the British film industry grew in value. On 3 January 1946, the *Kinematograph Weekly* reported that the industry was worth approximately £20 million more than it had been a year before. Share prices in the major British companies ABPC (Associated British Pictures Corporation), Odeon, Gaumont-British, and British and Dominion had risen very sharply.

During the war years, the Rank Organisation in particular had grown and grown. The vertically integrated company was, by 1946, as big as any of the Hollywood majors. It owned studios, cinemas, labs, newsreels and equipment manufacturers, had many production companies under its wing, was increasingly active abroad, was building up its own star system complete with publicity department – and was beginning to dominate UK distribution as well.

Since the mid-1930s, General Film Distributors, controlled by

Rank, had been the dominant British distribution company. Film-makers grumbled about the influence that the distributors exercised on which movies were made. 'They were virtually in charge of production, story, cast and presentation,' David Lean later complained in the *Penguin Film Review*. Films were financed through distributors' advances. Lean wrote of hair-raising afternoons in Soho screening rooms in which these distributors would look at early cuts of films they had invested in – and would regularly demand wholesale changes. The film-makers resented what they regarded as an arrogant belief by distributors that only they knew what would work at the box office. 'People who sell and exhibit think that the producers and directors are wild and woolly men who don't know what the public wants,' Lean concluded.[24]

There is an obvious irony here. As evidenced by the minutes of their meetings, the distributors felt beleaguered. They were intensely suspicious that they were being hoodwinked by producers misrepresenting their films, and by exhibitors falsifying box-office returns. They, though, were regarded with the same suspicion by other sectors of the industry.

There were murmurings that Rank was beginning to exercise a monopolistic hold on the industry. President of the Board of Trade Stafford Cripps declared in early 1946:

> I have decided to seek undertakings that the three major circuits [Gaumont-British, Odeon and ABC] will allot a proportion of screen time to the films of independent producers as an addition to the amount of screen time which they must already allocate to British films under the 1938 Act [...] The selection of films for this purpose will rest in the hands of an independent board to be appointed by myself.

Read through the trade press from the period and you encounter many clashing and contradictory points of view. There was a new-found national pride in British cinema and a sense that British audiences wanted to see home-grown movies. At the same time, there was also an exasperation at the austerity of the war years and a craving for the escapism that Hollywood still provided. Independent exhibitors were lobbying to be allowed to play fewer British films than the big circuits did – hardly an endorsement of local movies. There were anyway far too few British films to go round.

Postwar Britain was reeling from chronic shortages of the most basic goods and materials. 'Britain is confronted with an industrial crisis so serious that this dislocation makes the interference of the Luftwaffe seem trivial in comparison,' an editorial in the *Kinematograph Weekly* lamented.[25] Thanks to the national fuel emergency, cinemas were unable to open before 4pm. Studios at Shepherd's Bush and Islington both had to close down and Ealing was operating on a small generator.

One film which captures the mood of the times, although not set in Britain but in bombed-out, rubble-strewn postwar Vienna, is Carol Reed's *The Third Man*. Scripted by Graham Greene, this is a story about an American writer of dime westerns called Holly Martins who comes to the city to visit his old friend Harry Lime. No sooner has Martins arrived than he discovers his old friend has apparently been hit and killed by a car. Martins then learns that Lime was wrapped up in a penicillin-smuggling racket and that children are dying agonising deaths as a result of his scam. Lime turns out not to be as dead as Martins had first thought. The film was produced by Alexander Korda together with *Gone with the Wind*'s David O. Selznick. It was shot on location in Vienna and at Shepperton Studios. Orson Welles played Harry Lime, 'the disarmingly shameless scoundrel', as the character was styled by the *Monthly Film Bulletin*.

Quite apart from its exhaustively chronicled qualities as a thriller, *The Third Man* caught the mood of Britain in the late 1940s: the disillusionment and deprivation. This was an era of austerity (even bread was rationed), black markets, spivs and bureaucratic intervention in every area of life.

The genius of the film lay in its credentials both as a highly entertaining mass-market thriller and as an 'art' film, complete with heavily stylised chiaroscuro lighting from cinematographer Robert Krasker and its famously atmospheric zither music from Anton Karas. As the *Daily Mail* wrote of its director Reed, he had both won the 'approval of the highbrows' and 'given the ninepennies a storming entertainment'.

The Third Man also offered an example of the collaborative but very strained relationship between the British film industry and its partners in Hollywood. Inevitably, the two egotistical producers Korda and Selznick fell out over the movie. Korda bitterly resented Selznick's interference. He had commissioned Greene's screenplay in the first place and had given the American producer the US distribution rights in return for financial support and help in luring Hollywood stars. The film was distributed by British Lion in the UK and premiered at the Plaza Theatre in London's West End to enthusiastic reviews. However, as historian Charles Drazin noted, Selznick still insisted on previewing it in the US and then cutting it based on the responses of the preview audience.[26]

Karas had been discovered in Vienna by director Reed, busking with his zither. His music, which plays over the credits, was crucial to the film's atmosphere. It also spawned one of the UK film industry's first 'tie-in' albums. As *Billboard* magazine reported, 'the disc has been one of England's top-sellers on the English Decca label, reportedly going 400,000 in two months.'[27]

Ironically, Arthur Jarratt, the boss of the distributor British Lion (and later president of the KRS), had tried to have the Karas music removed prior to release. He sent a telegram to Reed praising the movie but requesting: 'please take off the banjo.'

The Third Man opened in London (the first place in the world to open the film) in early autumn 1949, just six months after Laurence Olivier's *Hamlet* had become the first non-US film to win the Best Picture Oscar. This was a golden era for ambitious, artistically adventurous British cinema. Alongside Reed and Olivier, David Lean was doing exceptional work (*Oliver Twist, Great Expectations*), as were Michael Powell and Emeric Pressburger with features as bold as *A Matter of Life and Death, Black Narcissus* and *The Red Shoes*.

Reed's movie was very well reviewed at the time, and is one of those films whose reputation has, if anything, grown – it topped the 'BFI 100' poll of British films in 1999 and remains on many UK and US critics' all-time favourite/masterpiece lists.

With *Odd Man Out* and *The Fallen Idol* also released in the 1940s, Carol Reed enjoyed a formidable reputation. *The Third Man* was an instant hit on its initial release in Europe and the US in 1949/50, and it was one of British cinema's biggest box-office successes in 1949.

10. Masterpiece: Just days after Carol Reed's film had opened in London's West End in September 1949, it played at 'special pre-release screenings' around the UK before going on general release on 3 October. Suburban and provincial cinemas rebooked it two or three times, while it continued to play in the West End, where takings actually rose week on week. In January 1950, *The Third Man* was launched in Scotland with a midnight performance at Edinburgh's Regal cinema, for which queues reportedly formed over three hours before the start.

Film poster (top) – source: Getty Images/Movie Poster Image Art
© StudioCanal UK Ltd; photograph – source: BFI Stills

The irony, as ever, was that just as Reed, Powell and Pressburger, and David Lean were making what are still regarded as some of the greatest films in British cinema history, the British film industry as a whole was again threatening to stall.

British Lion had been in existence as a distribution company since the 1920s but Korda had taken it over in 1946. At that time, there was huge optimism about the ability of British films to compete in the international marketplace and Korda was keen to create his own film company to match the one that J. Arthur Rank had been building. Korda had revived his old production company London Film Productions but needed to make new distribution arrangements as he no longer had a stake in United Artists (which had distributed his earlier movies with success). As Karol Kulik, another of Korda's biographers, notes, British Lion had survived and even prospered in a market dominated by the 'larger American and Rank-owned distribution companies' thanks to its contract with the small but prolific Hollywood 'Poverty Row' studio Republic, which turned out westerns and low-budget action movies in their droves.[28]

Korda saw the British Lion Film Corporation as a vehicle for his own empire-building. Having acquired a controlling interest in the company in January 1946, he went on to negotiate British Lion's purchase of a 74 per cent stake in Sound City (Films) Ltd, the production company which owned Shepperton Studios, and he contracted with Fox to distribute his films in the US. The hitch was that his big-budget postwar movies like *An Ideal Husband* (1947), *Anna Karenina* (1948) and *Bonnie Prince Charlie* (1948) were damp squibs at the box office.

In the late 1940s, a trade war broke out between the British film industry and its American partners. The British economy was in a parlous state after six years of war. The postwar government led by Prime Minister Clement Attlee was desperate to stop money leaking away on luxury imports. In 1947, the British Exchequer had therefore introduced an '*ad valorem*' tax that entitled it to 75 per cent of Hollywood movies' earnings in the British marketplace. Inevitably, the Americans cried foul. They protested that such a tax was illegal and reacted by putting an embargo on US films coming to Britain.

Given that an estimated 80 per cent of playing time in British cinemas was given over to US films and British production was languishing with an output of under 50 features a year, it was clear that distributors and exhibitors were facing a nightmarish situation. Soon, if the embargo held, there would be nothing to play in British cinemas. Rank responded by going on a patriotic production drive, announcing he would spend $40 million on 47 new features in 1948. Korda likewise ramped up production, announcing he would spend $20 million on 13 new features.

In the event, in the spring of 1948, the Hollywood embargo was ended. Rank was left in a difficult position when it came to deciding what to show in his cinemas. He had dozens of new British films but was competing against a huge backlog of Hollywood product – and the audiences in his own theatres seemed to prefer the American movies. The enthusiasm for British movies that had been so evident at the end of the war was already beginning to dissipate.

Korda, meanwhile, ran into acute financial difficulty. British Lion needed to be bailed out by the National Film Finance Corporation with a £2 million loan (subsequently increased to £3 million). Public funds were being pumped into a privately run distribution company. As Kulik points out, this provoked 'much adverse criticism both within and outside the industry'.[29]

The tenor of the criticism underlined the relatively low regard in which distributors were held and some common misunderstandings as to what they did. To the critics, it seemed perverse to be giving money to distributors rather than to the producers and directors who actually made the movies. What their complaints overlooked was the pivotal part that distribution companies played in the commissioning as well as the releasing of films. On a practical level, lending the money to British Lion made more sense than devising criteria to hand it out piecemeal to the various producers working with the company. In effect, the government was using British Lion as a national production fund. It was a predecessor to the various state-backed film financing initiatives – the BFI Production Board or the funds run by the UK Film Council – established in later years. In theory, such a company would be more daring and independent in its decisions than the executives at Rank and ABPC where, as many independent filmmakers were wont to grumble, hard-nosed executives with no interest whatsoever in the art of cinema took upon themselves the right to decide which films would be made and which ones rejected.

In the run-up to the 1948 Films Act, there were calls for entertainment tax to be abolished and for the money to be invested in production and distribution instead. In 1950, the government introduced the Eady Levy, which was firstly run as a voluntary tax on a proportion of the price of cinema tickets. Half was kept by the exhibitors and half went to producers of the films in the UK. This arrangement was designed to prevent the levy counting as a subsidy under the General Agreement on Tariffs and Trade (GATT), to which competitors could have objected. (The Eady Levy became compulsory in 1957 and remained in place until 1985.)

Countering the prevailing gloom caused by the Hollywood boycott and the problems faced by Rank and Korda, producer Michael Balcon, managing director of Ealing Studios, went for the funny bone. Balcon told the trade press in late 1947 that comedy, 'badly neglected' by the British studios in the war years, was 'going to make a comeback'. The films the studio was about to make included such cast-iron classics as *Passport to Pimlico*, *Whisky Galore* and *Kind Hearts and Coronets*.

In spite of the prevailing mood of crisis in 1947, the trade press noted a 'considerable increase in the size of renters' release programmes'. Exhibitors were offered 628 feature films during the year – around 12 a week – of which 155 were reissues. This compared to 561 films (89 reissues) in 1946, 547 films (101 reissues) in 1945, and 553 films (110 reissues) in 1944. What these statistics underline is that considerable numbers of films were being released throughout the war years. In 1948, there were almost 5,000 cinemas in the UK with one cinema seat for every 10 people in the population. By 1946, British pictures averaged £694 at the box office compared to £583 for foreign films.[30]

In spite of the austerity, the ongoing bickering between exhibitors and distributors (the former continued to complain about rental prices throughout the decade) and the tensions between the British film industry and Hollywood, there was still a widespread and very bullish belief that the cinema business would continue to grow. In fact, as the distributors were very quickly going to find out, the business was already beginning its long and steady decline.

CHAPTER 5

Trouble in Store

In the spring of 1939, when the committee of the KRS came together to discuss 'television', the mood was relatively sanguine. The distributors present were concerned about the possible effect of TV on their businesses but they were also confident that they could keep this new potential rival at bay. There didn't seem to be any real trouble in store.

The CEA had come up with the suggestion that the daily limit of films on TV 'should not exceed 20 minutes'. For the distributors, the key question was what the government was planning. They met the Postmaster General George Tryon in May 1939 to air their concerns. At that stage, no one was even sure whether television would be restricted to 'home sets' or whether the government would allow its 'diffusion' to paying audiences. In the case of the latter option, the distributors worried that they would be facing new and unfair competition – but they also saw a potential opportunity to expand their own businesses.

It was already almost three years since the BBC had launched the first regular high-definition television service in November 1936. Not that television was new. Even further back, in 1925, Selfridges department store in Oxford Street, London, had staged public demonstrations of the medium. As historian Mark Aldridge notes, TV wasn't then seen as a competitor to the cinema. Rather, it was an intriguing new device.[1]

From 1936 onwards, the BBC began transmitting two hours of material every day. Typical fare included some musical comedy, some juggling and items of British Movietone News. Early broadcasts were produced by Dallas Bower, who had worked as a sound technician on Alfred Hitchcock's *Blackmail* (the first British talkie) in 1929 and who later had the idea for Laurence Olivier's wartime film of *Henry V*, on which he was an associate producer.

Bower had realised earlier than almost anyone else that cinema and television were on a collision course. In a 1934 article, he wrote: 'for purposes of entertainment television must be synonymous with film.'[2]

'The establishment of universal television, so assiduously dreaded by cinema hall and newspaper proprietors, will do for broadcasting what sound did for silent cinema,' Bower suggested in his 1936 book, *Plan for Cinema*. 'What is entertainment television if it is not cinema in the home?' he asked. 'The television receiver, as addition to and part of the broadcast receiver, visually is identical with the amateur ciné screen.' He predicted confidently that TV would consist of 'the dialogue film in the main'.[3]

Just because Bower's observations were accurate, it didn't mean that others were keen to endorse them. There was a degree of ostrich-like self-deception in the film industry's attitude toward TV.

In the mid-1930s, Bower pointed out, quite correctly, that big cinemas would be looking to offer their audience spectacle and colour. They needed, he suggested, 'an alternative to the kind of entertainment they provide at present. It would be much too similar to television otherwise.'[4]

What is intriguing about Bower's predictions is that they were made at a time when British filmgoing was on a very rapid upward curve. A decade later, when British cinemagoing reached its peak of 1.6 billion, no one seemed too concerned about the threat from the new medium.

The war helped. The Brits were too busy fighting Hitler to devote time to refining TV technology and expanding the television audience. Even so, the spectre of television was always there, flickering ominously in the back of distributors' minds. In 1946, J. Arthur Rank told the 'Television Advisory Committee' that television, with 'the comparatively small number of receiving sets in private houses', did not yet affect the industry. 'But with the technical and other advances which may reasonably be expected in British television in the future, the film industry foresees the possibility of encroachment.'[5]

At one stage, the visionary young Rank technician and art director David Rawnsley had encouraged Rank to use TV to make movies through a new company, Television Film Production Ltd. He advocated film-making on an assembly-line principle with 10 to 15 minutes being shot every day instead of the 1.5 to 2 minutes that was generally achieved on British film sets of the time.

'Where I have had ridicule from film people at the suggestion that we might make a feature in a fortnight after 6 months' preparation, at a cost of between £20,000 and £30,000, I have had the reverse attitude from television people,' Rawnsley wrote.[6] His idea was for quick, inexpensive movies for TV, using standard interiors assembled from 'a few basic units' that, as a colleague at the Rank Organisation observed, could be 'stored away for next time'. His ideas fed into what was to become known as 'Independent Frame'. He aimed to use special effects, miniatures and split screen instead of relying on lengthy and expensive set building. The ideas were visionary but the films made through the process, *Poet's Pub*, *Warning to Wantons* and *Stop Press Girl* among them, seemed to audiences and critics to be stilted and artificial. Rawnsley's utopian dream of film and TV industries coming together in harmony turned out to be very misplaced.

By the late 1940s, the fear of the new medium was intensifying. Rank's idea that the film industry would have its own TV studios where TV programmes would be 'prepared for public showing' was accurate enough in its way but failed to acknowledge the destructive effect TV might have on the film industry. As Asa Briggs notes, in 1947 and 1948, both he and Alexander Korda were far more interested in 'showing large screen television in the cinema circuits they controlled than in selling films to the BBC'.[7]

Their blithe optimism that cinema attendances would continue to rise was soon shattered. 'The British public has lost £12,000,000 of the £30,000,000 which it invested in British film production during the twelve months ending in March 1947,' trade paper *Kinematograph Weekly* announced in a dour news report as share prices in film companies dipped.[8]

At the same time, as the *Pelican Cinema Book* 1951 noted, 'forests of television aerials' were 'sprouting in every town and suburb'.

Distributors just needed to raise their eyes and look at the rooftops to realise just how rapidly television was spreading. There were already 2 million TV licences in 1953, up from 800,000 in 1951 – and there would be 12 million a decade later.[9] In the same period, cinema audiences were declining, falling from the giddy heights of 1.6 billion in 1946 to only 500,000 by the early 1960s.

The BBC's epic, seven-hour broadcast of the Queen's coronation at Westminster Abbey in June 1953 helped to drive public acquisition of TV sets.

The coronation was shown to audiences in cinemas, hospitals and church halls as well as on TV. (It was an early example of what would later be called event releasing.) Many neighbours would crowd into homes with a TV set to watch the coronation as it happened, in all its 405-line monochrome glory, a huge novelty for a gigantic audience. The sheer drama and excitement for families in watching TV for the first time is well captured in John Boorman's autobiographical film *Queen and Country* (2014). We see the father on the roof, fiddling with the aerial, and his family below calling out to him just when a steady image has been achieved. The image quality may be poor but the very fact the TV is working at all is considered a cause for celebration.

If the encroachment of the BBC wasn't enough to frighten the film business, further alarm was felt when, after much debate, Parliament passed a Television Bill in 1954 that ushered in the beginnings of independent television. The ITA service began in September 1955.

Big film companies like the Rank Organisation and Granada Theatres were members of consortia bidding to run some of the regional ITV channels on offer. When Tyne Tees was launched in January 1959, the film producer Sydney Box was on its board. However, the fact that film companies were pragmatic enough to want to be involved in television didn't lessen their alarm at what was happening to their own businesses.

By the end of the decade, ITV channels covered 90 per cent of the population, and offered popular alternatives to the more formal BBC fare. ITV had success with half-hour prime-time swashbuckling dramas (for example, *The Adventures of Robin Hood*), as well as US imports such as cop shows and westerns, which all helped to keep older family audiences at home and away from cinemas. This, in turn, helped to propel teenagers to the cinemas, if only because they wanted to escape their mums and dads. The rise of the teen audience was at least a small consolation for the dip in cinemagoing among other demographics.

It was dispiriting how quickly the optimism that the British film industry felt at the end of World War II vanished. Austerity, the trade war with the US (detailed in the previous chapter) and the bickering over quotas all contributed to a mounting sense of uneasiness. There was a production slump after the artificial boom of 1948 when the studios rushed to make British movies to counter the American embargo. Exhibitors failed by a huge distance to hit their quota targets for showing British films. In 1948, there were a startling 1,608 exhibitor quota defaults, up from 1,328 in 1947.

Film-makers showed signs of losing their sense of direction. During the war years, they had had a sense of purpose. After the war, they couldn't identify which subjects they should tackle – and at what cost.

'I have the feeling that picture makers generally are floundering for want of some emotional mainspring,' suggested *Great Expectations* producer Anthony Havelock-Allan during a round table on British films organised by *Sight and Sound* magazine in May 1950. He continued:

> The situation for the Independent is that he is to make films wholly in this country, he is tremendously limited in subject matter by the economic factors. He knows – or very soon finds out – that there is a top cost figure beyond which, as an Independent Producer, he is taking an enormous risk. The figure is in fact so low that only if he is confident that he has a very exceptional subject can he really honestly go into production here.[10]

Havelock-Allan was identifying the economic straitjacket in which British film-makers were increasingly confined. Their domestic market wasn't big enough for them to be able to recoup the costs of ambitious, biggish-budget films. Their chances of finding audiences (and profit) abroad were uncertain too. Their perspective therefore narrowed. The artistic extravagance and visionary quality of movies like Carol Reed's

The Third Man, David Lean's *Oliver Twist* and Powell and Pressburger's *The Red Shoes* and *A Matter of Life and Death* gave way to a more conservative approach. This was in itself paradoxical and potentially self-defeating. At a time when the rhetoric was all about making big, widescreen colour movies that television couldn't compete with, the British were instead producing a large number of modestly budgeted domestic dramas and comedies.

Rank, which had supported extravagant and visionary films from Lean and Powell as well as mega-budget flops like musical *London Town* (1946) and Gabriel Pascal's ill-fated Shaw adaptation *Caesar and Cleopatra* (1945), was becoming far more conservative in its filmmaking policy. 'You will notice that certain producers and directors are no longer with us. I have told our creative artists that their creative freedom must be related to the economic side. The two must be blended,' J. Arthur Rank told a CEA Conference in 1948.

A special debate was held at the British Film Academy at which it was acknowledged that 'a widespread television service' might eliminate any need for the cinema at all.[11]

Echoing Dallas Bower, the industry looked to cinema's unique properties, most importantly the cinema's screen size and the fact that filmgoing was a public activity. R. K. Neilson Baxter put the matter succinctly when he told the British Film Academy:

> Television does not lend itself – and I question whether it ever will – to the same vastness of approach that the film can achieve. You could not put, say, *The Covered Wagon* on television because those wonderful long shots of the wagons winding across the plain just wouldn't mean a thing.[12]

The 1950s was a decade of new formats – Eastmancolor, 3D, CinemaScope – that would show off films like *The Covered Wagon* to best effect.

Spyros Skouras, president of Twentieth Century Fox, drove hard for a new widescreen format. Skouras paid French inventor Henri Chrétien a reported $2 million for his process, which became known as CinemaScope. In Britain, it was up to Fox's UK distribution team to convince the exhibitors that they needed to equip their cinemas to show the first CinemaScope movies – sword-and-sandal epic *The Robe* and *How to Marry a Millionaire* among them. This was an uphill business that required concessions and imaginative thinking. 'We set about it by making guarantees on product and in certain cases we made a contribution,' Fox's UK managing director Percy Livingstone later recalled.[13]

The Rank Organisation dragged its feet in accepting the format in its cinemas. The Rank philosophy in the 1950s under its very exacting managing director (and former accountant) John Davis was to make films as cheaply and efficiently as possible. It was a source of great pride to Davis that, by 1954, feature films were costing between £125,000 and £200,000, 'as against double those figures'. The attitude toward new widescreen formats was clearly that they were an extravagance.

Fox, though, realised that certain cinemas had been starved of product and would embrace CinemaScope if Fox guaranteed them a regular supply of prestigious films. The Granada chain quickly came on board, as did the Essoldo circuit, on the understanding that they would be guaranteed product for two years.

Rank eventually accepted CinemaScope in its theatres. Even Davis acknowledged that certain films were best seen on the big screen. 'If they are shown on the small television screen they lose much of their quality and definition, and in fact give people the impression that films are not good. Thus we depreciate the quality of our own goods.' However, the Rank boss also refused to accept there was any need for the film industry to be afraid of television. He predicted that TV would 'take its place in modern life without causing the destruction of the film industry', and also that the film industry would continue 'to develop and supply the bulk of the people with their entertainment'.[14]

Distributors and exhibitors were far less philosophical. Their attitude toward TV quickly hardened. In 1958, they formed FIDO – the Film Industry Defence Organisation. The idea was that FIDO (backed by the CEA, the British Film Producers' Association, the Federation of British Film Makers and the Association of Specialised Film Producers) would buy rights to films to prevent them being sold on to TV. This was an expensive business but FIDO raised money by imposing a small levy on cinema admissions. By the mid-1960s, FIDO was estimated to have spent '£2 million for the removal of 925 films from broadcast'.[15]

For some distributors, FIDO became an important source of revenue. As Sue Harper and Vincent Porter note in their study of British cinema in the 1950s, British Lion received £316,000 for agreeing not to sell on movies to broadcasters – income which helped the company move into profit.[16]

In the archives of the distributors' trade organisation, there are dozens of letters giving details of 'Deeds of Covenant' with FIDO. As security (and in return for FIDO's money), the distributors assigned UK TV rights to the organisation.

For all the short-term successes, the film industry's efforts to keep TV at bay couldn't help but rekindle memories of King Canute, sitting on his throne and telling the waves to retreat.

Wary about falling audiences and the threat from TV, the big distributors consolidated during the 1950s. As James Higgins, then working for MGM and eventually to become president of SFD, noted, this was a period in which alignment and barring became even more important: 'The Odeon and the ABC people would have an unofficial agreement that they wouldn't take films from the unaligned distributors. If you fell out with ABC and tried to take it to Rank, Rank wouldn't take your films.'[17]

The major West End cinemas had 'bars' for sometimes up to a year on films going outside that particular place. There was a new emphasis on 'big' movies like *Quo Vadis* (released with an X certificate and which stayed in British cinemas for over a year) and *The Robe*. Distributors and exhibitors were determined to make an event out of the releases of such films – and that might mean keeping them on in big West End cinemas for small eternities. Higgins noted:

> If you booked the film for the Odeon Leicester Square and it was a major film, they would insist on having a bar – that you couldn't sell it to any other cinemas in the area for six weeks or a year. Normally speaking, all the major circuit cinemas in the key cities had bars that allowed them to play in the centre

before anyone in the suburbs could play. And all the provincial cinemas had bars by certain of the major cities (the outskirts) and amongst themselves, they would bar each other.[18]

Inevitably, some of the smaller players called foul. The Hollywood studios, facing their own struggles with TV as well as the far-reaching impact of a 1948 Supreme Court decision enforcing a separation of cinema holdings from production and distribution, produced fewer films. As a result, some cinemas were struggling for product. This led to a prolonged debate between distributors and exhibitors over their goals and business practices.

Seemingly stating the obvious, the Joint Committee of the CEA and the KRS pointed out in a private report that 'the function of the renter and one of the reasons for his existence [is] that he is continually devising means with his exhibitor customers to see that outstanding films are given opportunities of earning more money'.[19]

To the independents, it seemed that the barring and alignment systems were preventing audiences from seeing the best films – and thereby potentially reducing profits.

It was apparent there was a resentment of the influence that the two major players, Rank and ABPC, held over the industry.

The Plant Report into Distribution and Exhibition of Cinematograph Films (published in 1949) was commissioned by the UK government's Board of Trade to look into these grievances. Its preamble stated: 'The fundamental contention throughout our Report is that the introduction of more active competitive trading at each stage in the process of film distribution and exhibition is an essential condition for any real revival or prosperity in the industry.'

The report called for more prints of films, to speed up their showing on general release; for relaxation of the barring system; and for distributors to be required to accept the 'highest bid' and to be obliged to rent films to cinemas with the greatest box-office potential (regardless of alignment).

Perhaps most worrying for the KRS members was the report's suggestion that 'a distribution charge of 15 per cent of the receipts after deduction of disbursements is considered adequate for films of average merit, excluding the terms of any financial agreement between producer and distributor'.

Most of the recommendations appear to have been disregarded completely.

Rank's distribution arm, General Film Distributors, was charging 50 per cent rentals – a figure which exhibitors complained was far too high. 'Arthur Rank is virtually dictator of the industry,' leading exhibitor Harry Mears complained. 'Rank ignores the CEA although he is a member of it. He never consults us. Rank already dictates to the press.'[20] Exhibitors described the Rank Organisation as 'a millstone round the neck of the film industry'.[21]

There was equal antagonism toward ABPC. Years later, in 1987, producer Michael Relph wrote an article about the 1950s in British cinema in which he bemoaned the way Rank's MD John Davis and ABPC's Robert Clark 'used to sit at opposite ends of the Film Producers' Association Board Table and dictate the policy of the British film industry to suit the interests of Rank and ABC'.[22]

The KRS/CEA private report, though, demanded a reality check. Stating that 'the theory that exceptional films are wandering about in numbers failing to find the necessary number of playing dates is plausible but not borne out by reality', the report countered the idea that independent cinemas were being starved of product because of the programming policies of the two major companies. The report argued that extended runs of 'outstanding' films in key cinemas wasn't preventing these films from being seen by the public at large. The cinemas were reacting to public demand.

It was common sense that cinemas in smaller towns needed more frequent changes of programming. Once a film had been screened for a few days, the likelihood was that everyone would have seen it. You could keep *Quo Vadis* or *The Robe* playing for months on end in big London cinemas but there was no economic reason for holding any movie for longer than a week in a rural town with a population of a few thousand.

Cinemagoers paying premium prices to see big new movies in West End cinemas might book tickets in advance and would be likely to turn up on time. In regional cinemas, filmgoing habits were very different.

In 1950, Rank's Odeon and Gaumont-British cinemas together with ABPC's circuit of ABC cinemas accounted for 20 per cent of the cinemas 'and 33 per cent of the country's total seating capacity'.[23] That hardly constituted a monopoly. Critics complained about the 'inflexibility' of Rank and ABPC programming. Both booked films into cinemas for six-day runs, with old films screened on Sundays.

There were some striking regional variations. London audiences, especially those visiting the West End, saw films first. However, 'over a quarter of the films shown in the independent cinemas that dominated the four northern regions were over six months old and nearly one in ten was over a year old.'[24] It can also be guessed that print quality would have deteriorated markedly by the time films reached outlying regions.

Cinemagoing was clearly in decline. There were now many other competing leisure activities alongside TV. Car ownership was increasing. Households were more likely to have central heating. No longer was cinema a place to go to escape into the warmth. By the late 1950s, Harper and Porter note, 'half of British housewives never went to the cinema at all' and 'younger men' were becoming the bedrock of the audience. Cinemas were closing, especially small, independent theatres. However, a sense of perspective is required. Cinemagoing may not have been at 1946 levels but this was still a huge business.

'Television was still not the threat that it later became. It was still transmitting only at limited hours during the day and cinema-going was still something that most people did at least once a week and sometimes twice. So there was a good living to be earned,' British Lion's John Hogarth noted of the early 1950s.[25] Not that Hogarth painted a flattering picture of the cinemagoing experience. In his description, this wasn't an escape to a world of luxury and opulence. With patrons smoking heavily, it was a venture into the Stygian gloom:

> Very often, in addition to the feature you had a second feature, and shorts, and a newsreel. In those days a programme would be running continuously and you could come in and go out whenever you wanted to. And people didn't book, I mean there was no such thing as advance booking and there was no such

thing as, 'I must arrive at half past seven because that's when the film starts.' People used to walk in ten minutes before the end, see the end of a mystery and sit through it again. I mean, you think my goodness what a peculiar way of going on, but that's what people did. That's if you could see the screen because the screen would be observed through a thick blanket of smoke and you'd sit there with your eyes streaming because of the denseness of the smoke. And I can remember during some very heavy London fogs, when the combination of smoke and fog coming in from the outside was such that you really couldn't see the screen. And I can remember being in one cinema where they had to stop the show because the screen was obliterated entirely by the fug that was in there, it was really quite extraordinary.[26]

Bizarrely, the biggest new British star of the CinemaScope era wasn't a Marilyn Monroe-like buxom blonde or an action hero. It was diminutive British comedian Norman Wisdom from an impoverished London background, who made his debut in the very modestly budgeted *Trouble in Store* (1953).

Rank had put Wisdom, an established TV and stage comedian and singer, under contract in 1952 but hadn't known what to do with him. The flyweight boxing champion of the British army in India, Wisdom was very nimble and good at pratfalls. He combined elements of Charlie Chaplin's anarchic loner with the cheery goofiness of 1930s and 1940s star George Formby.

Wisdom had a 'little boy lost' quality and his films came infused with a sentimentality that critics of the time found all too sickly. *Trouble in Store*, co-starring Margaret Rutherford, was a modestly budgeted black-and-white comedy with nothing whatsoever extravagant about it. The Rank Organisation didn't have especially high expectations of it but, from its very first scenes of Wisdom being knocked off his bicycle by the supercilious Jerry Desmonde, it touched a nerve. Wisdom used often to tell the story of how he was ignored by the Rank chiefs outside the film's first preview at the Odeon Camden Town, but was treated by them with reverence by the end of the final reel, when they realised the spectators had loved the film.

11. A little bit of Wisdom: The UK release poster for *Trouble in Store* conveyed a welcome promise of laughter. The on-set photograph of Norman Wisdom with co-star Margaret Rutherford was taken by Bert Hardy for *Picture Post* magazine, whose accompanying editorial asked whether Wisdom would be 'Another Charlie Chaplin'.

Poster – source: BFI Stills; photograph by Bert Hardy – source: Getty Images

The comedian played a clerk in 'Burridges', a West End department store. Like Chaplin, he had an immediately identifiable outfit – a suit that was tight-fitting and too short for him, and a cap. He was the 'gump', the lovable loser/everyman put upon and tormented by managers and bureaucrats. *Trouble in Store* played relentlessly on class differences. Wisdom rode a bicycle and worked in the basement. Desmonde, as the boss of the department store, drove an expensive car and gave orders from his office upstairs. Some of the jokes (slapstick with soda streams and the like) would have seemed old-fashioned in the days of Mack Sennett – and yet British audiences loved the film (the most popular movie of the year at the British box office). The film combined knockabout comedy with sentimental crooning (Wisdom performing 'Don't laugh at me ('cause I'm a fool)' as if he were Mario Lanza).

Wisdom won the BAFTA for Most Promising Newcomer in Film in 1954, following the success of *Trouble in Store*. The Rank Organisation may have treated him with Jerry Desmonde-like disdain but the publicity department appreciated his willingness to get involved in promoting his films, dressing up as the characters he played, whether milkmen or coppers. This support from stars has of course always been extremely helpful to distributors in generating local and national publicity.

Over the next decade, Wisdom films like *One Good Turn* (1955), *The Square Peg* (1958) and *The Bulldog Breed* (1960) became staples at the box office. In the early 1960s, they were still performing on a par with blockbusters such as the James Bond movies. Their appeal for the Rank Organisation was that they were a known quantity and therefore easy to produce and distribute. Each new film was a variation on its predecessor but Wisdom never strayed too far from type. To his admirers (notably his producer Hugh Stewart), he was a clown with acrobatic skills to rival those of Buster Keaton. To the critics in the broadsheets, he was an abomination. They referred witheringly to his 'odious sentimentality', his 'gags, grimaces and goo'. They called him an 'ignorant and offensive nuisance' or 'nauseating' or 'repulsive'. There was obvious class bias in their criticisms – a contempt for a populist comedian with a huge mass appeal not only in Britain but as far afield as Soviet Russia and Albania.

From the British distributors' point of view, Wisdom was the perfect star for his era. He was dependable. Rank and ABPC were taking a formulaic and (to their detractors) conservative approach to the business in a turbulent and transitional period. Look through the list of the most popular British films of the 1950s and what is striking is how many of them were comedies that were parts of franchises. There were *Carry On* films from ABPC, for example *Carry On Nurse*, the biggest British hit of 1959. At Rank, alongside Wisdom, there were the slightly more upmarket 'Doctor' films: *Doctor in the House* (1954), *Doctor at Sea* (1955), *Doctor at Large* (1957) and *Doctor in Love* (1960). Then, there was the schooldays farce *The Happiest Days of Your Life* (1950), which spawned the later *St Trinian's* films.

Alongside the comedies, war movies – nostalgic evocations of Britain's finest hours a decade or just over before – were also solid box-office earners. *The Cruel Sea* (1953), *The Dam Busters* (1955), *Reach for the Sky* (1956) and *Sink the Bismarck!* (1960) were all among the most popular British films of their years. Britain's star system of the 1950s reflected the practical, no-nonsense approach to distribution. The big names under contract to Rank included plenty of tweed-jacketed chaps like Dirk Bogarde, Kenneth More and Jack Hawkins. This may have been the era of James Dean and Marlon Brando in the US but British cinema wasn't yet interested in rebellious youth culture, method acting or rock'n'roll. Instead of kids in leather jackets racing motorbikes or performing suicidal stunts in cars, British cinema offered the gentle comedy of *Genevieve* (1953) in which various well-spoken types raced vintage cars from London to Brighton.

There was evidence of a gaping generational divide. The industry wasn't properly catering for what was becoming a crucial part of its audience – namely the teen market. Cinema owners and local authorities were disturbed by the behaviour of youngsters at screenings of films like *Blackboard Jungle* (1955) and *Rock around the Clock* (1956). Their instinct wasn't to welcome the new wave of rock-'n'-roll and teen-rebel movies but to try to ban them.

Blackboard Jungle had initially been refused a certificate. Its UK distributor, MGM, objected and eventually a cut version was released with an X certificate.

Meanwhile, the alleged 'teenage rioting' at some screenings of *Rock around the Clock*, as reported by the popular press at the time, provided excellent publicity. It helped alert distributors and exhibitors to the fact that the teenage audience existed and, gradually, to change approaches to marketing and publicity.

Inevitably, the industry's attitude toward television softened. The language used by the KRS council in a 1956 statement was instructive. The distributors' body declared that its members would 'not co-operate in any television programmes which offered valuable prizes and which were calculated to attract the public away from the cinema'.[27] At the same time, though, Sir David Griffiths, the KRS president, struck a more emollient tone when he stated that the renters were 'perfectly prepared to back television programmes which they considered to be helpful'.[28] The renters were willing to allow clips of movies to be used on TV shows in which critics discussed the new releases.

The most obvious help that television could provide the film industry was financial. As the decade wore on, some prominent producers, John Woolf and Daniel Angel among them, began to sell their movies to commercial TV. FIDO's endeavours to stop distributors from selling movies to television from 1958 onward simply interrupted and delayed a shift in the business that was inevitable.

Throughout the decade, disputes rumbled between the distributors and exhibitors about 'break figures', basically the cost of running the cinema (bills, staff wages, etc.) divided by the number of seats. Only once the basic outlay had been recouped would money begin to flow back to the distributor. The distributors didn't like the way in which the break figures were calculated. The low-level attrition between the two sectors of the industry remained as constant in the 1950s as it had been in 1915, when the KRS was formed. There was huge resentment on both sides at the amount of entertainment tax they were forced to pay. The government was taking vast amounts from the tax, first introduced in 1916 and only scrapped in 1960. For example, from 1945's gross box-office revenue of £115 million, £41 million went on the tax, compared with the £17 million taken by American film companies.[29] Although the tax was levied on other forms of entertainment, the cinema yielded 93 per cent of total entertainment-tax receipts at the end of the war. These figures underlined the absolutely central place that cinema enjoyed in British cultural life.

Another source of attrition between the bodies were the quotas for the showing of home-made fare. The 1948 Film Act had set these at 45 per cent for first features and 25 per cent for supporting fare. Predictably, many exhibitors defaulted and many of the supporting films made were of dubious quality. In 1950, the quota for first features was reduced to 30 per cent but the supporting programme was left at 25 per cent. Over 2,000 cinemas failed to reach the target but few were fined. The idea behind the quota legislation was to boost British production. This simply wasn't happening. With too little material to go round, the industry was forced to improvise. Distributors sometimes tried to persuade the smaller exhibitors to take second features that had already played on the major circuits as 'main attractions'. As Steve Chibnall and Brian McFarlane note in their study *The British 'B' Film*, at the 1952 CEA summer conference, one leading exhibitor described the supporting feature quota as 'a filthy racket', designed to 'peddle trash' to exhibitors and extract money from the Eady Levy (a tax on box-office receipts which was used to help boost production).[30]

A change in the 1950s that had nothing to do with colour or size of screen, entertainment tax, quotas or the Eady Levy, was the introduction of the X category. The Censorship Consultative Committee met in January 1951 to discuss the new certificate.

The BBFC was quick off the mark in responding to the more controversial subject matter in films. At first, the X certificate was for 16 and over only (raised to 18+ in 1970 when a new classification regime was launched). The new X incorporated the H (for Horror) certificate that had existed since the 1930s, but also took account of sex/nudity, drugs and what was regarded as anti-social behaviour.

Some of the decisions as to what constituted X films still seem baffling in hindsight. Sword-and-sandal saga *Quo Vadis*, for example, was an early X movie at a time when the BBFC was fretting about such matters as rioting in cinemas and teenage misbehaviour.

INSIDE THE POSTER VIEWING COMMITTEE

For distributors trying to alert the public to their latest movies, putting the most striking poster in the most prominent location has always been a matter of simple common sense. The poster provides information (release date, screening details) but it can also tantalise and excite potential cinemagoers.

Posters are seen in very public places – on buses, on billboards and in railway stations. They are subject to laws of public decency. In the era of the new age-restrictive X certificate, that is also often where the problems started.

In the 1950s, the Kinematograph Renters' Society set up its own 'Poster Viewing Committee'. This panel included film distributors, exhibitors, media owners, the British Board of Film Censors, local politicians and transport chiefs. Their job was to survey new posters and to check that they wouldn't cause offence.

The first meeting of the KRS Poster Viewing Committee (its name was later to change) was held on Monday 16 November 1958.

A few weeks before, the KRS had received a letter from a Mr Mallatratt, secretary of the Joint Censorship Committee of the Poster Advertising Industry, stating (as the KRS records recall) 'that at a meeting called to consider a theatre poster (at which no film industry representative was present), it had been decided to recommend that all pictorial horror posters, whether for plays or films, should be banned forthwith'.

The KRS reacted with outrage at a decision that had been taken so hastily and with so little consultation, Mallatratt backtracked, agreeing to give the KRS time to form a committee that would ensure that movie posters conformed to agreed definitions of public decency.

In support of the new committee, the BBFC, under its secretary John Trevelyan, added a clause to its agreement with distributors. 'The Publisher agrees that no Pictorial Poster shall be issued or used which is objectionable or that illustrates a scene or incident which is not included in the certified version of the film.'

The American members of the KRS agreed to disband their own publicity censorship committee and to support the new committee.

With the new X certificate, an elaborate game of cat and mouse was played out between the poster committee and the distributors as attitudes began to change over what was and wasn't 'objectionable'.

In the late 1950s, the British Transport Commission was threatening to refuse to display any poster with an X certificate. Ironically, for some distributors, a poster being banned by the Transport Commission could actually be regarded as 'good' publicity. It could give a film a whiff of scandal that might entice a certain type of viewer.

There is a mix of poignance and comedy in the deliberations of the Poster Viewing Committee. This was a case of various middle-aged men in suits meeting in an office to scrutinise the designs for posters which, over the course of the 1960s and 1970s, became ever more outrageous.

Read through the records of the meetings and you can't help but feel sympathy for the long-suffering committee members who were never quite sure of their footing.

Some of the early disputes seemed relatively innocuous. For example, the committee was upset over the 1960 film *The Trials of Oscar Wilde* (starring Peter Finch as the playwright and produced by a pre-James Bond Albert R. Broccoli), on the grounds that the poster flaunted its X certificate in association with the words 'Adults Only!' This was a statement of fact – the film was intended for adult viewers only – but the committee members refused to allow the artwork to draw too much attention to the age restriction or to use it for marketing purposes.

Homosexuality was still illegal at the time, one reason why the film became a controversial release taken only by a few cinemas. *The Trials of Oscar Wilde* was a 'respectable' period drama with high production values and well-known actors. Many of the films whose posters the committee pored over in subsequent years were less salubrious.

Sometimes, in these early years, the committee's grounds for complaint verged on the pedantic. For example, confronted with two captions for United Artists' 1960 horror film *Macumba Love*, the committee members approved 'Thrill to the Demon-Rites of the Witch Goddess' but rejected 'Weird, Shocking Savagery in Native Jungle Haunts'.

With US drama *From the Terrace* (1960), starring a youthful Paul Newman, the problem with the poster was one of sexual suggestion.

They approved the artwork on condition that the poster be altered to show the male figure wearing trousers rather than pyjamas and the 'indication of a pillow' removed. They didn't like the implication of 'illicit relationships between married persons'.

With a 1960s exploitation film called *Come to Bed Madame*, the problem was not so much the poster as the very title – but the committee discovered this had already been approved by the BBFC.

By the late 1960s, the committee seemed under siege. Distributors were springing up who specialised in exploitation: companies like New Realm, Cinecenta, Target, Variety and Border Film. Older firms like Butcher's, who could trace their history back to the early silent era, were also releasing genre movies.

Much of the committee's work involved re-dressing characters in posters who had too many buttons undone, or had rips in their trousers or tattoos of butterflies on their inner legs or were striking poses that were too suggestive.

When artwork was rejected by the committee, distributors would make small amendments and send it back. The exasperation the committee members felt at being confronted again and again with the same imagery and slogans they had already rejected was obvious. In records of an August 1970 meeting, committee member Mr H. H. Mallatratt is quoted as curtly observing that the title of one exploitation pic, *Do You Want to Remain a Virgin Forever*, had 'already been objected on at least three occasions'. That did not stop the distributor from submitting it again, and again.

'Sensuous, corrupt, perverted' was rejected for Cinecenta's *Complicated Girl* (1969), an Italian exploitation movie starring Catherine Spaak. Much debate followed on the use of pants in the original artwork in this film. These pants were eventually deemed permissible, on the understanding that they 'must be of distinctive colouring'.

'Violent passion… jealous lovers' were fine as captions for another exploitation film, *The Subject is Sex*, released at almost exactly the same time.

'Salacious' and 'sadistic' were not allowed on the film *Come Back Peter* (1969). After discussion, they were replaced with the alternatives 'seductive' and 'sizzling', with which the committee had no problem at all.

Many of the posters had a similar quality to saucy seaside postcards. You could imagine them being the subjects of Max Miller monologues or songs.

Warner–Pathé fell foul of the poster committee for its caption for its 1969 feature *The Arrangement*, directed by Elia Kazan and starring Faye Dunaway. 'Most arrangements are made in bed' was the offending line this time round. The committee didn't approve of the sight of a girl's buttocks on the poster either.

The poster committee did not always distinguish between art and pornography. The suggested poster for Ken Russell's D. H. Lawrence adaptation *Women in Love* (1969) was rejected on the grounds that it showed two naked men wrestling.

Russell's 1970 Tchaikovsky biopic, *The Music Lovers*, also encountered problems with the poster committee. Its original poster was rejected 'on the grounds that the unclothed female lying in the foreground invited graffiti'. Mr Berman, representing the film's distributors, United Artists, protested against the decision. He showed the committee posters for other subjects 'which in his opinion were as open to graffiti and which had been approved'. Berman also contested that the poster was 'in good taste and could be considered a work of art'. However, as the KRS notes make clear, 'the committee were not agreeable to reverse their original decision.'

United Artists was more fortunate with its Richard Brooks movie *The Happy Ending* (1969), starring an Oscar-nominated Jean Simmons as a repressed housewife with an overbearing and neglectful husband. 'She's got everything a woman could want… she's still looking for the happy ending' was approved. If this was a covert reference to female orgasm, the viewing committee members either didn't notice or didn't care.

There was often the sense that the posters were more raunchy than the films they represented. Distributors felt themselves obliged to push at the limits of what was permissible.

Some cinemas had set up as 'clubs' in order to show uncensored films. The KRS records have details of complaints from one of these, Cinecenta, that had opened up a venue on Tottenham Court Road. The Cinecenta Club wanted to advertise its films on the London

Underground with posters that would observe the same rules as those for X-certificate films. London Transport would not allow this – an anomaly in the view of Cinecenta boss Mr Houlihan given that the posters were no worse than those for other X films.

Cinecenta's films continued to be regarded with the gravest misgivings by the viewing committee. One, *What We Learnt at School Today*, had poster and press advertisements showing 'the legs of a girl with her skirt showing but also her pants half way down her legs'. Unsurprisingly, this illustration was deemed 'completely unacceptable'. Fellow distributor New Realm also had the knack of aggravating the committee with its selection of ever-smuttier poster ideas.

Another typical New Realm title, *Swedish Fly Girls*, revealed the linguistic contortions that committee members were sometimes forced to perform. The film, about a promiscuous Danish air stewardess, originally had the catchline 'We dare not tell you what goes on when these girls take off'. This was not approved. A second catchline, 'The girls who always say yes', was approved but New Realm contacted the editor of the *Evening Standard* to try to persuade him to accept the original catchline. This was a forlorn endeavour. The editor was a member of the committee and was obliged to stick by its decisions.

Any imagery of blood in posters was frowned on. Committee members seemingly suffered from arachnophobia, moving quickly to reject an image of horror film *Dr Phibes Rises Again* (1972), which showed an image of a spider crawling across a woman's face close to her eye.

By the early 1980s, the spate of sexploitation movies was drying up. Such fare was more likely now to be consumed on video than in cinemas. The Poster Viewing Committee continued to meet every Tuesday morning at 10am but its burden was lightening. There is a note of weary exasperation in its members' response to Italian movie *Caligula and Messalina* (1982), an 'orgy of lust!' as the poster put it. The members dutifully called for the omission of the word 'depravity', which was still as frowned on as two decades before. The members also 'expressed concern over the area of the poster containing several pairs of entangled legs'. It was noted that London Transport was 'reserving its opinion for the present'.

London Transport quickly rejected Russ Meyer movie *Cherry, Harry and Raquel*, which had been made in 1970 but which Tigon was releasing as part of a treble bill in the UK in 1982. As ever, committee members had useful and very thoroughgoing recommendations about what changes needed to be made to the artwork to secure approval. 'The woman on the left hand side of the poster [...] should be confined to one frame and her bust should be slightly "deflated". The nipple of the girl in the section for "Vixen" should be covered or air brushed out.'

The members also had qualms when confronted with Cannon exploitation movie *A Little Sex*. They agreed that 'the man's head should not be positioned in the woman's cleavage'.

To the outsider, it can't help but seem strange that senior industry executives with important jobs were spending so much time worrying over the positioning and prominence of nipples in Russ Meyer movies or where men's heads were positioned in relation to cleavages in Cannon films. However, there was money and opportunity riding on their decisions.

Most distributors accepted that it was in their commercial interest to abide by viewing-committee decisions and to get their artwork and posters seen. Some newcomers – most notably Palace Pictures – simply ignored the committee. This, though, was a dangerous policy. The major cinema chains supported the committee's work and were ready to reject films from distributors who didn't follow Advertising Viewing Committee (AVC) recommendations about posters and artwork. Newspapers, meanwhile, would not accept advertisements from Palace Pictures unless they had first been approved by the committee.

With the abolition of the Greater London Council (GLC) in 1986, the London boroughs took over responsibility for licensing cinemas.

The GLC had had an informal understanding with the AVC. 'Providing the poster committee operated responsibly the GLC would not initiate their own arrangements for censoring publicity material associated with the film industry.'

This arrangement didn't change. What was different was the number and type of posters being submitted. There was a move away from exploitation fare – and therefore far fewer contentious X-rated films for the committee to approve.

The Advertising Viewing Committee is still in existence today, tasked with 'approving display materials for 18-certificate films'. When it was first set up, fault lines were opening in British cinema as in British society as a whole. In the 1960s, these would cause major changes in the type of films that were made – and in the way that they were distributed.[31]

CHAPTER 6

Dr No

In 1959, when British Lion was releasing Jack Clayton's X-rated movie *Room at the Top* in British cinemas, the film's producers, Romulus, decided to hold a preview screening at an unprepossessing cinema, the Bruce Grove, in North London, substituting it for a Hammer horror film. The preview was a disaster. The audience didn't know what it was seeing in advance – and reacted with dismay.

Romulus was run by John and James Woolf, producers who had distribution in their blood. They were the sons of C. M. Woolf, a former president of the Kinematograph Renters' Society and the founder of General Film Distributors. Woolf had died in 1942 and GFD had long since metamorphosed into Rank Film Distribution. Rank, like ABC, had little interest in showing X films, even those produced by the Woolfs. That was why the brothers were testing out the film at the Bruce Grove in Tottenham as they looked for cinemas which might book the film. As John Woolf recalled many years later, 'the audience booed at the showing and poor Jack Clayton (the director) was in tears, this being his first feature film.'[1] The spectators had come to see Frankenstein and were infuriated at being 'fobbed off with social realism'.

Distributors and producers had sensed that audiences' tastes were beginning to change. There was a new permissiveness in the air and a sense of youthful rebelliousness. This was hinted at both in the mayhem during screenings of *Rock around the Clock* and in the heated debates in the press about 'angry young men' following the eventual success of John Osborne's fiery play *Look Back in Anger*, which had premiered at the Royal Court Theatre in London in 1956 under the direction of Tony Richardson to reviews that were, at least initially, very mixed.

With a distributor's acumen, John Woolf felt he had spotted a gap in the market. One evening in the spring of 1957, he had been watching the current-affairs programme *Panorama* on the BBC. The presenter was Woodrow Wyatt, a former Labour MP during the Attlee government and eventually to become an ardent Thatcherite in the 1970s and 1980s. Wyatt was shown interviewing a group of housewives in Bradford about a book their local librarian had written. The librarian was novelist John Braine and the book was *Room at the Top*. 'They [the housewives] made the book sound quite sensational. I told my brother about it and we got hold of the proofs from the publishers,' Woolf later remembered.[2]

There were obvious reasons why a film version seemed like a good idea. The story was set in the North of England – and some distributors suspected audiences were growing tired of too many Home Counties comedies starring Dirk Bogarde and Donald Sinden. Its main character, the ruthlessly careerist working-class hero Joe Lampton, reflected the aspirations of many youngsters, frustrated with the way their opportunities were still being stifled by an oppressive class system. What's more, the book featured illicit sex. Joe Lampton falls in love with and has an affair with an older woman, even as he is busy seducing and marrying the boss's daughter. *Room at the Top* was, as its deliberately titillating posters proclaimed, 'a savage story of lust and ambition'. The image on the poster was of a half-naked Lampton (played by Laurence Harvey) with his head nestling on the breast of the very glamorous and enigmatic French actress Simone Signoret, who played the older woman.

Even so, when the film was completed, the Woolfs were worried initially that they had a disaster on their hands. British cinemagoers – and those further afield – seemed very wary about the new fad for social realism. Tony Richardson's film version of *Look Back in Anger*, also released in 1959, a month or two after *Room at the Top*, did very poor business at the box office. 'It got good reviews everywhere and died in 51 countries,' its producer Harry Saltzman later remembered. It was distributed by Warner Bros., screened in ABC cinemas and had a major British star in Richard Burton. Nonetheless, the British public didn't seem interested. Nor, if the Tottenham preview was taken as the measure, were they interested in *Room at the Top*.

Woolf later talked about his alarm when he turned *Room at the Top* over to censors and it came back with a red slip (meaning they had turned it down). The only certificate they would give it was an X and that meant the Rank circuit simply wouldn't book it. Woolf immediately rushed over to complain to John Trevelyan, secretary of the British Board of Film Censors. To Woolf's surprise, Trevelyan, credited for 'the most extensive liberalisation' in the history of the BBFC, turned out to be a firm fan of *Room at the Top*. 'He said it was exactly the film they [the BBFC] wanted to establish the X Certificate and that it was a brilliant film.' In other words, the X, at least in this case, was a badge of honour rather than a mark of shame.[3]

Heartened by Trevelyan's encouragement, distributors British Lion booked *Room at the Top* into an independent West End venue, the Plaza on Lower Regent Street. The critics loved the film and, on the back of their reviews, the ABC chain took the film. In this case, ABC's bookers were clearly able to overcome their wariness about the film's X certificate and its potential affront to family values in the era of Norman Wisdom, *Carry On* and *Doctor in the House* films. *Room at the Top* had achieved critical respectability – and the whiff of scandal that the X rating still brought turned out to be an invaluable marketing tool. *Room at the Top* was the fourth most popular film at the UK box office in 1959.

The success of *Room at the Top* was significant on several different levels. Firstly, it proved that films about ruthless, womanising loners could be successful at the box office – a lesson that certainly didn't go unnoticed by the producers of a certain spy-movie franchise that was to be launched a year or two later. (Laurence Harvey, who played Joe Lampton, was later talked about as a potential James Bond.) The success also suggested that there was at least some appetite after all for kitchen-sink movies set in regional towns a long way from London. The film ushered in a new maturity when it came to dealing with sex. This was acknowledged by Albert Finney, star of the similarly frank *Saturday Night and Sunday Morning* (1960), in a 1982 *Guardian* interview:

I remember in terms of the sex, there were great discussions because the law then was that you had to have one foot on the floor, like in snooker. I think in fact *Room at the Top* was the first British film, which was made about a year before, two years before *Saturday Night*, which kind of intimated that two consenting adults had actually done something in bed together that we didn't see, that, if you knew what was what, you put two and two together.[4]

The film also showed independent producers and distributors managing to release a film successfully without having to kowtow to the major circuits. This was an era in which several independent companies were launched. Romulus had been in business since 1948 but it was now followed by Woodfall Films, founded by Tony Richardson and John Osborne; Beaver Films, founded by Richard Attenborough and Bryan Forbes; and Bryanston, a consortium formed by Michael Balcon and other producers in 1959 after the closure of Ealing Studios. The idea behind Bryanston was that individual partners paid a fee to join and were then given production support through the National Film Finance Corporation. In 1961, Bryanston struck a partnership with the British arm of American company Seven Arts Productions. This gave it the resources to make not just modest British movies but films on the scale of Alexander Mackendrick's *Sammy Going South* (1963), shot in CinemaScope and Eastmancolor in Africa with a big-name (albeit ageing) Hollywood star in Edward G. Robinson.

By this stage, British Lion had merged distribution operations with Columbia. Bryanston appointed John Hogarth (who had lost his job at British Lion in the merger) as their producers' rep. With what he later called 'a certain amount of devilment', he arranged for Bryanston's films to be distributed through British Lion Columbia, as the company was now called. He didn't hide his pleasure at being able to dictate terms to his former bosses.[5]

During this period, trade paper the *Kinematograph Weekly* wrote with enthusiasm of 'a new pattern of production and distribution in which creative individuals have as much say as impersonal mammoth corporations'.[6]

Distributors and exhibitors were heartened by the April 1960 decision of the Chancellor of the Exchequer, a full 44 years after it was introduced as a temporary measure in 1916, finally to abolish entertainment tax. British cinema's arguments that this was an invidious and unfair burden on its operations were finally heeded.

For all the vigour of the new production companies, these were not balmy times for the industry. Admissions were continuing to fall and costs to increase. In January 1960, Rank and ABC had jointly decided to raise ticket prices. They complained that attendances had been hit by the 'long, hot summer' of 1959 (a familiar grumble among exhibitors in slow summers) and that they were losing revenue.

Obviously, hiking up ticket prices wasn't likely to stem the leaking away of audiences. It was a moot point as to whether the industry benefited from the abolition of entertainment tax in the way that everyone had hoped. As John Spraos wrote in his 1962 study, *The Decline of the Cinema: An Economist's Report*, the 1959 Finance Act had already provided for the refunding of the first £20 of a cinema's weekly tax bill. 'This had entirely freed from Entertainments Duty about half the cinemas operating at the time. The final abolition of the tax therefore benefited only the remaining cinemas.'

Spraos predicted correctly that there would be wholesale closures of smaller cinemas. He had some dismaying data at his fingertips which pointed out that these smaller cinemas were struggling badly. 9.5 per cent of 'singleton' (as he called single-screen independent venues) cinemas were losing over £2,000 a year – a huge figure relatively – and 33.3 per cent of 'singletons' were loss-making.

The chains, meanwhile, were much better equipped to withstand the economic squalls of the time. As Spraos noted, they could offer 'a large market' to any film they screened and this put them in a position to drive 'hard bargains' with the distributors.[7]

In a bid to keep struggling cinemas open, a 'National Circuit' was set up. 'This differs from other releasing circuits in that it is not a mere extension of a chain. It is a collection of deprived cinemas which are not in competition with each other and which offer a ready market for films not pre-empted for Rank or ABC release.'[8]

The problem was that the cinemas huddling together to form the

National Circuit still weren't in a position to compete with Rank and ABC. The circuit, Spraos noted, 'has no bargaining strength because even if it is granted that it has many ribs, it has no backbone […] in the light of this it is no exaggeration to say that the cinemas in The National Circuit have no future.'[9]

During the 1950s, the number of cinemas in the UK shrank by around 25 per cent. Third-run cinemas, which showed films a considerable time after their original release, suffered the most. These were the cinemas with the least expensive tickets, and their disappearance and 'the complete extinction of the very cheap cinema', as Spraos noted, 'hit severely the lowest income groups'. Admissions prices had risen sharply throughout the 1950s, from an average of 1.51 shillings in 1950 to 2.51 in 1960. Spraos claimed that distributors were faring better than their exhibitor partners. There were fewer American movies than in the heyday of the Hollywood studios and that meant demand was high. The distributors were able to insist on minimum hire terms of 25 to 30 per cent of net takings for the hire of films regardless of the 'financial position of a cinema'.[10]

The distributors were cast in an unflattering light as being so determined to secure favourable hire terms that they didn't worry about cinemas going out of business as a result. 'Major distributors seem to know the percentages negotiated by their rivals with respect to every film and every cinema,' Spraos suggested. 'This must have a restraining effect with renters with an unpopular film on their hands who might feel tempted to offer it at bargain rates.'[11]

Spraos didn't provide evidence for his assertions, which seemed to imply a degree of collusion. He all but accused the distributors of putting their short-term interests ahead of the long-term well-being of the industry and argued that cinema closures hurt everybody. It may have been true that distributors had some idea about their competitors' terms. The market was the market and they would have a natural curiosity about their rivals' business methods. That, though, was very different from conspiring together to set prices. Nor was it in their interest to see cinemas being closed down. After all, the exhibitors were their customers. The distributors' own costs were rising. Their campaign spending strategies were changing as commercial television expanded and TV advertising became a possibility alongside press and radio.

Fifty years on, the criticisms seem misplaced. The very idea that led to the KRS being set up in 1915 in the first place was to push for solidarity among the distributor members. The KRS was never going to approve of individual distributors cutting one-off deals with struggling cinemas. It was up to the exhibitors' body, the Cinema Exhibitors' Association, to intervene and negotiate on behalf of its members if their livelihoods were under threat.

'Fair Shares Is Basis for Negotiation Agree CEA/KRS' was a headline in the trade press in April 1960.[12] However, 45 years after the setting up of the KRS in 1915 and 48 years on from the founding of the CEA in 1912, the two trade bodies were still at loggerheads, with very different ideas of how revenues should be split. The exhibitors still resented the percentage of box-office takings that the distributors clawed back. The distributors still didn't trust the exhibitors to send in accurate box-office returns. In this period, the KRS employed around 20 ticket inspectors who would roam the country, entering cinemas incognito – not so they could watch the movies but so they could check the number of spectators present.[13] These inspectors would buy a ticket and keep the stub, which they would then forward to the distributor of the film in question. That distributor was then able to check that the number of that specific ticket appeared in the box-office returns. If it did not, legal action might well follow.

Thanks to these inspectors, the Kinematograph Renters' Society became involved in a very famous legal case, one still often cited today. Byrne v. Kinematograph Renters' Society took place in 1958. In this case, the judge ruled that it was 'not trespass' for KRS inspectors to gain entry to the plaintiff's two cinemas by buying a ticket not to see a film but simply to count the number of patrons in the auditorium. The inspectors made a report to the joint committee of the KRS and CEA about the discrepancies in the cinema owner's box-office returns. There was an inquiry, which the cinema owner was invited to attend, and the KRS eventually recommended that its members no longer supply films to him pending an investigation by an accountant nominated by them. The cinema owner reacted by bringing legal action alleging conspiracy and claiming damages on the grounds that the proceedings before the joint committee were 'contrary to natural justice'.

It was an involved and complicated case. The judge, Justice Harman, agreed there was no allegation of dishonesty or fraud against the plaintiff and that, by stopping supplying his cinemas with films, the KRS 'had brought about a punishment altogether disproportionate to the offence'. In effect, the cinema owner was losing his livelihood. Nonetheless, the judge ruled against his claim for conspiracy 'because there were no unlawful means used and the predominant purpose of the defendants was not to injure the plaintiff but to protect their trade interests'.

Byrne's case against the KRS was only one of many, many similar disputes between cinema owners and the distributors' trade body. It is still cited in law journals today. This is not because of any interest within the legal community in the predicament of the cinema owner. It is considered an important ruling on the principles of 'natural justice' and how they apply in private law proceedings.

In a passage much quoted in law schools, Harman had described natural justice as he saw it in legal terms. 'First, I think that the person accused should know the nature of the accusation made; secondly, that he should be given an opportunity to state his case; and thirdly, of course, that the tribunal should act in good faith.'[14]

The KRS had met these requirements. However, the very fact that the case had been brought at all pointed to the increasing tensions in the film business. What was clear to everyone was that cinema in the UK was no longer the 'essential social habit of the age which slaughtered all competitors', as historian A. J. P. Taylor had described it in 1930s Britain. The business was in desperate competition for public attention with other leisure activities. Admissions were down to 500.8 million in 1960, a massive drop on the 1.1 billion attendances British cinema had achieved as recently as 1956.

The very role of cinema was being questioned. Theatres were being repurposed as bingo halls, dance venues and bowling alleys – or perhaps more appropriately as churches. Rank 'turned two large London cinemas, the Odeon Hackney Road and the Gaumont Peckham over to bingo in May 1961'.[15] Over the following years many Odeons and Gaumonts endured the same grisly fate, under the banner of Top Rank Social Clubs. Sometimes, the venues would show films on one day and stage bingo the next – but the bingo invariably seemed to prevail.

The 'kitchen sink' films of the early 1960s give a sense of changing approaches to leisure. The antagonism toward television is always palpable. As film historian Charles Barr has noted, *Saturday Night and Sunday Morning* (1960), *The Loneliness of the Long Distance Runner* (1962) and *A Kind of Loving* (1962) all feature scenes in which characters watch television as if hypnotised and being brainwashed.[16] The young heroes, for example Finney's Arthur Seaton in *Saturday Night and Sunday Morning*, want to escape the stifling domesticity of home, hearth and TV. 'Don't let the bastards grind you down' is Arthur's famous motto and television is part of what he is chafing against. We see him in the fairground, we see him in the pub – but Arthur doesn't seem to have any time for cinemagoing.

Harry Saltzman, the flamboyant Canadian producer of *Look Back in Anger*, didn't seem too abashed by the failure of the film and was on the lookout for other properties. 'What Harry was able to exude in abundance was potential. You always knew he [Saltzman] would somehow, somewhere discover the magic carpet that would transport you to riches,' director Tony Richardson observed of him. As Richardson also noted, before he produced *Look Back in Anger*, Saltzman 'hadn't a bean'.[17] That didn't put him off in the slightest. As a movie producer, he projected an image of power and affluence and that mattered more than the actual state of his bank balance.

In the end, Richardson grew exasperated with his producer and Saltzman was voted out of Woodfall midway through the making of *Saturday Night And Sunday Morning*, which Richardson produced, and was left with only an executive-producer credit. Saltzman, though, continued to hustle. He managed to come up with the money to buy a six-month option on the James Bond thrillers. (It helped that he shared a lawyer, Brian Lewis, with their author, Ian Fleming.) Saltzman didn't have the money to make a Bond movie. With his option fast running out, he took a meeting, brokered by writer Wolf Mankowitz, with American producer Albert R. "Cubby" Broccoli. In his memoir,

Broccoli claimed that Saltzman was more interested in persuading him to co-produce a film about a scarecrow, *Rapture in my Rags*, than in making Bond movies. However, Saltzman and Broccoli eventually agreed to a 50/50 partnership and set up production company Eon together in 1961.

The Bond films were financed by their distributor, United Artists. UA Chairman Arthur Krim agreed to stump up $1 million for the production of *Dr No*. (The agreed budget in UK currency was actually £321,227.)

Thunderball had originally been earmarked as the first of the Broccoli/Saltzman Bond movies and a script had been commissioned. That project, though, was postponed because of a dispute with producer Kevin McClory, with whom Fleming and fellow writer Jack Whittingham had collaborated on a treatment for a Bond movie in the late 1950s. McClory claimed that Fleming had drawn on that treatment when writing the novel *Thunderball* and had thereby begun a legal wrangle that would simmer on for many decades. It was not settled until 2013, when MGM and Danjaq (the holding company of Eon) acquired the Bond-related rights of the McClory estate, which in turn enabled the title *Spectre* to be used in Eon's 24th official Bond film.

Almost inevitably, *Dr No* ran over budget. Its 'star', the relatively unknown young Scottish actor and former bodybuilder Sean Connery, best known for his role in action drama *Hell Drivers* and whimsical Disney fable *Darby O'Gill and the Little People*, was paid only £6,000, a very modest amount. Lois Maxwell earned £200 for her two days' work in the studio as Moneypenny and Bernard Lee was paid £250 for his two days of studio work as James Bond's boss at MI6, M. The overall cast budget was only £21,064. The director, Terence Young, was paid £15,000, a relatively high figure, because he had decided to forgo any profit participation.[18]

One reason the budget crept up was the producers' proactive approach toward publicity. Even before *Dr No* went into production, they were taking ads in the trade press and trying to plant promotional stories in the newspapers.

Dr No began shooting in Jamaica in January 1962 and soon ran over budget. Bad weather, what Saltzman referred to as 'ulcer-making' production difficulties and the scale of production designer Ken Adam's sets – which had been budgeted at an absurdly low level – ensured that the film didn't keep to the original plans. It didn't help, either, that director Terence Young, at least according to Saltzman, insisted on a 'grand seigneur' way of living and 'spent money personally like water' during his time in Jamaica.

By February 1962, in a letter to Film Finances, the production's completion guarantors, Saltzman had taken to blaming the locals. 'The biggest problem is the "mañana" attitude of the local people and the fact that they do not keep their promises to their contracts and this has caused quite costly delays.'[19]

In the end, in April 1962, Film Finances 'took over' Dr No, so concerned had they become about the overspending. The producers were still in charge but now the film guarantors insisted on signing off on every item of expenditure as they tried to steer the film toward completion. As Charles Drazin notes, distributors UA accepted the intervention from Film Finances and used it as a 'shield' to protect them from having to provide extra money for the production. Even with Film Finances monitoring every piece of expenditure, Dr No came in £81,449 over budget.[20]

Given their initial enthusiasm for the Bond movies and their absolutely crucial role in making then possible, distributors United Artists were strangely tentative in their initial treatment of Dr No. They regarded the film as a test case and, in Drazin's words, were prepared to 'take a gamble but only at minimum risk'. Their distribution agreement from April 1962 stipulated that any future Bond movies should be in black and white unless they gave their approval for colour and that they should retain a right of veto on everything from director and screenwriter to cast and schedule. At that early stage, before Dr No had been released, the producers weren't in a position to contest these draconian strictures.

Dr No received its world premiere in October 1962 at the London Pavilion in Piccadilly Circus. Fleming and Connery were in attendance. Coincidentally, it was in the very same week that The Saint starring Roger Moore began its first series on ITV.

Dr No triggered a boom in spy movies, with Our Man Flint and Matt Helm films as well as the Harry Palmer series soon following. Bond also

12. Nobody does it better: The multi-faceted campaign supporting the release of *Dr No* successfully engaged a mass audience – and helped to change cinema. In 1962, cinema managers playing *Dr No* were encouraged to work with local book stores to highlight the frequently reprinted tie-in paperback edition of Ian Fleming's best-selling novel.

Source: *Dr No* original UK release materials reproduced by kind permission of Eon Productions Ltd. *Dr No* © 1962 Danjaq, LLC and United Artists Corporation. All rights reserved. 007 Gun Symbol Logo © 1962 Danjaq, LLC and United Artists Corporation. All rights reserved. Image photography by Tim Whitby (Getty Images/FDA).

spawned *The Man from UNCLE* and other shows on TV. And *Dr No* contributed to a racier, pacier style of action movie (editing by Peter Hunt), with extensive use of real locations (at a time when people didn't travel so much).

Fortunately for Film Finances and UA, *Dr No* was a huge hit, grossing over $6 million on its initial release and eventually far, far more. James Bond, the 'extraordinary gentleman spy' with the licence to kill 'when he chooses… where he chooses… whom he chooses' chimed with audiences in Britain and everywhere else. The Bond films were larger-than-life, exotic adventures, with ambitious production design and generally excellent international casts – the production money is 'up there on the screen', as Broccoli himself used to say. The iconic elements of the series – the gun-barrel ident, Dick Maibaum's taut script, Maurice Binder's animated main titles sequence, John Barry's interpretation of the Bond theme, Bond himself introduced at a casino gaming table – were all already there in the very first film.

John Brosnan, writing in *James Bond in the Cinema*, pointed to the mixed critical reaction to *Dr No*.

> The Vatican immediately issued a warning about the film [a special communiqué warning about its moral standpoint], and *Time*'s reviewer was distinctly unimpressed. The critics who attended the first press showing were apparently equally divided in their opinions. In the 'for' camp were Alexander Walker and Dilys Powell, while the 'against' camp included Derek Hill, Penelope Gilliat and Thomas Wiseman, who noted with disgust in the *Sunday Express* that 'Bond's methods and morals were indistinguishable from the villain's.' While the critics may have been divided, the cinemagoing public were unanimous in their support.[21]

Broccoli, though, rued the way its US distribution was handled. The film was released in North America in May 1963. 'Several of the UA bookers who saw the picture privately in our projection room expressed some doubt that they could sell a picture in the major US cities with "a Limey truck driver playing the lead,"' Broccoli recalled in his memoir *When the Snow Melts*. Instead of opening *Dr No* in key cities, UA released it in drive-in cinemas in Oklahoma and Texas. 'Moreover, they sold it on very low terms for a Bond picture. They took "frightened" money, scared it wouldn't do the business.'[22]

Ironically, the suave British spy was an immediate hit with the rough-and-ready drive-in audiences. The metropolitan critics liked Bond too. UA later had the 'chutzpah' (in Broccoli's words) to claim that the low-key release strategy had been intentional all along – a way of slowly drumming up interest in a movie that didn't seem to have obvious hooks for an American audience. UA had even complained about the casting of Connery. Nonetheless, the company had put up the money for Bond in exchange for distribution rights.

UA also financed *Tom Jones* (1963), Tony Richardson's riotous adaptation of the Henry Fielding novel that Richardson's usual backers at Bryanston, their distributors at British Lion/Columbia, had shied away from on cost grounds. Just as with *Dr No*, UA hit the jackpot. Just as with *Dr No*, the distributor wasn't at all sure what it had, at least at first. The two films cost roughly the same amount to make. 'The head of British distribution for United Artists saw the finished cut. He pronounced disaster: the film would be lucky if it made £40,000 worldwide,' Richardson recalled in his autobiography, *Long Distance Runner*.[23] (The same UA exec who had had such little confidence in *Tom Jones* reportedly responded to the news that the company had signed the Beatles for their first film with the remark, 'but who's going to star?')

Neither Bond nor the New Wave films really catered for what had become the biggest part of the British cinemagoing audience: the teenage market. There were 5 million teenagers in Britain in 1960 and 60 per cent of them went to the cinema at least once a week, as

13. Cheers! Film distributor Monty Morton (far left) and Richard Lester (second right) attending a film awards ceremony in 1965. Morton was KRS president for practically two decades, the 1960s and 1970s.

Photograph courtesy of Variety, the Children's Charity.

against only '13 per cent of the adult population' and '50 per cent of the adults never went at all.'[24]

In the case of *Tom Jones*, a literary adaptation set in eighteenth-century Britain somehow chimed perfectly with the youth audience and turned into one of the first flagship films for 'Swinging Britain'. It posted box-office returns of around $40 million on its $1 million budget.

The Beatles' first film, *A Hard Day's Night* (1964), was directed by British-based American Richard Lester for United Artists in a wildly energetic and zany style which likewise caught the spirit of the times – and the film made over $12 million at the global box office on a reported budget of $189,000.

Distributors were behind the British New Wave films of the early 1960s too. As Alexander Walker's *Hollywood England: The British Film Industry in the Sixties* points out, producer Joseph Janni received 100 per cent financing for *A Kind of Loving* (1962) and *Billy Liar* (1963) from production–distribution company Anglo-Amalgamated. Meanwhile, plenty of American companies had noticed the runaway successes UA had achieved with *Dr No* and *Tom Jones*. UA had opened a London production office in 1961 with George H. Ornstein in charge. By the mid-1960s, several of the other US majors had followed suit.

At the same time, independent distributors such as Kenneth Rive of Gala specialised in importing European New Wave films from directors like François Truffaut and Ingmar Bergman and were trying to develop an audience, at least in London, by screening them at cinemas in Mayfair and Tottenham Court Road. Rive was close friends with the directors whose movies he represented. He had an apartment in Paris in the same building in which Truffaut lived (reportedly with shared bathroom facilities).

North-London born, Rive is credited with introducing subtitled European art-house cinema to UK audiences through Gala Films, formed in 1958. One early coup was persuading the Soviet government to channel Russian films to the UK through his company. Rive's father was a cinematographer. He had been a child actor himself. A glance at his career clearly illustrates his pragmatism as well as his passion for films

14. A passion for cinema: Kenneth Rive (1918–2002) was a leading influence on the development of postwar art-house cinema. Like many colleagues, he was also a keen supporter of entertainment charities and spent a year in the 1960s as Chief Barker of Variety.

Photograph courtesy of Variety, the Children's Charity

from European directors like Truffaut and Bergman. He had his own West End cinemas – the Berkeley and the Continental – and so was not reliant on the whims of bookers for screens on which to reach the all-important London audience.

Rive, like other leading UK indie distributors of his era, was prepared to make strategic alliances with everyone from the BBC (he wanted to be able to sell on his Truffaut and Bergman movies to TV) to Cannon, the very flashy, mainstream-oriented company set up by Israeli mavericks Menahem Golan and Yoram Globus in the 1970s.

These appeared to be boom times, with a new generation of young British stars emerging (Connery, Michael Caine, Albert Finney, Susannah York, Julie Christie, etc.) and a seemingly voracious appetite for new British movies at home and abroad. Thanks to the injection of American money, the earnings of British producers, directors and actors had all shot up. One American company alone, Universal, is estimated to have spent an astronomical $30 million on its British films (among them *Charlie Bubbles*, *A Countess from Hong Kong*, *Fahrenheit 451* and *Can Hieronymus Merkin Ever Forget Mercy Humppe and Find True Happiness?*) Its London-based boss, Jay Kanter, was smart and well respected. However, when none of the films at all turned into a box-office hit, Kanter resigned in 1969, and Universal abruptly moved its production activities back to Hollywood. It was a lesson for the British. They couldn't rely on the whims of Hollywood financiers to underpin their own industry.

From the perspective of most producers and distributors, the business remained as much a struggle as ever. Exhibition was still dominated by the Rank and ABC circuits. Alexander Walker cites figures which suggest that at the start of 1960s, the average return to distributors from films released on the Rank circuit was £90,000; the return on the ABC circuit was £80,000; the return on National Circuit, which folded in 1961 anyway, was barely £35,000. Walker commented:

> When distributors' fees, print costs, publicity and advertising came off these sums, the butter left on the bread was hardly enough to be tasted and needed some subsidy spread on it from the Eady Levy to keep many a producer from starvation [...] Only in the most exceptional cases could a British-made film hope to make a profit inside Britain.[25]

Some of those in distribution and exhibition were much older than the new audience they were catering for and had little understanding of the teen market. 'It is an industry of old men and nowhere is its age more apparent than among exhibitors,' critic Ian Cameron wrote in a waspish article in the *Spectator* entitled 'Saving the cinema'.[26]

The problem of barring remained. The chief bookers at Rank and ABC held enormous power, as Cameron pointed out:

> When a British film is likely to obtain two-thirds of its earn-ings in Britain, a Rank or ABC release is absolutely essential. Before a film has any chance of finding backers, it needs a distributor, and before most distributors will agree to handle a film, they are liable to consult the circuits to see if there will be a market for it. So the two men who are the circuit bookers come to have a profound influence on the whole of British film production.

Cameron also noted that the circuits themselves were 'doing very nicely, thank you' in spite of the chronic problems facing the rest of the industry. Rank and ABPC were paying their shareholders gener-ous dividends. The consolidation of Odeons and Gaumonts and the closing of unprofitable cinemas meant that the circuits had plenty of films to choose from. 'They are in the happy position of having access to more new films than they need.'

Michael Balcon had pointed out that independent producers were invariably given the 'poorest play-dates' at the most inconvenient times.

The net result was that producers had to wait for what often seemed like a small eternity for their films to be given screen time – and for the chance to recoup the money they had invested (and borrowed) to make the films in the first place. It didn't help either that when 'big' movies like *Ben-Hur* or *The Sound of Music* came along, they would play for weeks or months on end – eating up yet more of the precious screen time that might have been available to British productions.

Cameron's article made it clear that the independent exhibitors were being equally roughly treated. Not that he displayed too much sympathy for them:

> Exhibitors are in general the most backward, bone-headed element in the industry. Hardly any of them have the ability or the courage to pick their own programmes. Instead they rely blindly on the advice of trade papers and demand only more films like their past successes. It is exactly this backward-looking policy (which extends in reduced degree to distributors and producers and stems from a lack of any real feeling for the cinema) that tends to sap any vitality that could help the cinema to survive.[27]

The government's attempts at intervening to curb the monopolistic tendencies of Rank and ABC and to set the industry on a sounder footing were feeble in the extreme. In October 1966, the Monopolies Commission published a report, *The Supply of Films for Exhibition in Cinemas*. The report was commissioned in the first place because there was a widely held perception across the industry that the two major circuits risked squeezing the life out of independent British cinema. However, while the report identified the industry's problems clearly enough, it came up with next to no measures with which to alleviate those problems. 'It [the report] roundly condemns the film industry as monopolistic, restrictive and rigid in structure, dominated by Rank and AB Pictures, and operating in numerous ways against the public interest,' Nicholas Davenport noted in the *Spectator*.[28] 'Yet this is the industry which Parliament has been asked to subsidise.'

The report pointed out what had long been common knowledge, namely that Rank and ABPC made it a general practice to book films from tied distributors and that each refused to deal with distributors who supplied the other.

The Kinematograph Renters' Society was criticised in the report, albeit simply because it had continued to pursue the same policies which it had first embraced when it was founded 50 years before. The KRS continued to prevent exhibitors from booking films on behalf of other cinemas and it did not generally support the use of cinemas for purposes other than showing movies. As ever, the society was simply trying to protect its members' interests – the hitch as far as the commission was concerned was that those interests weren't always the same as those of other sectors of the industry.

The commission decided against the dismantling of the two major circuits on the grounds that doing so would cause so much upheaval that the industry would suffer more than it gained. At a time when exhibition generally was in a parlous state, it seemed to the commission to make sense to preserve the two cinema chains. After all, whatever the grumbles of independent producers and cinema owners, Odeon and ABC were at least profitable. The circuits argued that their profitability lay at least partly in their booking practices. They needed to be allowed the right to choose what to show. The producers, meanwhile, argued that the reason their films weren't profitable was precisely because the circuits wouldn't book them. It was a chicken-and-egg-style stand-off.

The commission called for more flexible programming with 'limited or partial' circuit bookings for films of limited appeal. However, as Alexander Walker noted, 'the status quo had been sanctioned, the monopolistic interests safeguarded.' The pattern of British distribution and exhibition was to be left unchanged for more than a decade, until the beginning of the multiplex era in the early 1980s.[29]

LIVERPOOL JOHN MOORES UNIVERSITY
LEARNING SERVICES

In the meantime, British cinemas themselves, especially smaller independent ones, were often in shocking states of disrepair. Their owners had neglected to invest in their upkeep and modernisation when business had been good. Now, when business was bad, they couldn't afford to make any improvements. British director Mike Leigh gave a vivid description of his local 'flea pit', the Tolmer in Tolmer Square near Euston, when he was living in the area in the 1960s. 'The thing about the Tolmer was that it remained for many years the cheapest cinema in Britain,' he recalled. 'It was crummy in the extreme, the projection was awful, there was a section where you did not sit because that was where the brownouts and tramps sat and they drenched the seats with piss.' At least, Leigh conceded after watching art-house epic *The Leopard* at the Tolmer, the programming was adventurous and unpredictable.[30]

According to BFI Screenonline, from a postwar total of 4,700, the number of British cinemas had declined to 3,050 at the end of 1960 and to 1,971 at the end of 1965. By the mid-1960s, there were only enough mainstream films to provide weekly releases for two chains: ABC and Rank (combining Odeon and Gaumont). 'Occasional attempts were made to play films for a fortnight or longer on general release but audiences, from habit, tended to flock to them in the first week.'

This difficult period witnessed the rise of 'double bills', with a distributor releasing two films that complemented each other on the same programme. The Bond films were often rereleased as double bills during the 1960s and 1970s, adding significantly to their original box-office takes.

The 1970s was to be a horrendously difficult decade for British distribution, by common consensus a nadir, but it was still one in which some unlikely new opportunities were to emerge, at least in the independent distribution sector.

CHAPTER 7

Star Wars

The first edition of the trade magazine *Screen International*, published on 6 September 1975, makes revealing reading. The magazine billed itself as 'the paper of the entertainment industry'. Its history, if unpicked in full, stretched right back to the earliest days of the silent era and beyond. *Screen International* was the offspring of *Cinema TV Today*, which was itself spawned by *Today's Cinema*. That publication had taken over its rival *Kine Weekly* in 1971. *Kine Weekly* traced its own history under that name back to 1907 but was itself the offspring of the *Optical Magic Lantern and Photographic Enlarger*, founded in 1889.

As its family tree makes apparent, this was a venerable and respected film magazine with a very long history indeed. On the cover of its latest incarnation, *Screen* featured a photograph. 'Nadiuska's our girl Friday' ran the headline accompanying an image of an actress in a skimpy negligee.[1] According to her biographical entry on the film website IMDb, the Bavarian-born beauty, who didn't use a surname, was a 'queen of softcore movies in Italy and Spain'. As she tried to reinvent herself as a serious, mainstream actress, she was appearing alongside British comic actors Leslie Phillips, Terry-Thomas and Frank Thornton (Captain Peacock from comedy *Are You Being Served?*) in a new EMI-backed romp called *Spanish Fly*.

A respected British film industry trade paper was showing off a glamour model on the front page of its relaunch issue. The editor, veteran film journalist Peter Noble, promised 'an all round show business weekly', but what that initial issue revealed was the doldrums into which British cinema had fallen in the mid-1970s.

The magazine published a 'London's Top 10' of the most success-ful films that week at the West End box office. This was headed by Clint Eastwood's mountaineering drama *The Eiger Sanction* and also included the Paul Newman detective thriller *The Drowning Pool,* John Frankenheimer's *French Connection 2*, Disney rerelease *Lady and the Tramp*, and a couple of the big-budget disaster movies then in vogue, *Earthquake* and *The Towering Inferno.* The only mainstream British film in the list was Ken Russell's rock musical *Tommy*, featuring the Who and distributed by Columbia.

The list seemed conventional enough but what was mildly sur-prising was the presence of two softcore porn films in the top ten. *Emmanuelle* was the number five film in London that week although it was only screening at one cinema, the Prince Charles behind Leicester Square. Its distributors, New Realm, achieved astonishing success with the film, pursuing the same strategy that Fox had with *The Sound of Music* a few years before, namely leaving it to play undisturbed for week after week.

Doing almost as well at the box office was *The Happy Hooker*, an erotic comedy based on the autobiography of prostitute Xaviera Hollander (played by Lynn Redgrave). 'Be a Happy Booker... Book the Happy Hooker!' was the message on an ad a few pages into the magazine from the distributors, Scotia-Barber, trying to encourage cinemas to rent the film.[2]

Scotia-Barber was a relatively mainstream distributor which han-dled children's films (*Charlotte's Web*) and star-driven US films (*The Tamarind Seed*, with Julie Andrews and Omar Sharif), but, reflecting the times, it also released its share of exploitation fare. Another of its releases around this period was Don Sharp's *Psychomania/ The Death Wheelers*, a zombie biker movie starring Beryl Reid and George Sanders.

What is clear from that first issue of *Screen International* is that in British film distribution of the 1970s, the lines between mainstream and exploitation fare had become utterly blurred. On the front page of the magazine, there is an ad from Cinema International Corporation (CIC), the British-based international distribution partnership between US studios Paramount and Universal. CIC, launched in 1973, billed itself as 'the largest international motion picture distribution company in the world'. CIC operated the Empire Leicester Square and Plaza Lower Regent Street as its West End showcase cinemas. (When MGM joined as a third partner, CIC became UIP in the early 1980s.) The CIC release slate in September 1975 is revealing. Alongside *The Eiger Sanction*, *Jaws* and *Earthquake* and a revival of *Gone with the Wind*, its other main films in British cinemas included the notorious, Dino De Laurentiis-produced exploitation picture *Mandingo*, dismissed by influential US critic Roger Ebert as 'racist trash', and a risqué American drama aimed at an adult audience, Jacqueline Susann's *Once Is Not Enough*. (The author's name was one of its selling points and was therefore incorporated in the title.) 'In fact, it's been a pretty disastrous year altogether,' the main story on *Screen International*'s front page cheerily informed its readers, but it predicted that after its 'fairly barren summer', British film production was about to 'jerk' back into gear.[3]

By this stage, it appeared that the idea that filmgoing was an activity for everyone, young and old, had been largely abandoned in Britain. In the spring of 1971, the *Evening Standard* had published a survey of 50 cinemas in the London area to see what they were showing. As the newspaper's film critic, Alexander Walker, pointed out, 'of the 60 films viewed by two dozen researchers, 31 had X Certificates [banned to under 18s], 12 had AA [14–16 year olds], 5 were A [more suitable for older children] and a mere 12 were U [general audiences].'[4]

The early part of the decade had seen long and wearisome debates about censorship and whether or not films were corrupting public morals. Three features in particular stirred up very angry feelings: Ken Russell's *The Devils* (1971), Sam Peckinpah's *Straw Dogs* (1971) and Stanley Kubrick's *A Clockwork Orange* (1971). The releases of these three films, and the problems they all caused for the BBFC, have been exhaustively chronicled elsewhere. What is sometimes less acknowledged is the way the British film industry was ignoring a large part of its traditional audience. UK producers and distributors were primarily targeting teenagers and young adults, by then 'the most reliable box office group' in Walker's words, but paying little attention to anyone else. 'I think the British cinema rather correctly mirrors a nation that has ceased to believe in itself, is confused and fatigued, divided and without imagination,' Lindsay Anderson, one of the most waspish and perceptive film-makers of the era, commented in 1974.[5]

The loss of confidence had been exacerbated by the failure of the highly respected Bryan Forbes to turn Elstree Studios into a profitable British operation. Forbes, director of early 1960s classics *Whistle Down the Wind* (1961) and *The L-Shaped Room* (1962), had been appointed by Bernard Delfont at EMI to run Elstree. He had artistic vision, a three-year mandate, a revolving fund of £4 million and a passionate commitment to British film-making. He was avowedly against what he called 'the pornography of violence'.[6] During his time at Elstree, the productions he oversaw included Lionel Jeffries's version of *The Railway Children* (1970) and Reginald Mills's *The Tales of Beatrix Potter* (1971). Forbes lost his job after just over two years for reasons that are still debated. Some cited the box-office failure of the films he green-lit. Others pointed to what his bosses perceived to be a conflict of interest when he directed a film himself, *The Raging Moon* (1971), while running the studio that was financing and producing it. Whatever the case, when he left Elstree, British film-makers lost a sympathetic and visionary patron. Planned projects by such directors as Michael Powell and Richard Attenborough were quickly shelved.

With opportunities elsewhere contracting, some of the best-known and most experienced of these film-makers were delving into the murky world of sex comedies.

The director/producer team of Ralph Thomas and Betty Box, who had made the 'Doctor' comedies and such films as *The Clouded Yellow* and *A Tale of Two Cities*, started off the decade with the egregious *Percy* (1970). This was a sex comedy about a penis transplant. Hywel Bennett played the man whose 'part' is mutilated in an accident and who receives the replacement, thereby becoming very well endowed. The film, released by EMI/MGM, featured plenty of familiar faces from mainstream British film and TV, among them character actor Denholm Elliott and Swedish actress and future Bond girl Britt Ekland. There was music by the Kinks and even a cameo by footballer George Best. It was a box-office success, in the top ten of British films of the year, but did nothing to enhance the reputations of the film-makers behind it. Nor did the flaccid sequel, *Percy's Progress* (1974).

Ralph Thomas and Betty Box had long made their films for the Rank Organisation. As Rank retrenched and tastes changed, they turned for support to Nat Cohen at EMI. Son of a kosher butcher from the East End of London, Cohen (as Thomas's son Jeremy Thomas puts it) 'liked bawdy'.[7]

Another industry veteran, Val Guest, who co-wrote Will Hay comedies in the 1930s, and directed British cinema classics *The Quatermass Experiment* (1955) and *The Day the Earth Caught Fire* (1961), was reduced to making *Au Pair Girls* (1972) and *Confessions of a Window Cleaner* (1973). The latter, distributed by Columbia, was a substantial box-office hit.

'Was I proud of them?' Guest addressed his surprising foray into soft porn in an interview late in his career in typically pragmatic and unapologetic fashion. 'Not in the slightest. They were just something that happened in a long career. There are lots of other films I made that I wasn't proud of, and some of those are still making money too.'[8]

Well-known film-makers and established distributors were catering for what seemed to be a huge new appetite for exploitation fare. There were also new opportunities for independent distributors. Variety Film Distributors released *The Amorous Milkman* and *Flesh Gordon*. Production and distribution outfit Tigon, which had backed horror classic *Witchfinder General* (1968), released a steady diet of sex films throughout the 1970s, including *Come Play with Me* (1977), the most famous of the movies starring 'adult' actress Mary Millington. Eagle Films released another Millington title, *Eskimo Nell* (1975), directed by Martin Campbell, who went on to make *The Mask of Zorro* (1998) as well as two James Bond films, notable for launching both Pierce Brosnan and Daniel Craig into the role, with huge success on each occasion.

Joan Collins, a Rank contract artist in the 1970s, enjoyed enormous box-office success, along with atrocious reviews, by starring as highly sexed London socialite Fontaine Khaled in *The Stud* (1978) and *The Bitch* (1979). The two films were underwritten by George Walker, a colourful former boxer and petty East End gangster turned tycoon and founder of the Brent Walker property company. Attracted by the glamour of the film business as well as the opportunity it provided for financial sharp practice, Walker had set up Brent Walker Film Distribution Ltd and briefly went on to run Elstree Studios. He had met Collins at a lunch in Cannes and had offered to finance the films, based on bestselling novels by Collins's sister, Jackie Collins.

The World 'Gala' Premiere of *The Bitch* was held at the Rialto Cinema in the West End. (The cinema, which had had many different operators including ABC and Fox and which had been one of the first British theatres to show movies in CinemaScope, was run by Brent Walker between 1977 and 1982.) Collins didn't seem especially embarrassed at this foray into sex films, which would pave the way for her to become a global star in US soap opera *Dynasty*. 'I've done a lot of horror films and you can't get much lower than that, scrubbing blood off a white carpet,' she told an interviewer, as if sex was at least a small step up on horror.[9]

This was an X-rated sex film and yet was handled by distributors Brent Walker, and treated by the mainstream media, as if it was just another star-studded British movie. Collins turned up at the premiere with fur draped round her neck, looking more like Gloria Swanson in *Sunset Boulevard* than Mary Millington in *Eskimo Nell*.

One of the few enthusiastic reviewers of *The Bitch* in the magazine *Felix* wrote:

> The film is cool and sharp. Real Saturday night entertainment [...] A classy comment on London's night life [...] and guaranteed to add to the satisfaction of living in London. 50 per cent of the film is based on some form of sex. 25 per cent is filled with the stars thinking about sex. In the remaining 25 per cent, they are allowed to recover.[10]

The film is said to have outperformed its predecessor, *The Stud*, and to have made well over $20 million at the box office.

Nonetheless, as the example of Hammer films showed, sex didn't necessarily sell. Hammer horror was one of British cinema's most well-known 'brands' but, by the early 1970s, Hammer was making films like *The Vampire Lovers* (1970) and *Lust for a Vampire* (1971) which were nicknamed 'bloodshed and bosoms' movies. In trying to make horror hip and graphic both in terms of sex and violence, Hammer risked losing its identity – and its audience.

Alongside the sex films, the 1970s was the decade of TV spin-offs. *On the Buses* (1971), also produced by Hammer, was based on a creaky sitcom set around a bus depot. It was made for a reported £90,000 and generated over £1 million at the box office. Film versions of *Dad's Army* (1971), derived from a long-running comedy about the British Home Guard during World War II; *Bless This House* (1971), a family suburban sitcom with Sid James as the smirking but long-suffering husband and father; and *Steptoe and Son* (1972), taken from a sitcom about a feckless father and son working in the rag-and-bone business, were likewise box-office successes.

The old Rank/ABC duopoly remained in control of the majority of the country's cinemas, albeit that both companies were striking new alliances of their own. EMI had taken over ABPC in 1969. It had entered into a co-production agreement with MGM in April 1970 – and this in turn had spawned a new distribution arm, MGM–EMI Distributors. (It proved a short-lived venture as MGM soon became a partner in CIC.) Rank had strengthened yet further its distribution partnership with Fox.

To some, the approach to distribution seemed unnecessarily rigid. David Puttnam recalls that, in the early 1970s, when he was a youthful producer working on rock-'n'-roll drama *That'll Be the Day* with distribution company Anglo-Amalgamated/EMI (under producer/distributor Nat Cohen), he was given 10 per cent of the budget (a standard figure) to spend on the promotion of the film. Realising that this would not be enough to make an impact, Puttnam went straight to the record company Ronco Music to ask them partially to finance the film. David Essex, Ringo Starr, Keith Moon and Billy Fury, all big-name music stars, headlined the cast. A tie-in album was planned anyway and was being promoted on TV. Puttnam piggybacked on the album campaign to push the film. The budget for the campaign was far more than that for the entire movie.

'Because I came out of advertising, I was able to re-think for myself the shibboleths that had attached themselves to film distribution,'

Puttnam comments regarding the decision to use advertising and music industry techniques to sell his movies.[11]

Puttnam's anecdotes about the early 1970s underline the formulaic nature of UK distribution in that period – the 10 per cent of budget spent on marketing, the rigidly systematic way in which the distributors licensed their films to cinemas and provided the posters and advertising blocks for local papers. In the Exhibitor Campaign Books which distributors compiled at the time, there was a section with small pre-approved, ready-made adverts which could be dropped into local papers.

The major cinema companies, Rank (which owned the Odeon chain) and ABC-EMI (owner of the ABC chain), dominated British exhibition in the early 1970s. Distributors were 'aligned' with one or the other. This meant that the companies' chief 'bookers', Bob Webster, managing director of EMI Cinemas, and George Pinches, the head of exhibition at Rank, exercised enormous power. 'It was worse than a duopoly because it was an uncompetitive duopoly,' Puttnam says of the two all-powerful companies. 'It was absolutely formulaic and there was no one sitting there, saying what is right for this movie. You fell into a cookie cutter.'

Puttnam was part of a new generation of British film-makers coming into the industry from the world of advertising. This included such maverick figures as Alan Parker (director of *Bugsy Malone* and *Midnight Express*) and Ridley Scott (director of *The Duellists* and *Alien*). One characteristic they shared was the attention they paid to the marketing and distribution of their work. Parker, a very talented and very caustic cartoonist, oversaw every aspect of his films and was one of the few directors ready to bite back when critics attacked him. Parker even helped change the way posters were shown in cinemas. For many years, 'quads' (as standard British posters were called) had been folded and circulated in envelopes. Parker, riding high in the 1980s, complained that they should be displayed in cinemas in pristine condition – hence leading to the National Screen Service (and others) dispatching quads rolled up in tubes.

There was a sense of unease and often downright hostility between generations. 'A sick film made by sick people for sick audiences' was the description of Nic Roeg's *Bad Timing* (1980) given by one senior Rank distribution executive. Such an animus against the film wouldn't have mattered so much if it hadn't happened to be the case that Rank itself was distributing the film. Roeg's Vienna-set movie was a dark romantic psychodrama that touched on necrophilia, not a subject that Rank's bookers seemed especially enthusiastic about. There was an obvious irony. Rank, the company set up by a Methodist flour magnate, had initially refused to show X films as a matter of principle but, in British cinema of the 1970s, X films were part of the staple diet. 'They took the Gong Man off the front of the film. The [Rank] trademark was taken off the front of the film,' the film's producer Jeremy Thomas recalls. 'Morality got in the way. They misunderstood the film.'[12]

The early 1970s is regarded now as one of the golden moments in American cinema. This was a period in which visionary directors and producers were briefly given their head – when the lunatics really were able to take over the asylum, as had been quipped about United Artists. Stars like Charlie Chaplin and Mary Pickford and directors like D. W. Griffith didn't just make the films but took the business decisions too. It is the period covered in Peter Biskind's book *Easy Riders, Raging Bulls*. A new generation of adventurous film-makers led by such figures as Dennis Hopper, Bob Rafelson, Martin Scorsese, Francis Ford Coppola, Hal Ashby, Roman Polanski and others were turning out exceptional work under the patronage of benign and indulgent studio bosses. Films like *Taxi Driver*, *Five Easy Pieces*, *The Godfather*, *Coming Home* and *Chinatown* were certainly more dynamic and innovative than dismal British TV spin-offs like *Rising Damp* and *On the Buses*.

One of this new generation was Steven Spielberg. His 1975 *Jaws* was to have far-reaching effects on cinemagoing both in the US and UK. *Jaws* is generally acknowledged as the first of the big summer 'tentpole' blockbusters that have done so much to drive box office ever since. Rather than being given the traditional platform release, opening first in the big cities and building up word of mouth (an apt phrase in the case of *Jaws*), the film was launched on 500 screens simultaneously. This was an unprecedented number. In the words of trade paper *Variety*'s reviewer, *Jaws* was 'an artistic and commercial smash'.

The director, Spielberg, himself was later strangely bashful about the new style of distribution he and his shark had helped usher in. In an interview he gave to the *Los Angeles Times* in late 1998, Spielberg expressed nostalgia for an older, 'sweeter' time in Hollywood history:

> When I first got started, there didn't seem to be this kind of hysteria and true nail-biting anxiety before a film opened. Films opened quietly, there weren't full page ads touting the three day box office in the trades. It just didn't seem as frantic as today. I would love it if studios stopped boasting about how much money their movies made. It would be so wonderful if it didn't become the Olympics every Monday of every holiday weekend.

This sounded a little like Dr Frankenstein bemoaning the fact that his monster hadn't turned out quite as he had wished. By the late 1990s, print and advertising costs for big Hollywood movies were reported to be well over $50 million. (The costs of releasing films in the UK also crept up. In 2014, writer and producer Stephen Follows calculated that the average film budgeted over £10 million cost £2.4 million to distribute in Britain while the average film budgeted over £500,000 cost £40,000.)

One of the key weapons in Universal's *Jaws* publicity offensive was TV advertising. This was an extraordinarily expensive way to reach potential cinemagoers but, it turned out, eventually, to be a hugely effective one.

Earlier examples of TV advertising had been distinctly mixed. Hollywood had shunned small-screen slots on the basis that they were extremely costly. Before the release of *Jaws*, rival studio Columbia had bought 42 prime-time spots for Charles Bronson vehicle *Breakout* at a reported cost of $3.5 million.[13] The investment failed to help the film make much headway at the box office. However, with *Jaws*, Universal peppered the main TV networks with 30-second ads for the film during the three nights before its release. The Peter Benchley book on which the film was based was already a bestseller and the studio was able to turn *Jaws* into a nationwide phenomenon. The film was released in midsummer in the US and reached London six months later, on Boxing Day 1975. It had been passed uncut by the BBFC with an A certificate, which meant that it was accessible to the teen audience. (In essence, this was a family 'horror' movie.)

Two years later, a film shot at Elstree Studios in London was to trump *Jaws* and further revolutionise distribution strategy: George Lucas's *Star Wars* (1977).

It took a little while for Lucas's film to turn into a phenomenon. *Time* magazine described *Star Wars* as 'the year's best movie' and many critics liked it. But the trade expected little from it. Its production at Elstree had been under the radar as far as Hollywood was concerned. At the time, US exhibitors showed little interest in sci-fi adventures for families. Fox could only book the film into 43 US cinemas in May 1977 (a wide US release at the time would have been 400+ screens). It expanded rapidly on audience reaction, reaching 1,044 screens in August and played continuously into 1978. Fox managed to book it in May into Grauman's Chinese Theatre on Hollywood Boulevard because another film intended for the slot wasn't completed in time. It played there for four weeks, then became the first film in the 50 years of that famous cinema to be rebooked to play there during its initial release.

In the US, *Star Wars* ended up overhauling *Jaws* as the top-grosser of all time. It was a news story before it opened in the UK, which helped to build anticipation. The film opened in the UK on Tuesday, 27 December 1977 at the Dominion Tottenham Court Road and the Leicester Square Theatre, both operated by Rank. In its first week at those two screens it grossed a new record of £117,690. After four weeks at just those two screens (where there were literally queues around the block for unsold tickets), it broadened to 12 key cities around the UK, and a further 16 cinemas in the Greater London area the week afterwards – which seemed a normal pattern at that time.

Star Wars was a hugely successful film in its own right but it had added significance in what it spawned – and continues to spawn. It transformed approaches toward merchandising. 'In a way, this film was designed around toys,' Lucas acknowledged around the time of the film's initial release. 'I actually make toys. If I make money, it will be from toys.'[14]

15. The Force is strong with this one: Blockbuster queues outside American cinemas were replicated when *Star Wars* later opened in the UK and around the world.

Photograph: Getty Images/Paul Slade.
Star Wars TM & © Lucasfilm Ltd. All rights reserved.

Lucas hadn't just directed a movie. He had created a new fictional world with endless possibilities. The film was just the starting point. As Lucas went on to make more and more sequels, his company LucasArts began to license video games, toys, sweets, computer games, drinks, stationery and, of course, plenty of light sabres.

Prior to *Star Wars*, distributors had been generally wary about merchandising for feature films. Whereas TV series might play for years and years, films had a limited shelf life. It seemed risky in the extreme to mass-produce toys and comic books inspired by films that, after their initial releases, would pass out of circulation (and popular memory) until some of them re-emerged on TV. There were exceptions. Corgi had produced a die-cast model of James Bond's Aston Martin DB5 from *Goldfinger* with huge success a decade earlier; that model is still on sale today. Disney characters had merchandising programmes. Bond and Disney had the advantage of being full-blown brands with a pre-existing level of recognition that most one-off movies couldn't come close to matching.

Star Wars, like *Jaws*, was released in the UK at Christmas time. The BBC carried reports which underlined how quickly Lucas's sci-fi epic had turned into a full-blown phenomenon. Young and old queued from early in the morning at the Dominion and Leicester Square cinemas, where *Star Wars* was first being shown, desperate to grab 'non-reserved tickets' to see the film, which was otherwise fully booked up until March of 1978. The BBC pointed out that the 'build-up and hype' over the movie, which had been released in the US seven months earlier, had led to 'store wars', with products 'including T-shirts, sweets, jigsaw puzzles, watches and food'. There were books and comics to accompany the film and touts were selling black-market tickets with a face value of £2.20 for £30.

Jaws, *Star Wars* and a still regular supply of James Bond movies kept British cinemas afloat in what was a decade of steady decline. In 1978, when the cinemas had the force of *Star Wars* with them, attendances rose a little, to 126.1 million, up from 103.5 million the year before, but the figure was still low. This was a period just before the VHS revolution. The only way to watch movies at home was either when they were broadcast on television or to buy 8mm copies – and so, in theory at least, audiences should still have been venturing out to cinemas.

'The mid-Seventies coincided with the lowest point in British film-making,' Alexander Walker notes in his book *National Heroes* as if this was an undisputed fact.[15] There were some visionary talents making movies in the UK, among them Nic Roeg (whose credits included *Don't Look Now* and *The Man Who Fell to Earth*), Ken Russell (*The Devils*) and expat American Joseph Losey (*The Romantic Englishwoman*). Another expat, Stanley Kubrick, was British cinema's genius-in-residence. Meanwhile, British companies were backing some very upscale Hollywood films. EMI, under its managing director Michael Deeley, developed the script for and helped finance Michael Cimino's multiple Oscar winner *The Deer Hunter* (1978) while at the same time backing the markedly less successful Sam Peckinpah film *Convoy* (1978) starring Kris Kristofferson.

However, distributors often seemed at a loss as to what to do with films that weren't TV spin-offs.

The cautionary tale of the release of horror movie *The Wicker Man* is a case in point. The film, about a policeman investigating pagan goings-on on a remote Scottish island, had been financed by British Lion, then under the control of young tycoon John Bentley, 'a takeover and break-up merchant' as he was styled by the press.

The unions were wary that Bentley was going to end film production at Shepperton (then run by British Lion). 'In order to prove to the unions that Shepperton and British Lion were still in business, he [Bentley] hunted around on his desk for a script that they could make into a film,' director Robin Hardy later explained, revealing how his cult horror movie was financed. 'We were the lucky ones. He signed a cheque and we made the film.'[16]

Unfortunately for Hardy, before *The Wicker Man* was released, British Lion had been taken over again. The new regime didn't care for the film at all. 'They planned simply never to show it,' Hardy claimed.

With *The Wicker Man* languishing on the shelf, the film's star Christopher Lee (who called *The Wicker Man* 'the best-scripted film I ever took part in') helped save the film from being buried. According to Hardy, 'Christopher, not an easily bowed chap, put the film under his arm as it were and went off to Paris to submit it to the Festival du Film Fantastique.' It won a prize and its critical reputation began to grow.

Nonetheless, when *The Wicker Man* was released in the UK, it had been 'butchered' (in Hardy's words). The running time had been cut to less than 90 minutes and the film was put out as the bottom half of a double bill with Nic Roeg's *Don't Look Now.*

On the one hand, for cinephiles and horror fans, this was a tremendous double bill. On the other, the impression lingered that both films were being tossed away carelessly. Double bills were a way for distributors to help keep cinema screens filled, whilst offering audiences a good deal, but they were also seen as a way of squeezing a little extra juice out of films that had already been released. During the 1970s, there were pairings of such features as *On the Buses* and *Up Pompeii*; *The Italian Job* and *Monte Carlo or Bust*; and *Blazing Saddles* and *Confessions of a Window Cleaner.* Hammer horror films were paired together as were classic Bond movies, for example *From Russia with Love* and *Thunderball.*

VIDEO DRONE

There was a low-level murmur that, by the late 1970s, was too loud for film distributors in the UK and US to ignore. Home video was coming.

Jack Valenti, the president of the Motion Picture Association of America (the lobby group and trade association that represented the interests of the Hollywood studios), offered a very stark warning about the havoc that video would wreak on the international film business.

In a typically emotional and ever so slightly overblown speech, Valenti told Congress:

> American films and television dominate the screens of the world and that just didn't happen. It happened because of the quality and calibre and the imagination and the way people construct fragile imaginings that we call the American film [...] But now we are facing a very new and a very troubling assault on our fiscal security, on our very economic life and we are facing it from a thing called the video cassette recorder and its necessary companion called the blank tape. And it is like a great tidal wave

just off the shore. This video cassette recorder and the blank tape threaten profoundly the life-sustaining protection, I guess you would call it, on which copyright owners depend, on which film people depend, on which television people depend and it is called copyright.[17]

Valenti's fear – shared by the film industry in the UK – was that films were going to be 'eroded in value' by being copied onto blank cassettes and then watched by the public inside their homes. Their makers' intellectual property was going to be stolen. He didn't explain fully how this was going to happen but there was a whiff of jingoism to his remarks. The hardware on which the cassettes was going to be played was manufactured by America's most bitter trade rival, Japan. Film-making was the one field in which the US still easily outstripped the Japanese but, Valenti predicted, this one American-made product that 'the Japanese, skilled beyond all comparison in their conquest of world trade, are unable to duplicate or to displace' was about to be stolen. The only purpose he could see in VHS recorders was copying 'copyrighted material that belonged to other people'.

Distributors in the UK were likewise apprehensive about the advent of VHS and its rival format Betamax, at least at first. As one industry expert noted in *Billboard* in late 1979,

> a number of people who bought VTRs bought them to watch porno but porno is itself transitional. Eventually, it all looks the same and if you have an expensive piece of equipment sitting there, there's a great deal of incentive to use it for more than that.[18]

Billboard pointed out that big, prestigious Hollywood films like *M*A*S*H*, *Patton* and *The Sound of Music* were the top-sellers among the 'non-porno' products in the new market for pre-recorded tapes. Old classics like *The African Queen* and *Citizen Kane* were also selling well.

In spite of Valenti's dire warnings, film distributors began to realise that video was a potential source of extra revenue as much as a deadly new rival. The Hollywood studios either launched their own video-distribution arms or took over companies already active in the retail video business. Some of the more far-sighted executives realised that the nature of the video market would change very quickly. In those early years, older titles accounted for a very large market share for the simple reason that they were the films that were most readily available. 'With time, newer and newer product will become available,' Twentieth Century Fox exec Steve Roberts told the trade press. 'Consequently, the market share for the older films will decrease dramatically.'[19]

The execs were talking in excited terms about the prospect that video would soon potentially 'have a 5 per cent penetration' among the 74 million US homes reckoned in 1979 to have TVs.

In this early period of home video, pre-recorded films were extremely expensive – they cost as much as $70 for a single movie. The more perceptive distributors realised, though, that it was inevitable prices would come down and video recorders would become almost as commonplace as TVs themselves.

The first commercial VHS player, the JVC HR-3300EK, was launched in the UK in 1978 at the then astronomical price of £799.[20] 'If you missed it on BBC or ITV, see it on JVC,' read the slogan on the ads for the new machine.

Once the hardware became available and affordable, the software (namely the movies) soon followed. Video shops became a familiar part of every British high street. There were both independently owned outlets and stores that were part of big chains. (Blockbuster launched in the mid-1980s.) At first, the market was primarily for rental titles for the simple reason that pre-recorded tapes were still so expensive.

UK distributors were quick to get into the video market – but in the early days, the UK video business was largely unregulated. The pioneers in video distribution tended to be companies dealing with exploitation fare.

One adventurous new outfit was VIPCO (Video Instant Picture Company). Company founder Mike Lee had been selling video machines at a store on Oxford Street. He thought he saw a gap in the market and so rang distributors whose numbers he found in the Yellow Pages to ask if they had any films they could license to him for video after or instead of cinema release. What was available was exploitation fare – films like *Hot Sex in Bangkok* and *Caged Women*. These films sold well. With the profits, VIPCO invested in slightly more upmarket fare. This included Abel Ferrara's cult horror movie *The Driller Killer*, which the company released in 1982.

Ferrara is a respected, if very maverick, film-maker whose work has shown in festivals like Cannes and Venice. However, when the film was released on video in the UK, VIPCO marketed it with a lurid ingenuity worthy of Hollywood B-movie ballyhoo merchant, William Castle (famous for electrocuting cinemagoers during screenings of his 1959 film, *The Tingler*). The cover image, also used in advertising, was of a bearded man screaming in agony as a drill penetrates deep into his forehead and blood cascades down over his eye and toward his mouth. 'The blood runs in rivers… and the drill keeps tearing through flesh and bone,' ran the slogan on the poster. 'As the streaming drill closes on its victim you don't really believe what you are seeing… until blood starts pouring and another tearing scream joins the drill. A steel stomach is required to watch the final scenes of mayhem.'

VIPCO's shock tactics were effective, but only in the short term. Its films were released without certification from the BBFC. In the early, lawless days of video distribution in the UK, that was part of their appeal. Some distributors took pride in being beyond the censors' control.

There was a certain inevitability about the uproar that soon followed. The British press took almost as much pleasure in decrying 'video nasties' as their distributors did in hyping them up. The *Daily Mail* was especially vociferous, warning in headlines of the 'rape of our children's minds' and encouraging politicians to 'ban video sadism now'. Moral crusader Mary Whitehouse, the founder and president of the National Viewers' and Listeners' Association and a very prominent campaigner against obscenity, was also quick to attack video nasties, which she described as 'appalling and utter filth'. It didn't help that one distributor, Go Video, had reportedly secretly sent her a copy of *Cannibal Holocaust* (1980) in the hope she would fulminate against it and thereby raise its profile.

Several films (including *The Driller Killer*) were prosecuted under the 1959 Obscene Publications Act (which had been amended hastily to include films and to make this possible). Tapes were impounded and one distributor, David Hamilton-Grant, was given an 18-month prison sentence for distributing the Italian slasher movie *Nightmares in a Damaged Brain* (1981). In 1983, over 70 films were put on a list drawn up by the Director of Public Prosecutions as violating the Obscene Publications Act and over half of these were prosecuted. The list included films by Sam Raimi, Wes Craven and Andy Warhol as well as plenty of low-grade Italian genre fare.

The furore led eventually to the passing of the Video Recordings Act 1984, which decreed that videos being sold or rented would have to be classified. (In 1985, the BBFC was appointed to undertake the job of certifying the videos, using the same categories as it did with films for theatrical release.)

The Kinematograph Renters' Society, which changed its name in 1979 to the Society of Film Distributors (SFD), was heavily involved in the debates around censorship and obscenity. A delegation of distributors led by SFD president Percy Livingstone had given evidence to the so-called 'Williams' Committee on Obscenity and Film Censorship' in 1979.

Eventually, all the din about video nasties died down. In the US, in spite of Jack Valenti's dire warnings that home video was going to destroy the film business, video became a vital source of revenue for the Hollywood studios. (Valenti had made similarly grim predictions about the damage the cable TV business would do to cinema – and he was equally inaccurate about that as well.) Film-makers were learning to work with partners they had formerly seen as sworn enemies. This was underlined in 1974 when United Artists agreed to license a package of six Bond movies to British TV – an act that would have been considered treachery by film distributors only a few years before.

With the growth of the video market, the UK's distributors and exhibitors realised they needed to make a compelling new argument to their customers as to why they should make the effort to see films on the big screen.

In this period, 007 was still doing his part for the British box office. After the height of 'Bondmania' in the mid-1960s, the series soared to new heights in the late 1970s with *The Spy Who Loved Me* and *Moonraker* (itself influenced by *Star Wars*), two huge productions that rivalled anything being made in the world at the time (with epic Ken Adam production design, and big, televised world premieres from the Odeon Leicester Square).

The *Star Wars* series was also gaining traction. In 1978, the original film won seven Academy Awards, giving it critical respectability. It was nominated for five BAFTAs and won two – a considerable achievement given that most BAFTAs in the 1970s went to US films such as *One Flew Over the Cuckoo's Nest*, *The Godfather*, *Butch Cassidy and the Sundance Kid*, *Annie Hall*, *Cabaret* and *Alice Doesn't Live Here Anymore*, and so it was in prestigious company.

The example of audiences queuing on a freezing January morning to see *Star Wars* or turning up in huge numbers to watch the latest Bond movie suggested the demand was still there – at least for certain kinds of films.

The old system clearly wasn't working. There was still a duopoly, between Rank and EMI. This wasn't a free or flexible market. Barring systems were still in place and the major distributors remained aligned with one or other of the circuits. In spite of all the inquiries about and government reports on exhibition practices in previous years, nothing much seemed to have changed. Films that did strong business in London's West End cinemas could take a small eternity to filter outward to cinemas in other parts of the country. The cinemas themselves were looking threadbare. There was a sense of déjà vu when, in the summer of 1980, the Monopolies and Mergers Commission announced that it intended to explore how films were booked into the Rank and EMI circuits.

It wasn't the government that cracked the problem of the lack of competition in British exhibition. As it turned out, the real revolution would begin a few years later in Milton Keynes in Buckinghamshire when an American company decided to open Britain's first multiplex.

CHAPTER 8

Chariots of Fire

Revolutions begin in surprising ways. In 1985, a newly built glass and red-steel pyramid was opened in Milton Keynes in Buckinghamshire. 'On the outside, it is not going to win any architectural awards. Like much of Milton Keynes, it is unashamedly functional,' announced a TV news reporter covering the opening of the new cinema, the Point. This was a 'multiplex'. It offered bars, a gym, a bingo hall, a brasserie and, so the report claimed, 'the world's first ten-screen cinema'. It was a moot point whether this really was the 'world's' first ten-screener but it was the first one in Britain and the local news reporters were keen to soup up their story.

The Point's owners, US chain AMC, had little understanding of the infighting or secret rules in the British market. Concepts like 'barring' and 'alignment' were foreign to them. AMC's history stretched back to the silent era. The company had been founded by the Dubinsky brothers, vaudeville performers who put on shows in the Midwest. Their stock-in-trade was melodramas or versions of Broadway hits which they performed in tents.

Exhausted by life on the road, the brothers bought the Regal Theatre in Kansas City, Missouri, and decided to move into the movie exhibition business. In little more than a decade, they had opened 40 cinemas in venues across the Midwest. Their business continued to grow.

The most prominent of the brothers, Edward Dubinsky, changed his name to Edward Durwood. With his death in 1960, his son Stan took over the running of the family company.

Stan's moment of epiphany came in 1962 when he was standing

in the lobby of the 600-seat Roxy Cinema in Kansas. At the time, audiences were dropping and attendance levels were so low that he had taken to closing off the balcony in order not to have to pay an usher to stay up there. As he later told the trade magazine *Variety*, he realised that, if he added a second screen, he could double his box office without having to pay the staff extra. Starting in the Kansas City area, he therefore began to build multiplex cinemas. The first one, the Parkway Twin, with two screens, opened in July 1963. It was a sign of things to come that its original programme consisted of just one film, *The Great Escape*, but now shown in two adjoining cinemas. Forty years later, when summer blockbusters were released, there would be the seemingly paradoxical situation of multiplexes, set up to increase choice, showing the same film on thousands of screens.

Stan changed the name of the company from Durwood Theatres to American Multi-Cinema (AMC) in 1968.

Gradually, the programming policy became more expansive. There weren't just two-screen cinemas but four-screen cinemas and then six-screen cinemas and then eight-screen cinemas. 'It was like punching a hole in the floor of your living room and oil coming out,' Mr Durwood later claimed. 'I figured I had about five years to run with the ball before the big guys would overtake me.'[1] The irony was that Durwood, the Midwestern exhibitor, became one of the big guys himself. Forty years later, long after his own death in 1992, the chain he founded was sold in 2012 to Chinese property company Dalian Wanda in a deal worth $2.6 billion.

Durwood didn't just want to offer his patrons greater choice. Another of the selling points of the new multiplexes was their luxury. Like the picture palaces of the 1930s, they offered comfort and modernity – comfortable seating and state-of-the-art sound and projection facilities. For example, he was later credited with introducing the first armrest cup holders in his cinemas.

The American showman saw Milton Keynes as the perfect place to launch AMC multiplexes internationally. It is telling that a concept thought up in Kansas City had its first British application in a 'New Town' in Buckinghamshire. The multiplex wasn't intended for the big-city audiences in London or New York. The idea behind it was that this was a new kind of cinema, accessible to everyone, not just those well off enough to pay West End prices.

British distributors and exhibitors at the time were largely ignorant about the history of multiplexes. As former SFD president James Higgins notes, films in the early 1980s were still released in a very traditional way:

> We used to work on those days on about fifty prints on a very successful film. It would go out in dribs and drabs. You'd go the first day to the West End, maybe it would be in the West End for four or five weeks and then you might go to the major key cities. It would be playing in the centre there for another three or four weeks before it was then allowed to go to the suburbs.[2]

'You'd only need a few prints to get the film opened,' veteran publicist Geraldine Moloney agrees. 'You could gauge the kind of attention it was getting and business it was generating and move it out from there.'[3] In short, the business ran very differently than it would 30 years later when *Harry Potter* movies would open on 1,200 screens simultaneously.

Independent film-makers trying to get screen time for their films had to negotiate with the head bookers at the two main chains. Producer Jeremy Thomas offers a wry description of his encounters with Rank's exhibition chief George Pinches when he was trying to get bookings for his films:

> I can just describe his office which may be the metaphor for the man. His office had nothing in it. It had nothing on the wall. It had nothing on the desk. It had a desk, two chairs, pale white walls and a lace curtain looking out onto a wall at the back of the Dominion Cinema. You'd go in through the back entrance of the Dominion building. That is where exhibition ran. George Pinches had a top-floor office but it was an office which was a square room with nothing in it.[4]

This austere man, Pinches, then in late middle age, was still determining the distribution fate of many British films.

If 1946 had been British cinema's annus mirabilis, the moment at which British cinemagoing reached an all-time peak, 1984 – the year before the opening of the Point in Milton Keynes – had been its annus horribilis, the point at which it fell to its absolute nadir. Look at the figures and you could be forgiven for thinking that cinemagoing was about to be snuffed out altogether in the country. Admissions had been at 1.6 billion in 1946. By 1984, that figure had fallen to a mere 54 million.

There was a certain irony in the choice of films screened at the Point when it opened. Alongside such Hollywood fare as *The Goonies* and *Back to the Future* was Stephen Frears's TV-backed *My Beautiful Laundrette*, a lowish-budget British film about a gay love affair between a white working-class man and an Asian. In future years, a familiar lament about multiplexes was that for all the choice they seemed to offer, their programming was resolutely mainstream. They didn't tend to show 'niche' fare like Frears's movie.

The Point had ten screens and its operators needed films to show on them. They had no understanding of the arcane rules about barring and alignment enforced by British distributors – and so simply ignored them.

At this point, in the mid-1980s, the main distributors in the UK were still aligned with one or other of the big cinema chains. United Artists, Fox and Disney all released their films through Odeon. Warner Bros. and CIC (Universal and Paramount) released through ABC. Some cinemas had twin or triple screens but these were on their old sites. Rather than invest in new theatres, the exhibitors had simply split the old buildings in two. It wasn't a satisfactory solution. Cinemagoers often grumbled that they could hear the movie on the adjoining screen. The cinemas themselves still seemed run-down. This was the beginning of a new age of populist Hollywood blockbusters led by films like the first *Star Wars* trilogy and the Indiana Jones cycle, but British cinemagoers were still often watching them in substandard conditions.

British distributor/exhibitor Peter Buckingham remembers a dispute between the ABC Bletchley and the Point over the UK release of *The Witches of Eastwick* (1987), distributed by Warner Bros. 'It [the

ABC] was a little twin cinema,' Buckingham recalls. 'Warners told them they were going to play it [*The Witches*] at The Point.' The ABC chain was aligned with Warner Bros. and expected the Point to be barred from showing the film. When this didn't happen, ABC pulled the film from its entire circuit. 'Warners then pieced together a release from all the independents. They didn't go to the Odeon, because that was on the other side [of the alignment system].' Buckingham booked the film at the Cameo in Edinburgh, a cinema he was then programming. The movie screened successfully there and at many other independent cinemas around the UK. 'It was at that point ABC threw in the towel.'[5]

With the arrival of AMC, which soon built further multiplexes in the Newcastle area, Warrington, Dudley and Telford and continued to expand right across Britain, the old releasing model was shattered. All of the distributors realised they needed their movies in the new multiplexes, regardless of their sensitivities about barring and alignment.

As more and more multiplexes were built, the market opened up. 'The biggest factor in breaking up the alignment and the barring system was the introduction of the multiplex system,' James Higgins, former SFD president, acknowledged in an interview for this book. The government's Monopolies and Mergers Commission had launched several investigations into how films were distributed through the two big cinema chains but hadn't managed to reform the system. AMC, with its new ten-screen cinemas, did the job instantly.

As Geraldine Moloney points out, the new multiplexes were offering an experience which conformed to the British public's fantasies about American culture. These new cinemas were big, shiny and clean. They had excellent projection facilities and sold popcorn by the bucketload. Older cinemagoers were reassured that they could pre-book their tickets and park their cars without inconvenience. The younger cinemagoers loved the brashness of it all.

'They [AMC] came in with a very American way of doing things,' Moloney recalls of the Point. 'Even before the cinema had opened, they were reaching out to the people in the shopping centre by giving free popcorn away.'[6] With their exuberant marketing, the US exhibitors had managed to build a customer base before the cinema had even opened its doors. The cinema was purpose-built, bright and shiny.

Even its ushers were in on the act, greeting customers with a smiley American-style enthusiasm that they didn't always encounter when they were going to movies at their local ABCs or Odeon. The Point went on to sell 2 million tickets in its first two years.

Independent exhibitors had long been complaining about the closed system – but now, at long last, the market was opened up.

In 1985, audiences began to rise again, increasing by around 18 million to 72 million. This wasn't just attributable to the Milton Keynes multiplex effect. It reflected the films being released. *Ghostbusters*, *Beverly Hills Cop*, *Gremlins* and the latest efforts from George Lucas and Steven Spielberg were helping to attract a new generation of filmgoers.

The British industry itself had rallied strongly to defend its interests. 1985 was designated British Film Year by the SFD, CEA and Association of Independent Producers (AIP) and there was intense lobbying and marketing on behalf of British cinema from senior industry figures led by director Richard Attenborough. This helped put the problems facing the industry in the public eye. There was also a British Film Year roadshow that travelled the country, drumming up enthusiasm for British movies. Meanwhile, Leicester Square launched its own 'Star Pavement', inaugurated in May 1985 by Sir John Mills, Dame Anna Neagle, Alan Bates, Charlton Heston and Omar Sharif. Each paving stone had a brass star on which a personality's name was engraved, set in the concrete alongside that star's handprints. (These plaques were all removed from Leicester Square in 2012 when it had a make-over by Westminster City Council.)

UK film distributors supported British Film Year fully. The 'All Industry Marketing (AIM) Committee' was founded in 1985 as a joint initiative by the then SFD and CEA to promote cinemagoing. With admissions having just plummeted the previous year to 54 million – the equivalent of barely one admission per head of population all year – there was some sense that cinema might die out, especially as home video soared. The industry formed AIM as a generic promotion vehicle which remains intact today (currently named Cinema First). It invested in film education and an early anti-piracy campaign.

Even given their support, the distributors couldn't hide a slight scepticism about what the initiative had achieved, at least in the short term. 'The British Film Year Road Show has been helpful to members in certain locations, but research indicated that admissions had not been materially affected by the presence of the Road Show in key cities,' concluded a 'Publicity Directors' Meeting' held in early 1986. The distributors noted that, although local press coverage 'had been good in certain instances', BFY 'lacked a national presence'.[7]

BFY had certainly worked in creating a debate about British cinema and in reminding the public and politicians alike of the problems it still faced.

The 1985 Films Act abolished the Eady Levy, the long-standing tax on box-office receipts that was supposed to generate extra funding for British production. The exhibitors welcomed its disappearance. (Producers were far less sanguine about the loss of a potential source of production finance. The levy could return some 8 per cent of the cinema ticket price to the producer of a qualifying (British) film to help with the next production.) This, though, was the Thatcher era and the Conservative government preached the gospel of deregulation and leaving industries to market forces.

Another important factor in the mini-renaissance in British cinema was that British films were being made that were winning awards at home and abroad. On a symbolic level, the four Oscars won by *Chariots of Fire* in 1982 were very important. The film's screenwriter, Colin Welland, told the audience at the Oscars that 'the British are coming!'

Chariots of Fire was an unlikely project for Hollywood to embrace. The film dramatised the stories of two British runners competing in the 1924 Olympic Games. As producer/financier Jake Eberts acknowledged,

> It takes quite a long time to explain what *Chariots of Fire* is about. It's about class, it's about anti-Semitism, it's about achievement, it's about the Church of England, it's about growing up, it's about university life. It's about all sorts of things jumbled together which you cannot paraphrase in a few lines.[8]

Producer David Puttnam had befriended the manager of the Odeon Haymarket, in central London, where *Chariots of Fire* opened in the late spring of 1981. 'I tried to make sure that all my movies opened there,' Puttnam said of the Haymarket venue. 'You didn't run the risks of the [1,800 seat] Odeon Leicester Square and you weren't as exposed. It [the Haymarket venue] was a 620-seater, in a good position. It became a lucky cinema for me.'[9]

The Haymarket cinema wasn't as sought after as Odeon's flagship Leicester Square venue. That gave Puttnam flexibility and more time for his films to find their audience.

Puttnam took a very close interest in the distribution and exhibition of his movies, arguing that doing so was simply a part of his work as a producer:

> I've insisted and will go to my grave insisting that this is a total industry. These silos for exhibition, distribution and production are really artificial. In the end, it is about seeing the product right the way through and therefore good producers ought to understand the constraints of exhibition. If you don't understand how exhibition works, you are not really a producer. You might as well call yourself a production manager. Understanding the whole business, soup to nuts, is something that I was very keen on.[10]

It was Puttnam who took the decision to include the Vangelis music. The Greek composer delivered his celebrated electronic theme when the film was already well-nigh complete. The only way that it could still be included was to put it over the opening and closing credits. With his advertising background, Puttnam was even responsible for the main poster for the film.

Chariots of Fire may have seemed to critics to be a quintessentially British film but it was distributed by Americans – by Fox internationally and by the Ladd Company/Warner Bros. in the United States. Puttnam told a Parliamentary committee of the British film industry that he had only managed to attract £17,000 of funding for the film from British sources.[11] 'I was very lucky because the team that took on *Chariots of Fire*, largely the Ladd Company more than Warner, loved the movie and drove it. I was in very good hands.'[12]

16. A winner all the way: *Chariots of Fire*'s iconic beach run, which opens and closes the film, is one of the most widely recognised and frequently imitated scenes in British cinema. Set in Kent, the run was shot in St Andrews, manufacturing a local connection to the Olympic Games which the town continues to celebrate. In June 2012, the Olympic torch was proudly carried through St Andrews on its journey to East London. At the film's royal charity premiere in London's Leicester Square in March 1981, the cast including Ben Cross (brilliantly cast as Harold Abrahams) were presented to Queen Elizabeth the Queen Mother. The quad posters designed for *Chariots of Fire* stylishly introduced its characters and drama, while also highlighting its haul of prestigious awards.

Poster – source: BFI Stills. UK release by Twentieth Century Fox;
photograph – source: Getty Images/Central Press

As the *New York Times* noted in an article on the marketing of *Chariots*, this was not an easy film to advertise.[13] The newspaper quoted Terry Semel, president of Warner Bros., summing up the challenges the film presented:

> The actors had prominent British or Scottish accents, none of them were recognizable name actors, it was a period movie – which would turn off men – and it was a sports movie – which would turn off women. And there was no real hook from an advertising standpoint. What could you show to turn people on?

There weren't trailers or obvious hooks that could convince exhibitors that this was a film they should book. The solution, the distributors decided in the end, was to show the entire movie. 'Why can't we just say, "Here's a good movie, go see for yourself?"' was the strategy thought up by Ashley Boone, the head of marketing for the Ladd Company.

The distributors booked *Chariots of Fire* into mainstream cinemas rather than art houses. It was opened very slowly, starting in a handful of cinemas in New York, Los Angeles and Toronto and building up word of mouth over a period of more than four months. Radio and newspaper ads flagged up the exceptional reviews it had been given. (There were different trailers cut for different cities using reviews from their local critics.) Only at the very end of the campaign, with the Oscars beckoning, did the TV advertising come in. This was a slow-burning and painstaking campaign. As one exec told the *New York Times*, 'We spent time on *Chariots of Fire*, not money.'

The version of *Chariots of Fire* released in the US was slightly different to the one that had been put out in the UK. A cricket scene had been removed and replaced with an encounter at a railway station.

Puttnam pays tribute to the artistry and ingenuity of the US distribution team as he reflects on its painstaking and ultimately very successful efforts to launch *Chariots* into the American market.

The best distributors understand that each film is an individual entity and tailor their marketing campaigns accordingly. 'Every single film has its own specific challenges, its own specific opportunities and its own specific audience,' Puttnam states.[14]

With production company Goldcrest in its pomp and films like *The Mission* and *The Killing Fields* being made along with costume dramas like *A Room with a View*, comedies such as *Gregory's Girl* and *Local Hero* and contemporary thrillers like *Mona Lisa*, there were at last films that the critics could champion. British cinema was clawing back its self-respect.

Not that the new multiplexes necessarily made it easier for such films to secure distribution. When AMC and its rivals opened up their new multi-screen theatres, smaller independent cinemas in their vicinity were sometimes forced to close.

The 1980s witnessed the flowering of a new generation of independent film-makers whose work was backed by the BFI Production Board and by British Screen. Peter Greenaway, Derek Jarman, Bill Douglas, Sally Potter and Terence Davies were making feature films. Their work was shown at art-house cinemas and regional film theatres.

There were a number of new distributors handling foreign-language and art-house fare, among them Tartan Films, founded in 1984; Artificial Eye, launched in 1976; Mainline Pictures; Contemporary, run by Charles and Kitty Cooper and set up in the 1950s; Electric Pictures; and Kenneth Rive's long-running Gala Distribution.

Some video distributors had taken the plunge into theatrical distribution, most notably Palace, founded by Stephen Woolley and Nik Powell in 1982 and which metamorphosed from a video company into a theatrical distributor the following year.

'To the veterans of the film distribution business – men and women who have, on the whole, sunk into a depressed lethargy over UK exhibition – Palace is something of an enigma,' Adrian Hodges wrote in *Stills* magazine.[15] Palace had moved into theatrical distribution primarily because that was the easiest way to secure the films that would work best on video. Their acquisitions of French cult movie *Diva* and US horror picture *The Evil Dead* turned out to be big box-office successes – and their cinema releases helped Palace to sell thousands of copies of the movies on VHS. The next step for Palace was becoming a production company as well, making such films as *The Company of Wolves* (1984) and *Mona Lisa* (1986).

Video was beginning to underpin the film business and to complicate debates about theatrical windows. In theory, exhibitors were still asking for films to be held back from television broadcast for three years (reduced from five years). In practice, this was becoming unsustainable. By the mid-1980s, as Alexander Walker notes in his book *Icons in the Fire*, 'more UK households owned a VCR than owned a car, or life insurance, or even their own home.'[16]

At the start of the 1980s, Rank had pulled out of production. The Cannon group, run by flamboyant Israeli businessmen Menahem Golan and Yoram Globus, took over Thorn EMI Screen Entertainment (TESE) in 1986. It was a matter of great pride to them that they managed to do so behind the backs of a disapproving British film industry. TESE had refused to sell to them but they simply acquired the company from Alan Bond, the Australian tycoon who had bought the company a week before, by paying him a premium on his investment.

There may have been just a whiff of anti-Semitism in the British film industry's attitude toward Golan and Globus, whom the old establishment figures regarded as vulgar opportunists. 'Cannon made no pretence of supporting an indigenous British film industry,' Walker noted of the company run by the Israeli cousins.[17] However, by the time of the Cannes Festival in May 1986, opinion had swung behind the Israelis. After all, they were the ones who seemed to have the money – and they owned 39 per cent of the screens in the UK. As the *Spectator* noted, they were buying drinks and giving interviews. They looked as if they were going to become the dominant figures in the British industry. That was why there was so much grovelling toward them, both by the trade press in Cannes and by the politicians back home.

The Tory government's Trade and Industry Secretary Paul Channon briefly threatened to refer the takeover to the Monopolies and Mergers Commission but eventually waved the deal through. Alexander Walker later wrote:

> The stupidest act of folly in film industry–government relations had been done: virtually half the British film industry had been sold to a pair of foreigners who, even as Channon nodded them through, were about to hit the economic crisis that led to their collapse less than three years later.[18]

Cannon at least paid lip service to the idea of cinema as an art form: the company bought Ken Rive's Gala. 'Yoram and Menahem had decided they wanted to have an artier side to the company,' recalls Sue Porter, a publicist at Cannon who went on to work for Gala. 'It was a very difficult relationship [between Gala and Cannon] because Menahem and Yoram didn't understand how you market world cinema and assumed they [art films] would take the same kind of box office that bigger mainstream films would.'[19] In the end, in 1989, Rive bought back his company (which had been operating under its own name anyway).

For all the optimism engendered by the success of *Chariots of Fire*, film production began to slow down during the latter part of the 1980s. The big companies were over-extending themselves. Goldcrest, seen as being at the vanguard of a renaissance in British film production, ended up with too many large budget movies – *Revolution*, *The Mission* and *Absolute Beginners* – shooting at once and eventually collapsed. So did Cannon and Palace.

The old Rank/ABC duopoly had been broken. There was a far richer selection of films being released in cinemas and on video than in the 1970s. Nonetheless, British production was stalling. The Eady support was gone. There was little private money coming into the industry. The public funders at the British Film Institute and British Screen had only limited resources.

Much of the best work by British film-makers during the 1980s was done for TV. Neil Jordan (with *Angel*), Peter Greenaway (with *The Draughtsman's Contract*), Alan Clarke (with *Rita, Sue and Bob Too*) and Stephen Frears (with *Walter* and *My Beautiful Laundrette*) were among the directors whose work was backed by new TV station Channel 4, launched in 1982, through its film arm, Film on Four. The hitch was that these films were originally intended to be shown on the small screen, which was why Channel 4 had commissioned them in the first place. The three-year holdback between a film's theatrical release and its TV premiere was a major obstacle for the broadcaster. The distributors were keen to release several of the Channel 4 films in cinemas and the film-makers behind them invariably wanted to see them on the big screen.

This led to complicated negotiations between Channel 4 and the Cinema Exhibitors' Association. Eventually, a compromise was reached. As long as the films had budgets of less than £1.25 million, the CEA agreed to allow them to be shown on British television shortly after their theatrical release ended.

The irony was very obvious. Television, for so long regarded by the British film industry as its nemesis, had joined video as its protector.

Satellite broadcasters BSB and Sky (merged in 1990 to form BSkyB) were opening up a new pay-TV market for films. (For cable and satellite, an initial 12-month window was in place.) It was instructive to see how distributors responded. There was little of the anger and fear that had greeted the growth of TV as a popular medium in the 1950s. 'After much discussion concerning the problems and difficulties it was affirmed that the industry should welcome and encourage satellite broadcasting as it has every prospect of broadening markets,' reads the note in the minutes of a Committee Meeting on Supplemental Video Markets in September 1981.[20] This was a turn-up, an acknowledgement that in the years to come, film distributors weren't just going to be concentrating on theatrical releasing as they had for the first 60 or more years of the society's existence. There was a growing acceptance of what would eventually be accepted as a truism among distributors of all but the biggest blockbusters. Theatrical was the 'engine that drove ancillary'. Instead of looking to cinema runs for immediate profits, distributors now were beginning to see the big-screen releases as a way of driving sales to video and TV, where the real profits could be made.

AN INSPECTOR CALLS

They were sometimes called 'secret shoppers'. They had a thankless job but one that the Society of Film Distributors considered to be of great importance. From the silent era almost to the present day, they were the ones who secretly attended cinema showings incognito so they could check that there were no irregularities. These were the 'inspectors'. They travelled the country. Whenever they bought a ticket, they would clip their half of it to their report. The other halves of the tickets would be retained on-site for some years for VAT purposes. Exhibitors entered the ticket numbers on the box-office return forms (or were supposed to), but they were taken on trust. The inspectors were on the lookout for 'irregularities' and any cinemas that were cheating on the returns were likely to be put on the restricted credit list.

During much of its history, Film Distributors' Association under its various names has attempted to support its members in 'vetting' cinemas. It has administered barring committees and has run comprehensive systems of credit controls. Distributors are all too aware that exhibitors benefit from (highly profitable) sales of drinks, sweets and popcorn; advance-booking fees; screen-advertising rates; and (more recently) 'upgrade' ticket costs for, say, VIP seating, 3D/IMAX films, and so on. It is only the box-office income that is shared with the distributor (and therefore accounted back to the producer/financier). The distributor does not participate in any other income, even though it is the distributor's campaign and the film itself that have driven audiences to the cinema. This explains the desire to ensure they weren't fiddled.

The inspectors weren't only doing their work on behalf of distributors. The owners of the cinemas were often equally keen to find out if there had been petty pilfering or sharp practice by their managers and ushers.

The FDA archives contain extensive records of the inspectors' investigations.[21] Their work was painstaking and was potentially monotonous. 'The Society had checked 9 performances on 7 days using 4 different checkers,' one inspector wrote to a cinema owner about goings-on at the Regal in Daventry in late 1992. 'We found that on one occasion the ticket sold to the checker was shown in the box-office returns as having been sold three days earlier.' The cinema was eventually closed 'due to heavy losses and lack of trustworthy management'.

When tickets did go astray, it wasn't just distributors who lost out. Customs and Excise and the cinema owners suffered too.

Generally, the checkers were sent into action when distributors had a cause for suspicion. If, for example, box-office returns on a specific film were lower than anticipated, the inspectors would be called. They were very thorough. For example, FDA has records of a 1993 case involving the Camden Parkway Cinema. The venue was visited on 11 different days in January. Thirty-three performances of films came under scrutiny. Six different checkers were used and, on five occasions, two separate checkers attended a single performance. This may have seemed an excessive reaction to what might have turned out to be petty pilfering but the inspectors soon discovered a shortfall of 35 per cent over the period they were checking. It turned out that the cinema owner had been admitting students without any tickets; that he was neglecting to print out daily returns (contrary to the society's Standard Conditions) and that he wasn't even trying to account for the complementary tickets he had been issuing. To exacerbate matters further, 'because of pressure of work, he had had to take a holiday,' and had left the cinema in the hands of a trainee manager who was even less competent than him. It was at this point that stock and equipment began to disappear.

The hapless cinema manager had been called into a committee meeting, quizzed by the distributor members and allowed to answer the charges against him. Then, he was asked to leave the room while the committee went through its findings. The upshot was that he received a bill for £4,500 plus VAT as restitution for 'rentals not paid'. The manager, boxed into a corner, accepted the decision and thanked the committee for its consideration.

The inspectors' work didn't yield many spectacular victories. Turning up '12 tickets at £2.50 unaccounted for' was the type of mini-triumph these Pooterish detectives might achieve. Whatever happened, there were always forms to fill in, letters to write. The investigators were never likely to stumble on major theft – 12 tickets incorrectly sold constituted a solid haul for an inspector. It didn't help, either, that many cinemas doubled up as bingo halls and that tickets then sold for films became mixed up with bingo tickets.

On 2 September 1987, an inspector made a special visit to the Cannon 1 in Oxford Street in Central London and spent from 1.10pm until 9pm there. The weather that day was warm and humid. The films showing were *Lethal Weapon*, *Who's That Girl* and *Full Metal Jacket*. At 1.45pm 51 patrons were in the cinema; there were 56 for the 4pm screening, approximately 106 at 6.45pm and 145 at 9pm. Projection and sound quality were fine. The tickets were issued correctly but the inspector grumbled that the afternoon started 11 minutes late and the evening programme a 'good 4 minutes early'.

In the FDA vaults, there is a comic, slightly forlorn note from one inspector, fretting that he has been to the same cinema, the Cannon in Turnpike Lane, 'no less than nine times' in recent months, primarily to cover screenings of *Superman IV*. He has been getting 'odd looks' from one staff member and is quite sure that he will soon be 'rumbled [...] despite my effecting a complete change of clothes every time'. After all, he and his inspector colleagues are 'the only people of mature years' in a cinema showing films aimed at kids and therefore 'stick out like sore thumbs'. The other adults there are accompanying children. In his reports, the investigator offers physical descriptions of the cashiers to assist potential identification later when their names were not known (no badges).

However humdrum their work, the inspectors played an important role in discouraging cinemas from indulging in sharp or illegal practices. Between January 1977 and early October 1980, 27 cases of staff fraud were discovered, 20 of them as 'a result of the Inspectors' own initiative', according to FDA records. There were police prosecutions, presumably with fines administered and jail sentences imposed (although this is not recorded), in seven of the cases.

Changing technology would reduce the need for the 'secret shoppers', but even in the computer age, the same suspicions between distributors and exhibitors still persisted. The relationship between production and distribution was also beginning to change; British cinema was entering a new era of 'distribution pull', not 'production push', a time when, for a short period at least, distribution was to be considered the most important part of the entire film-making process.

CHAPTER 9

Trainspotting

In late February 1996, posters and teaser ads began to appear all over the UK, announcing the imminent arrival of something called *Trainspotting*. There were images on bus shelters, billboards, newspapers and in magazines. At first, it wasn't quite clear what was being advertised. There was white lettering against an orange background with images of one of five scrawny characters looking defiantly and aggressively at passers-by. Many must have assumed they were advertising trainers, soft drinks or maybe a new indie record. The film connection wasn't trumpeted. Even the tag line – 'from the team that brought you *Shallow Grave*' – was kept in small print.

Trainspotting, directed by Danny Boyle, was an adaptation of Irvine Welsh's controversial, picaresque 1993 novel about a group of 'skaggies' (heroin addicts) from a poor part of Edinburgh. Despite the seemingly grim subject matter, the new picture was being marketed as if it was a zany Dick Lester-style youth movie from the early 1960s.

The film was released by PolyGram Filmed Entertainment, a movie company that had sprung out of a music outfit, PolyGram, owned by the huge Dutch electronics and technology company Philips. The team behind *Trainspotting*, director Boyle, Scottish producer Andrew Macdonald and screenwriter John Hodge, had collaborated on one previous feature, the low-budget thriller *Shallow Grave* (1994), also set in Edinburgh.

What was fascinating about the way that *Trainspotting* was released was that the film was marketed with tactics generally reserved for Britpop music.

Macdonald later explained the thinking behind the release strategy:

I was very sure that I wanted it to be a buddy movie. I wanted the imagery to be young and fashionable – to have an attitude. We hired guys called Stylorouge to come up with the concept for the poster. They normally work in the music business, they do Blur's covers, all that sort of stuff. They brought a different sort of concept to it.

PolyGram supported him fully in the attempt to make sure that *Trainspotting* didn't seem like just another 'dull drugs movie'.[1]

Trainspotting's cast wasn't especially well known – although its leads went on after its success to become international names and to appear in *Star Wars* and *James Bond* movies. What the posters made clear was that Ewan McGregor, as Renton; Robert Carlyle, as the film's psychopathic brawler, Begbie; Jonny Lee Miller, as Sick Boy; and Kelly Macdonald, as Diane, were young, good-looking, and had plenty of attitude. If the film couldn't be sold on the back of its stars, it helped that many of the leading Britpop bands of the era – Blur, Elastica, Pulp and Primal Scream among them – featured on the soundtrack. Not only did this ensure endless articles in style and music magazines, it also helped entice young British cinemagoers who generally avoided low-budget British movies.

Trainspotting's advertising/poster campaign looked very modern and edgy in part because it was photographic. It was at the end of the 1980s/start of the 1990s that film posters moved away from illustration and into digital design with photographs and Photoshopping. This changed the way films were presented to audiences – illustration quickly became very rare in campaigns.

When *Trainspotting* came out in cinemas, there were film, book and album campaigns all running in tandem. Andrew Macdonald had signed separate deals with EMI, which was releasing the soundtrack album; Minerva, Welsh's publishers; and Faber and Faber, publishers of Hodge's screenplay. The marketing teams from the three companies weren't keen to collaborate with one another but Macdonald encouraged them to sit down in a room together to brainstorm and to decide on such matters as cover images, publication dates and tie-in opportunities. The album 'plugged' the book, the book 'plugged' the

17. Choose your future, choose life: If *Trainspotting* re-energised British film-making, its poster revitalised British film advertising, too. Design consultancy Stylorouge confidently branded the campaign with the individual personalities of the five lead characters, eschewing a more traditional group shot. The gritty black-and-white photographs were taken on the day after the production's wrap party. With clinically clean typography suggesting pharmaceutical packaging as well as railway timetables, the campaign won awards and became famous in its own right.

Poster – source: BFI Stills © Channel Four International/DNA Films

album – and everything 'plugged the film'. There were *Trainspotting* mugs and T-shirts as well.

Just as when David Puttnam had borrowed ideas from advertising and the music business to promote *That'll Be the Day* in the early 1970s, this was an example of a young producer engaging knowledgeably and collaboratively in the distribution process.

Early on during production, Macdonald had begun courting the exhibitors. When *Trainspotting* was released in the spring of 1996, it arrived in cinemas on the same day as two other very high-profile films, Martin Scorsese's gangster picture *Casino* and Ang Lee's Jane Austen adaptation, *Sense and Sensibility*. The exhibitors convinced him *Trainspotting* could live with such competition. 'We invited them up to the set. They were the first people we invited to a screening, even when the film wasn't finished,' Macdonald later recalled. 'Their support and loyalty was very important. Exhibitors really love films – and they know about them.'[2]

PolyGram, meanwhile, had its own ideas about how to release the film. The company had earlier done very well with *Reservoir Dogs* and *The Usual Suspects*, two films set in America but sharing certain characteristics with *Trainspotting*. They too were films with energy and attitude and whose characters were brave but charismatic outsiders with potential cult appeal. They were also films that targeted an audience aged 18–30. PolyGram spent heavily on the film, investing over $1 million in the lead-up to the UK release and then intervening when the box office began to slide. The film was platformed for two weeks in key cities and then released across Britain. After an initial rush, admissions started dropping. 'That was due to new starts. Also, we were moving out of the big screens,' Chris Bailey, PolyGram's then head of UK Theatrical Distribution, told film trade magazine *Moving Pictures*. 'As a holding exercise, we decided to do TV advertising for the first time, highlighting the humour of the film. The effect of that spend was to hold that drop almost completely.'[3]

The *Trainspotting* campaign inspired many imitators. Cobra shoes ran a Trainer-spotting campaign. *Trainspotting*-style posters were used to support the rerelease of *Withnail and I*. Danny Boyle's film became the perfect emblem for a new brash and energetic style of distribution that British cinema was trying to embrace in the 1990s – the era of 'Cool Britannia'.

British production had been in a parlous state. 'The British film industry in 1990 seemed a sickly plant unlikely to survive the Millennium,' historian Robert Murphy wrote in the very first line of a book about British cinema in the 1990s.[4] Goldcrest and Palace Pictures had collapsed. Lowish-budget British films were still being made in reasonable numbers but few were performing well at the box office and some weren't even receiving distribution. Cinemagoing was increasing, passing the 100 million admissions mark in 1991 and continuing to rise, but US movies were dominating. Multiplexes became the dominant form of cinema viewing. As well as the larger sites (8–16 screens), some smaller multiplexes were built (5–6 screens) in smaller catchment areas. Developers would look for catchment areas of 0.5 million people within a 25-minute drive radius. From the old duopoly, the 1990s saw five substantial cinema operators in the UK: Rank's Odeon, Virgin Cinemas (which took over ABC for a few years until Cineworld came along), UCI (a Paramount/Universal JV, later merged with Odeon), Showcase (National Amusements) and Warner Village (which sold out to what became Vue and moved on to develop other underperforming territories). All multiplexes would take films on their release dates, so distributors' print runs (and budgets) increased markedly. The modern pattern of wide openings then declining returns/screens week by week for a run of a few weeks emerged at this time.

James Cameron's *True Lies*, *Terminator 2: Judgment Day* and, toward the end of the decade, *Titanic*, Roland Emmerich's *Independence Day* and Steven Spielberg's *Jurassic Park* were the films dominating at the box office. What was clear, James Bond excepted, was that there wasn't much room for British fare at the multiplexes.

The pivotal film-related event during the Thatcher era, one which would eventually have far-reaching consequences for the entire film industry including the distribution sector, had been the Downing Street film summit in the summer of 1990. Various UK film industry potentates met with Thatcher and Universal boss Lew Wasserman for a seminar. Proposals were made that eventually led to the setting up of a £5 million co-production fund. Lines of communication were opened up between the industry and government, and a few years later in 1994 – as David Puttnam wrote – 'at the urging of Richard Attenborough, the then Prime Minister, John Major, agreed to National Lottery funds being used to support film production.'[5]

Lottery money was to have an utterly transformative effect on British film, although it would take many years and plenty of controversy for its benefits to be felt. At first, it was the production sector that boomed. When the Lottery money came on tap in the autumn of 1995, administered by the Arts Council, a mini-production boom ensued. The films made were of very variable quality. 'Some films that we have put money into are pretty weak,' Carolyn Lambert, director of Lottery Film at the Arts Council, commented in 1998. 'British scripts go into production too soon. The typical four drafts – if you're very lucky – are simply not enough for a polished product.'[6]

There was such a rush to get projects into production that not much attention had been paid to how they would be released and by whom. Between April 1995 and May 1999, the Arts Council England was responsible for the allocation of Lottery funds in regard to British films. It awarded over £67 million to 79 features and £1.4 million to 49 short films.

Screen Finance reported in 1998 the startling fact that 'nearly 60 per cent of the films involving a UK producer that went into production in 1996 have yet to be screened at a UK cinema'.[7]

Trade journalists conjured up images of a 'film mountain' akin to the European Union's 'butter mountains' and 'milk lakes'. There were films being made that looked as if they would never be released. At the same time, the growing force in the British film industry in the 1990s was PolyGram Filmed Entertainment, a company that was distribution driven. PFE was the latest in a long line of British-based companies attempting to match the Hollywood studios. The mantra was all about vertical integration – about being involved in production, sales and distribution. PolyGram had a genius for marketing, demonstrated by its success with *Four Weddings and a Funeral* (which it launched in the US first), *The Usual Suspects* and *Trainspotting*. It had some of the best British production companies under its umbrella, Working Title and ITC Entertainment among them. The company started its own US distribution arm while opening offices across Europe as well.

PolyGram's philosophy became increasingly influential in government thinking about film. Its executives went on to hold key positions at other prominent companies. In theory, PFE helped put distribution at the heart of British public film policy. It became acknowledged that investment in production on its own would be ineffectual unless there was a way of getting films to audiences. When the government provided £156 million toward up to four 'lottery franchises' to invest in slates of films in 1997, the intention was to create a series of state-supported companies with the entrepreneurialism and flexibility shown by PolyGram in the private sector. Each applicant for the funding was supposed to combine production with distribution. The guidelines specified that 'the inclusion of credible plans for achieving theatrical distribution' would be one of the key criteria for assessing bids.

The tendering process sparked a mad scurry among British producers and distributors to form alliances in the hope of winning one of the franchises. Trade paper *Variety* reported 17 bidding consortia. Many of the main British distributors were involved, as were dozens of production companies, drawn together in what appeared to be marriages of convenience.

In May 1997, days after Labour leader Tony Blair had been elected prime minister for the first time, the results of the tender process were announced by the new Culture Secretary Chris Smith in a cinema on the Rue d'Antibes in Cannes. The entire British industry had decamped there for the film festival. In the event, only three awards were given, each receiving around £30 million over the six years of the franchise period.

One winner was the Film Consortium, involving various production companies together with the exhibitor Virgin Cinemas, Rank Film Distributors and BMG Video. Another was Pathé Pictures, the British offshoot of the giant French company. Pathé had its own distribution arm. The third was DNA, the company formed by *Trainspotting* producer Andrew Macdonald together with Duncan Kenworthy, producer of *Four Weddings and a Funeral.* They were the dream team of the moment. DNA's distribution partner was to be PolyGram. There were heavy rumours that a fourth consortium involving Oscar-winning producer Jeremy Thomas and leading independent British distributor Entertainment had been rejected at the last minute on the grounds that Thomas's films were too controversial and that he worked so often abroad.

The awards event was interrupted by the *Evening Standard*'s elderly but still combative film critic, Alexander Walker, who was sitting at the back of the cinema, like the uninvited guest at the wedding. He railed against the decision to give the Film Consortium public money on the grounds that one of its producer partners was a company called Scala, run by the team behind Palace Pictures. Palace, Walker reminded the audience, had gone bankrupt, leaving many of its smaller suppliers in the lurch. It may have been a fair point but nobody wanted to pay any attention to him. This seemed like the beginning of an era. It was the start of New Labour, the high point of 'Cool Britannia', when British music and fashion was causing an excitement among the Americans that had not been felt since 'Swinging London' in the 1960s. Everyone was looking forward while Walker was encouraging them to turn their heads back.

As it happened, the lottery franchise system began to fall apart within days of being set up. The first harbinger of doom came from one of the industry's oldest names. In April, Rank had sold its distribution arm, which traced its history right back to the 1930s, and its vast library to media company Carlton Communications (whose director of corporate affairs was the future Tory prime minister David Cameron). Carlton promised to remain in theatrical film distribution – but this wasn't a promise it could keep. In September, the company confirmed that it would be withdrawing from film distribution. Its real intention, underlined by its acquisitions of the ITC and Romulus Libraries, had been to acquire library titles for broadcast and for selling on DVD.

PolyGram itself hit the reefs by the end of the decade. It had expanded too quickly and made too little money to please its owners Philips, which, in 1998, hawked it off to drinks company Seagram, which already controlled Universal Pictures. Philips Chairman Cor Boonstra had talked to the press about getting rid of the 'bleeders', that is to say the parts of the Philips electronics empire that were causing red ink to leak across the company's balance sheet. He took a very short-term view. PFE boss Michael Kuhn had been planning on a much longer-term scenario, investing heavily in order to turn PolyGram into a distribution-driven film company with a global reach. Kuhn accepted that PFE might have to 'bleed' a little before this could be achieved. It was a clash in corporate strategy – one which PFE was bound to lose.

By the late 1990s, the bold new vision of a distribution-led British film industry appeared to be in tatters. The three lottery franchises had failed to deliver on their promises on either the number of films they would make or how they would deliver them to audiences. The Hollywood majors continued to account for at least three quarters of overall profits from British cinemas. Hollywood films were released on around 1,000 prints while British films went out on 70 if they were lucky. In 1997, Buena Vista, Fox, Columbia, UIP and Warner Bros. accounted for 78 per cent of total box office – and that figure would shoot up yet further with the closure, a year later, of PolyGram Filmed Entertainment (which had had a market share of 8.9 per cent).

At least there was a renewed appetite for cinemagoing. By 1997, admissions had risen to 137 million. As PFE's former president Stewart Till told a House of Commons committee in 2003:

> There has been a fascinating sea-change in the last eight years, when Britain has gone from being perhaps one of the more under-screened developed film markets to, perhaps, the best-screened on a worldwide basis. Undoubtedly, I would argue, the main reason that the UK box office has grown at such incredible rates over the last 10 to 15 years has been the emergence of good screens. I think the pendulum has swung from being under-screened and offering the consumer not enough availability of films in pretty unattractive environments to too much the other way, and I expect my exhibitor colleagues would say that where we are now is that Britain – from the exhibitor point of view, not from an industry point of view – being probably a little over-screened with higher staff costs and high rent and rates.[8]

Till's remarks were significant. He had been one of the moving forces behind *The Bigger Picture*, the 1998 government film-policy review group report into the film industry. The report compared the UK industry ('production-led and fragmented') unfavourably with that of the US ('distribution-led and integrated'). It called for a new approach, to be driven by marketing, sales and distribution. PolyGram had epitomised such an approach. 'The US industry is dominated by distribution-led integrated structures, the big studios, where the processes of development, production and distribution are financed and carried out by a single company,' the report observed.[9] This was stating the obvious: it was a remark that could have been made at any time in the past 50 years. However, the context was now different. When the report was delivered, it seemed as if PolyGram was ready to compete with the US studios on equal terms.

PFE was, at that stage, the de facto leader of the British film industry. However, it wasn't the only company that was trying to mirror the vertically integrated US studios by combining production and distribution. Film Four, the stand-alone film arm of broadcaster Channel 4, was trying to do something similar. Launched in its new guise in 1998, it invested in production; had its own foreign sales arm; was active in UK theatrical distribution – and it was also providing films to be shown on TV for its parent company. This, too, was a mini-studio with its own ultra-modern offices in Charlotte Street in London.

Like PolyGram, Film Four basked in some of the reflected *Trainspotting* and *Four Weddings and a Funeral* lustre, Channel 4 having invested in both movies.

Also like PolyGram, Film Four was eventually to be accused by its critics of over-expanding. The company struck a co-production deal with Warner Bros. in 2000. Together, they collaborated on two high-profile projects, wartime-set drama *Charlotte Gray* (2001) and *Death to Smoochy* (2002). When neither was successful, Film Four was forced to scale back, to close down its distribution and sales arms and to abandon the dream of becoming a mini-studio.

The Bigger Picture called for greater public investment in development, distribution and marketing.

In 1998, influenced by the Bigger Picture, the Labour government's then Culture Secretary, Chris Smith, called for British public film policy to be centralised in one institution. He later commented:

> There were about four or five different agencies all dealing with some aspect of the film industry and film-making, as well as some residual work being done through the Arts Council. I felt there was a need for two things. One was much greater coherence – hence the idea of bringing everything under one roof. Second, I wanted to make sure that we brought what one might call the artistic side of British film-making together with the more commercial side so that each could usefully feed off the other.[10]

Smith wanted a 'body with real clout' that could fund film-making and film initiatives while also pressing the government on the issues that mattered most for the film industry.

This new body was the Film Council (later the UK Film Council). PolyGram may have disappeared but much of its thinking was adopted by the Film Council as it set about pursuing its holy grail of a 'sustainable British film industry'.

In an interview with trade paper *Moving Pictures* just before its launch in 2000, the Film Council's chief executive, John Woodward, pointed to the 'almost complete disconnection' between production and distribution in the UK:

> We have a very, very large number of tiny little production companies, basically one-man bands operating round Soho. They have no capitalisation. They stagger from project to project. Their films go into production as soon as the money is there because the production company needs to get the money to pay their overhead. There's never enough money or time to do the fourth re-write or the fifth re-write, to polish.[11]

The examples of joined-up thinking were already there in PolyGram's successes (*Four Weddings and a Funeral, Trainspotting*) and in those of other British films (*The Full Monty* and, as we shall see in the next chapter, *Billy Elliot*).

Woodward was calling for the training of business-affairs executives. 'There's a problem with the lack of professional managers who understand managing and growing businesses,' he confided. 'It tends to be a guy in a leather jacket with a filoxfax, a mobile phone and a great idea who is interested in all sorts of things but not necessarily growing a company.'[12]

The new Film Council boss was able to identify the types of films he didn't want the Brits to carry on making. He spoke darkly of

> just hacking money into dozens and dozens of £2–3 million movies that are under-developed. Their budgets are so small they never have a star in them. Their production value is so low

that when they have an explosion, the explosions are too small, they don't attract distribution. They don't go into market with enough welly behind them. They barely make it to the cinema – when they do, it's on 20 prints, they last a long weekend and then they vanish.[13]

'We will never invest again in films like *Keep the Aspidistra Flying*,' one senior Film Council executive insisted in an interview with the author, pointing to a recent British costume drama that had proved a damp squib with critics and at the box office:

That is exactly what we want to get away from – that stolid notion of an English heritage film from a George Orwell novel but [that] actually is made so cheaply that there are never wide shots because they can't afford to dress the set that much. It doesn't have a star in it and is dreadfully turgid. People say oh it's going to be a great bit of art, like a Merchant Ivory film. You think, oh not it's not, it's a dog, nobody is going to see it.

The executive promised the Film Council was more interested in 'solidly commercial fare' than vanity projects from would-be 'auteurs'. The new body, he insisted, would not

give someone a million pounds to make a movie when you're certain in your heart that you're kissing goodbye to it [the money] and [only] the director and his family are going to watch it and several hundred people of the intelligentsia of north London are actually going to go.

Distribution was to be more central in public film policy but this didn't mean the Film Council was going to underwrite distributors' release costs. The Film Council, the executive pointed out, had roughly £60 million a year to spend.

'We can throw the entire budget […] into the market supporting distribution and we can lose the whole lot in three weekends and it wouldn't make a blind bit of difference to anything,' the executive said. 'The problems about distribution of British films in their own marketplace are structural ones.'

The Film Council had floated the idea of setting up a prints and advertising (P&A) fund to support distribution. This would eventually happen but, early on, the executive claimed, British distributors argued it would be a bad idea. The executive claimed:

> They [the distributors] said if you're dumb enough to set up a fund which is going to give us access to subsidised prints and advertising, we'll take it, sure, but you shouldn't kid yourself that that is going to change anything. [The distributors had told me that] we've got access to money. We've got lines of credit to the bank. When we have a good British film, we've got the money to strike the prints and we've got money to buy the advertising. The problem we've got is that there aren't enough good British films around.

An added gripe was that 'pay TV', namely BSkyB, was treating independent distributors so poorly. The satellite broadcaster tended to buy packages of films from the US studios and to invest very little in British or independent films from UK distributors. It was a commercially driven organisation with no public-service obligations.

In essence, the Film Council executive was identifying a problem which had existed almost since the Kinematograph Renters' Society was set up in 1915, namely that there was still the same massive divide in the marketplace between the major companies and the small British independents.

The executive's remarks were echoed by those made by Film Council chairman Alan Parker in a famous and controversial speech to the UK film industry in 2002. 'Production led by distribution, not the other way round. Pull, not push,' Parker encouraged his listeners. What rankled with many was his call for the UK industry to strengthen its 'traditional links with the American industry' and to 'abandon a Little England' vision of a UK industry – in other words (critics suggested), to throw in its lot with US distributors. If the British no longer had their own Rank or PolyGram, its producers should look to access the global market by working with American companies. Parker appointed Nigel Green of leading British independent distributor Entertainment to the UKFC Board and always supported British distributors who had broad, consumer-focused (commercially driven) ambition and perspective. It was clear, though, that he felt the best (and perhaps the only) way British films could reach global audiences was through an alliance with Hollywood. 'We have to stop defining success by how well British films perform in Milton Keynes. This is a big world – really successful British films like *Notting Hill* can make up to 85 per cent of their revenues outside the UK,' the Film Council chairman continued.

Parker's choice of Milton Keynes was curious. After all, the town was the home to Britain's first multiplex, and locally films that performed well there, in the face of intense competition from US blockbusters, had a very strong chance of success in the 'big world' too.

Britain's distributors reacted in ambivalent fashion to Parker's barnstorming speech. On the one hand, they welcomed his drawing attention to the fact that public film policy in the UK had 'always largely focused on production'. He was calling for a shift of emphasis which could surely only be to distributors' benefit. Parker was advocating tax breaks which would encourage distributors, both strong British ones and their US rivals, to release UK movies. 'We need distribution-led companies to carve out a British share of the $60 billion world market and we can't do this simply by staying at home,' Parker stated. He pointed out that film-making in Hollywood had always been distribution led:

> The formula used now by Hollywood majors is exactly the same as it has been for 80 years. The Hollywood studios' mathematics are simple: money spent on production is more than earned back in distribution, profits are taken and the balance is used to help finance the production and distribution of more films. Make no mistake, international distribution is where the real money is made in the film industry.[14]

What worried some of his listeners was the Film Council chairman's attempt to redefine Britishness. He was telling the industry not to worry about the 'nationality of money'. The one company in recent history that had stood out was, Parker suggested, PolyGram Filmed Entertainment. His speech didn't acknowledge that PolyGram, Film Four and a host of other predecessors from Goldcrest to Thorn EMI, from Rank to Korda, had come unstuck as a result of attempts to compete with Hollywood in the global film market and to build international film empires.

Parker was calling for the industry to 'abandon' its UK-oriented vision, delivering 'parochial British films'. On one level, he saw 'British' as a positive – the Britishness of the Richard Curtis/Bridget Jones/Working Title films distinguished them in the market place. To their detractors, the Working Title movies seemed a little ersatz. They presented an idealised, tourist-eye view of Britishness.

An alternative version of British film history to the one presented by Parker would point out that many of British cinema's biggest international successes had been little, local films. *Trainspotting* itself, the film rightly celebrated for the ingenuity with which it had been marketed and distributed, was a gritty local movie with a proudly parochial 'Little Scotland' attitude. In one of its most famous scenes, its lead character Renton (Ewan McGregor) yells out, 'It's shite being Scottish, we're the lowest of the low, the scum of the fucking earth' and bemoans the fact that the Scots are colonised by 'wankers' (that's to say, the English). It is fiery, witty and obscenity-laden rhetoric. International audiences may not have understood the context – the ongoing debate about Scottish independence, the huge resentment the Scottish people felt about having been governed for more than 15 years by a political party in Westminster that they hadn't voted for – but what the film had was authenticity. It wasn't trying to package picture-postcard, ersatz imagery of Britain for US consumption. From the Ealing comedies of the late 1940s to the films of Ken Loach and Mike Leigh half a century later, films with an intensely local flavour often turned out to be the ones with the widest international appeal.

That was certainly true of one of the biggest British box-office successes of the 1990s, *The Full Monty* (1997). The film was about a group of unemployed Sheffield steel workers who become male strippers in a bid to earn money and claw back some self-respect.

It was a film about a seemingly downbeat subject, without stars (although it did feature *Trainspotting*'s Robert Carlyle) and made on a very low budget. For its distributors, Fox Searchlight, this was part of its attraction. There was something innately appealing about its Little England, small-time quality. As Lindsay Law, head of Fox Searchlight, told the *New York Times*, it was a film 'that had no resemblance to our world or our lives. In this movie, the audience actually understands and loves these guys. You can't say that about too many other movies.'[15]

The film's screenwriter, Simon Beaufoy, made a similar point:

When we first showed it at the Sundance Film Festival 17 years ago, there were people coming out going: 'God, I loved that. I didn't understand a word they were saying but I loved it!' We scratched our heads over that but there is something about the characters and the story that is universally understood. It's about human nature and loss: loss of job, of pride, of dignity. It did fantastically in Brazil.[16]

Just as *The Full Monty*'s characters were bucking the economic odds, the film itself was performing its own David vs Goliath heroics at the international box office. Audiences relished its local, Little England flavour.

Depending on your point of view, the film's $260 million world-wide box-office gross on a budget of $3 million either underpinned Parker's arguments about a distribution-led industry or risked demol-ishing them. *The Full Monty* was the highest-grossing film in the UK of the entire decade with the sole exception of James Cameron's *Titanic* (1998). *The Full Monty* (UK box office £52.2 million) remains in the UK's all-time top 20 cinema releases, a huge achievement. The phenomenal success came about partly because the film was fed through Fox's global distribution system. This was a perfect example of Parker's mantra of distribution pull, production push. On the other hand, *The Full Monty* was a modest British movie which even broadcaster Channel 4 had declined to invest in (having initially commissioned the screenplay). This was a film about working-class men at a very low point in their lives. Beaufoy had been inspired to write the screenplay by observing unemployed workers in Sheffield wandering around the town with nothing to do. He hadn't been trying to make a film that viewed 'the world beyond the UK' (as Parker encouraged in his speech).

It is easy to disagree with parts of Parker's speech. His fellow film-maker Alex Cox excoriated him for putting about 'the outrageous lie that small companies never made great British features',[17] thereby ignoring the legacy of production outfits like Woodall and Ealing. Nonetheless, the speech was also visionary and prophetic. Parker had called for the reinvention of the UK as a

> film hub [...] a natural destination for international investment. A film hub which is a natural supplier of skills and services to the global film market. A film hub which consistently creates British films that attract worldwide distribution and large audience.

He called for tax incentives to lure the US studios to Britain.

The Full Monty had shown what a tiny-budget British film could achieve with a major US studio to finance, market and distribute it. At the start of the next decade, Warner Bros. attempted film-making in Britain on a far more ambitious scale and, with their distribution might, helped turn J. K. Rowling's Harry Potter novels into the biggest British-originated movie franchise since James Bond.

At the same time, the UK's distribution landscape was changing. From the formation of the Kinematograph Renters' Society in 1915 until the turn of the century, distribution had operated on a two-tier system. There were the big Hollywood players, and the smaller independents. Now, a third tier was added. The late 1990s and early 2000s saw the emergence of 'major' independents – UK distributors who were capable of competing head-on with the US studios. Some had significant backing from foreign partners. Some were British owned. What they shared was an ability to handle the kind of movies that, only a few years before, would have been released only by the US majors and the Rank/ABC duopoly.

Among the smaller independents, this was also a time of radical change. Buttressed by the growth of the DVD market and the new-found possibilities of digital distribution, a host of new players entered the marketplace. By 2010, Film Distributors' Association calculated that over 90 'suppliers' were releasing films in British cinemas. In theory, the economic logic was still daunting. Distributors' 'rentals' were lower in the UK than anywhere else in Europe, access to screens was limited (especially for art-house and foreign-language fare), broadcasters remained reluctant to buy film rights, piracy was widespread, and the competition for cinema bookings was ferocious. Nonetheless, UK distribution was entering one of its most dynamic periods.

CHAPTER 10

Billy Elliot

In the early 1990s, Will Clarke, a 22-year-old recent graduate, was taken on to do work experience at the Feature Film Company, the London-based distribution outfit that had been launched in 1991 by the plain-speaking Mick Southworth, a former booker for ABC and Cannon.

Clarke had run a film society at Greenwich University. He was passionate about film but had little real sense of how the industry worked. On his arrival, Southworth left him in charge of the office while the rest of the company decamped to Cannes for the festival.

'I fell in love with it straightaway,' Clarke recalls of that first exposure to the world of distribution. He noticed the similarities to his work at the student film society. He was again programming, marketing and putting up posters. 'It was just the getting your hands dirty, the nuts and bolts I loved.'[1]

Over the months, Southworth taught Clarke about contracts, 'print movement', how to deal with the labs (where the prints were duplicated) and how to work out transport costs. He was involved in publicity and marketing. He organised press screenings. One of the Feature Film Company's most notable early pick-ups was Steve James's acclaimed but very lengthy basketball documentary *Hoop Dreams*. 'It was bloody nine reels,' the distributor says, recalling having to carry the film in its cans to the screening venue in Soho where it was being shown to journalists, taking the cans down a long flight of stairs and then back up again. (The typical feature was five or six reels but *Hoop Dreams* was three hours long.)

Clarke was still in his twenties when he assumed responsibility for much of the day-to-day running of the company. In 1995, Mick

Southworth was headhunted to set up Film Four Distributors for Channel 4. Another of Clarke's slightly older colleagues, Rupert Preston, also left the company, founding a new independent distribution company, Metrodome, in 1997. With their departures, David Holloway, Feature Film Company's managing director, entrusted Clarke with keeping the company going. 'I threw myself into it,' Clarke recalls. 'Nobody was teaching me anything really. You had to be self-taught through trial and error.'

In 1996, Clarke oversaw the tenth-anniversary rerelease of cult movie *Withnail and I* (1987), an experience which underlined to the young distributor that it was still possible to find an audience for older movies. (He also helped rerelease *Quadrophenia* and *It's a Wonderful Life*.) *Withnail*, a rambling comic yarn about two feckless, heavy-drinking, out-of-work young actors in late-1960s London, hadn't done especially well in cinemas on its initial release. However, Clarke realised the film would appeal to the *Trainspotting* audience and to readers of 'New Lad' magazines. He arranged for the film to be cross-promoted with wine merchants Oddbins while publishers Bloomsbury brought out a book edition of the script. The end result was box-office takings of £600,000, more than the film had made on its original release.

Clarke was one of a number of young entrepreneurial types coming into UK distribution in the late 1990s. When they set up their own companies, they faced, a least initially, a crisis of credibility. Nobody took them seriously.

Optimum Releasing, Clarke's new company, was set up in 1999 with initial backing of £12,000 from investor Paul Higgins. ('He [Higgins] said later I could have got much more than that.')

The investor and the would-be distributor met in a pub. Clarke sketched out his plans for the company on the back of a beer mat. There would be an office for two people, Clarke himself and Danny Perkins (who had started his career as a marketing executive at the Feature Film Company in 1996 and agreed to join Clarke in the new venture).

Optimum ('Optimistic Releasing', as its sceptical rivals originally dubbed it) opened in a tiny office barely big enough to fit a printer, let alone Clarke and Perkins.

Clarke threw himself into building up his new company. 'It was my life,' the Optimum founder recalls. 'Every waking hour was put into either the acquisition or releasing of movies.'

Optimum was being run by two twenty-something entrepreneurs with no significant investment behind them:

> You don't have the influence to get cinema screens. Acquiring pictures, you are not taken as seriously because you don't have the deep pockets. From a publicity point of view, the newspapers will pick up the phone to certain distributors [...]. [I]t was just a real hard slog. You have to make every single penny go that extra yard.

Right from the outset, Clarke was determined that Optimum would offer cinemagoers a 'point of difference [...], either a film that is different or a way of releasing that is different'. The company had no chance of competing with the huge marketing machines of the studios or even those of its better-resourced British rivals. This was a tiny, flea-sized operation. However, Clarke and Perkins were looking for films that would intrigue the public and offer an alternative to the latest multiplex blockbuster. 'I had to find a film that would put us on the map. I had nothing. I had 12 grand,' Clarke recalls.

The company's first significant release was a theatrical reissue of a 50-year-old classic: Carol Reed's *The Third Man* (1949). Clarke and Perkins launched the black-and-white British masterpiece in the same week *Star Wars Episode 1: The Phantom Menace* arrived in UK cinemas. It was clever counter-programming, a self-conscious attempt to present Reed's movie as the David against the *Star Wars* Goliath. *The Third Man* (discussed earlier in the book) was famous for its mesmeric zither music. To promote it, Optimum hired zither players to tweak the strings outside selected cinemas.

The company had little money to spend on advertising but *The Third Man* was an acknowledged classic that hadn't been seen on cinema screens for a while. The critics gave it plentiful column inches – and they seemed to enjoy writing about the film as a respite from *Star Wars* mania. Their reviews were as effective in creating awareness of the rerelease as any conventional advertising campaign might have been.

The film raked in an impressive £320,000 from five prints and an outlay of £15,000 – more than the initial seed money for the company – on marketing.

Importantly for the company's future growth, *The Third Man* had been licensed from StudioCanal. The French major, the film arm of the Canal+ pay-TV channel, had been on an acquisition drive, snapping up library titles which encompassed many of the greatest movies in British cinema history. It owned the libraries of British Lion, Ealing Studios, EMI Films, London Films and the Associated British Pictures Corporation.

Along with *The Third Man*, Optimum also rereleased Jean-Luc Godard's *Breathless* (1960), a French New Wave classic likewise about to celebrate its fiftieth anniversary.

Through these rereleases, Clarke established a strong working relationship with StudioCanal exec Ron Halpern, who was responsible for the development and exploitation of remake rights, stage rights, theatrical reissues and special library events in StudioCanal's catalogue of 4,000 films.

These were the beginnings of the boom years of sell-through DVD. The rise and rise of the DVD market wrong-footed many in the industry. There were grim stories from the 1970s and 1980s of the US studios neglecting and even throwing away out-takes and rejected cuts of old films. British companies hadn't been any more attentive in preserving old materials.

Suddenly, in a new era of DVD extras and 'Director's Cut' new editions, such material was at an absolute premium. 'It [DVD] was definitely the saviour of my company because I started, quite early on, acquiring movies for DVD,' Clarke recalls.

In the early years, Optimum's titles were released through World Cinema, the company backed by Metro Tartan and Artificial Eye. Then, in 2004, Optimum Home Entertainment was launched.

In this period, at the turn of the century, independent UK distributors were struggling to sell their films to pay TV, where BSkyB had a virtual monopoly. Terrestrial broadcasters were losing their appetite for movies, showing them on new digital channels. (For example, foreign-language films bought by the BBC were most likely to find slots on BBC 4, which had been launched in 2002.) Very few indie movies made an impact at the theatrical box office. DVD therefore assumed a huge new importance in giving these distributors an opportunity of turning a profit.

The DVD market was very different from that for video rental in the 1980s and 1990s. Consumers weren't just looking for an action movie or romantic comedy to watch on their VHS overnight. They were prepared to pay a premium price for collectors' editions of films. The big DVD retailers had huge amounts of inventory. On the shelves of the HMV and Tower Records stores found on high streets all over Britain, Asian horror and kung fu discs shared space with World Cinema, old Hollywood classics, adult and action fare, kids' movies and animation, and all the latest mainstream releases.

Films were benefiting from the new buying habits of the so-called '50-quid man', characterised by journalist, music-business expert and publishing executive David Hepworth as

the guy we've all seen in Borders or HMV on a Friday after-noon, possibly after a drink or two, tie slightly undone, buying two CDs, a DVD and maybe a book – fifty quid's worth – and frantically computing how he's going to convince his partner that this is a really, really worthwhile investment.[2]

Optimum had been launched just as the DVD boom was beginning in earnest. In the early years, its titles were released through World Cinema, the company backed by Metro Tartan and Artificial Eye. Then in 2004 Optimum Home Entertainment was launched.

One of Optimum's most significant early acquisitions was Japanese animated feature *Spirited Away* by venerable director Hayao Miyazaki, the co-founder of Studio Ghibli. Critics had reacted with bafflement when the film was chosen in competition at the 2002 Berlin Film Festival. They seemed to think it was just a kids' movie. Clarke recalls seeing it in a near-empty cinema in Berlin. He pinched himself, struggling to understand why a film he immediately regarded as a masterpiece seemed to have stirred up such little public interest. The Optimum boss hurried around to the offices of French sales agent Wild Bunch, which had signed on to represent Studio Ghibli in the international market, and bought the film 'there and then'.

As it turned out, Miyazaki had some very influential fans, among them John Lasseter of Pixar. *Spirited Away* itself won the Golden Bear in Berlin and an Oscar as well. Back home in Japan, Studio Ghibli movies were easily as popular as those of Disney. Optimum, the tiny British company set up with £12,000, was now their distributor of choice. Clarke looked through the Ghibli catalogue and realised that most of its titles weren't available on DVD in the UK. Some of Miyazaki's finest work, from *Nausicaä of the Valley of the Wind* (1984) to *Princess Mononoke* (1997) and *My Neighbour Totoro* (1988), wasn't available on DVD in the UK. 'I acquired all of them from Disney, for all rights, for very little money, and I filled in the blanks,' he says of his attempts to gather together every major film made by Studio Ghibli. Optimum released some of the films theatrically. The company used new Studio Ghibli releases to whip up interest in the older titles, which were marketed on DVD at the same time. This became (at least by the standards of independent art-house distribution) 'a huge earner' for Optimum.

It wasn't just Asian kids' movies that Optimum was releasing. The company's Optimum Asia label also began to pick up Asian horror and martial-arts movies. The Home Entertainment operation had several other divisions (Optimum Classics, Optimum World), releasing films in almost every genre, both theatrically and on DVD.

Optimum started picking up Spanish and Latin American films from directors who, at that early stage, were little known outside their own domestic markets. One notable acquisition was the very raw Mexican portmanteau drama *Amores Perros* (2000), the first feature from the brilliant young director Alejandro González Iñárritu. This caused a censorship row in the UK because of a dog-fighting scene but it did eventually receive BBFC clearance.

The company took rights to a number of films from Guillermo del Toro, among them *Pan's Labyrinth*, and ventured into documentary, 'betting the shop' as Clarke puts it, on polemical US journalist and film-maker Michael Moore's *Fahrenheit 9/11*, which grossed over £6 million at the UK box office (a record-shattering figure for a documentary). 'People talk about making brands. No independent company really has a brand. Movies make a company's brand,' Clarke observes of the huge range of films Optimum was acquiring.

StudioCanal needed someone to release its vast library holdings in the UK – and Optimum was the obvious candidate. The sheer breadth of the young company's operations appealed to the French major.

In 2006, when Clarke was still only 34, he and Perkins decided to sell Optimum to StudioCanal. The price paid wasn't disclosed but was rumoured to be £25 million, an extraordinary figure given that the company had been founded seven years before with only £12,000 behind it.

Clarke and Perkins at Optimum weren't the only distributors starting companies from scratch. Throughout the 2000s, new entrants continued to crowd into the UK distribution sector.

There were now several British companies run by executives far younger than the long-in-the-tooth veterans who had dominated the sector for so long. Rupert Preston had launched Metrodome. In 2002, Eve Gabereau and Ed Fletcher had started Soda Pictures. In 2004, Dogwoof, which specialised at first in digital and then in feature-documentary releasing, was founded by ex-banker Andy Whittaker and his business partner, Anna Godas. Meanwhile, family-owned company and video specialist Arrow Films ventured into theatrical distribution. In 2006, Knatchbull Communications Group and Act Entertainment Group, owner of Curzon Cinemas, took over the UK's most respected art-house distributor, Artificial Eye, rebranding it as Curzon Artificial Eye under new CEO Philip Knatchbull.

The smooth, well-spoken former City exec Knatchbull was very different to Artificial Eye's hirsute, hard-drinking, Viking-like founder Andi Engel, a legendary figure in UK art-house distribution, who died in 2007.

In 2008, Pam Engel and Robert Beeson, who had been running Artificial Eye, started New Wave, an art-house company in the spirit of the old Artificial Eye.

Formerly a City banker (a fixed-income arbitrageur at Paribas), Simon Franks gave a fascinating interview to author Angus Finney for the 2010 book *The International Film Business*. Franks was still in his twenties when he left the City and set up Redbus Film Distribution in

1998, with support from Demon Internet founder Cliff Stanford. 'Now, although film is my passion – I see many films every week and have thousands of DVDs, a cinema in my home etc. – this had nothing to do with me being in the film business,' Franks told Finney.[3] Furthermore:

> What we looked for, firstly, was to avoid the wrong people in the wrong place who couldn't be unemotional and have perspective. The second thing was that people thought film was utterly random, and so serious UK people shunned it. No one had really sat down and said, okay, can you model films? Can you build a process in a risk-adjusted way as you can do in other businesses?

When he started his distribution company, Franks built 'a very complicated spreadsheet which tried to model returns' on the basis of budget sizes, actors and genre. He was taking what in hindsight might be described as the 'Moneyball' approach. (*Moneyball* was the Michael Lewis book, published in 2003, about the Oakland A's baseball team and its general manager, Billy Beane, who relied on hard data – statistical analysis – rather than the instincts or whims or coaches or scouts, to make decisions about recruitment and tactics.)

It helped, too, that the sell-through video market was still buoyant and that broadcasters were ready to buy Redbus movies. 'I think only once in our history in 12 years we made money at the theatrical stage of a film's life,' Franks told Finney. 'Independents don't have special terms [with exhibitors] because we don't have films that excite in advance as much as big studio fare.'

The Redbus story, as recounted in very colourful fashion by Franks to Finney, was full of reversals and upheavals as well as successes and inspired business decisions (among them the early one to hire almost all of PolyGram Filmed Entertainment's marketing team). It didn't quite prove the case that the application of Billy Beane-like 'sabermetrics' turned the company into an instant success. There were many instances in which Redbus teetered on the brink of catastrophe. At one stage, its bankers took away its overdraft facility. There was a merger with German company Helkon Media, then booming thanks to its Neuer Markt flotation.

Helkon boss Werner Koenig wanted to buy Redbus outright. Franks eventually sold him 51 per cent at what looked like a very generous price – $23 million – but when Koenig died in a skiing accident and Helkon itself skidded toward bankruptcy, Franks faced a Herculean struggle to regain control of his company. Eventually, in October 2005, he sold it again, this time to Lionsgate for a reported $35 million plus $7 million of stock. After all the twists and turns, what was left from the outfit he had set up in his spare bedroom was a major distributor which would go on to release films on the scale of *The Hunger Games* and *The Expendables*. It was now owned by a big North American parent but Franks had still helped shake up the UK distribution landscape.

Redbus and Optimum were both prepared to take on films that rival distributors had passed on, or often hadn't even considered. Some of the films turned into substantial theatrical successes. However, what was apparent to independent distributors handling modestly budgeted fare was that making profits from cinema screenings alone was well-nigh impossible. Their rental terms were likely to be low. Gaining access to the screens they wanted wasn't easy. With a dozen or more new films released in British cinemas almost every week, screen space was at a premium. Broadcasters were loath to show foreign-language films.

One key change evident from the 1990s onward was the blurring of lines between the US studios and the 'independents'. Many big-budget US studio films were co-financed by international partners (newly rich German distribution companies which had floated on the Neuer Markt or, later, by ambitious Indian media companies). All of a sudden, independent distributors in the UK and elsewhere were able to get their hands on star-driven, big-budget movies that, in the past, would have been handled only by the American majors. This was the era of what was called 'the new economics' in Hollywood.

British sales agent Graham King, who ran an LA-based company called Initial, turned up at the Mifed trade market in Milan in 2000, inviting European and Asian distributors to pre-buy Martin Scorsese's new feature *The Gangs of New York*. He had bought the international rights from Disney for $65 million. (The film was eventually to cost over $100 million.) King's challenge was to sell on these rights to buyers from all over the world – and thereby enable the film to be made. Here was a film with Leonardo DiCaprio, Daniel Day-Lewis and Cameron Diaz, who ranked among Hollywood's most prominent and bankable stars.

The opportunities for distributors were enormous – but so were the risks. The British company which benefited most from the new-found access to big-budget, star-driven movies was Entertainment, by then being run by its joint managing directors Nigel and Trevor Green. (Their father, Michael L. Green, founder of the company, died in 2003.)

This was a family business of long standing. Green Snr had come into the industry in 1934, working as a sales supervisor for United Artists before forming his own film export/import company in the late 1940s. With partner Joe Vegoda, he formed Regal Films International, specialising in marketing and selling films internationally, and later went into production with British Home Entertainment, supporting such movies as Stuart Burge's *Othello* (1965) and Franco Zeffirelli's *Romeo and Juliet* (1968). He formed Variety Film Distributors to release films in the UK market and continued to support production through Blackwater Film Productions. Entertainment Film Distributors was launched in 1978.

'His vision was to look at the market and see what the market required,' is how Trevor Green sums up his father's philosophy toward distribution.[4] In the course of his career, Michael Green released everything from Shakespeare adaptations to risqué spoof comedies (*Flesh Gordon*) and music movies (*The Buddy Holly Story*). What started as a family business eventually went on to release Hollywood blockbusters (most notably Peter Jackson's *The Lord of the Rings* trilogy).

Entertainment had already released such films as the Jim Carrey vehicle *The Mask* and *Rush Hour* starring Jackie Chan. Those films' US producer, New Line, which also produced the *Lord of the Rings* trilogy, had a long-standing relationship with Entertainment and trusted them.

The *Lord of the Rings* trilogy was a leap of faith for the UK distribution company, which, like its equivalents across Europe, was obliged to commit to releasing all three of the films before any of them had been completed. However, by early 2004, the BBC was reporting that Entertainment was 'the most profitable firm in the UK'.[5] The company's profits went up from £2.4 million in 2000 to £61.6 million in 2004, thereby topping the Profit Track 100 *Sunday Times* PWC survey.

'We had a relationship with New Line. Not all of New Line's films were blockbuster movies but we had the relationship and so when it came to *The Lord of the Rings*, we had the relationship' – Trevor Green keeps on repeating the word 'relationship' in discussing the New Line deal on Peter Jackson's three-film epic.[6] His point is clear. Entertainment had shown its loyalty in the way it had handled many earlier New Line movies, many of them on a far smaller scale than *The Lord of the Rings*. They always 'gave it a go'. If a producer they respected wanted a film to be seen in cinemas, they would 'back it 100 per cent' even though they knew it would almost certainly make more money on a straight-to-video release.

The company also had many 'ongoing partnerships' with producers and sales agents other than New Line. When those producers started making bigger movies, they would still come to Entertainment.

The Green brothers were pragmatic, private (they rarely spoke to the press), frugal in some respects but ready to put major resources behind the marketing of their releases. Through first-look and output deals, they had access to the best US independent fare. This gave them leverage with broadcasters. To the immense envy of their independent rivals, Entertainment was said to have an output deal with BSkyB, which controlled the lucrative pay-TV market. BSkyB licensed packages of films from the US studios and from Entertainment but would only acquire movies from the other UK distributors on a one-off, piecemeal basis.

At the same time as they released studio-level movies, the Green brothers were better than most of their British competitors at whipping up enthusiasm among cinemagoers for locally made films. For example, they did spectacular business with the cinema releases of the *Inbetweeners* movies, the raucous, lowish-budget feature spin-offs from a popular Channel 4 series about youngsters perched between youth and adulthood.

Art-house distributors sometimes sneered at Entertainment and implied that they had simply got lucky with their New Line deal. In truth, the Greens could distribute art-house movies just as well as these rivals. They had proved as much back in the early 1990s when they released Jane Campion's Cannes Palme d'Or winner *The Piano*

(1993). This was a moody, New Zealand-set costume drama about a mute Scottish woman (played by Holly Hunter) who has a fling with a taciturn forester (played by method actor Harvey Keitel).

As distributor/exhibitor Peter Buckingham recalls, Entertainment released *The Piano* on 90 screens. 'You don't do that! Ninety screens on an art movie. You go out on *ten*!' Entertainment also invested heavily in outdoor poster advertising – something only generally done on big blockbuster movies. The net result was that the film became a big hit. 'They blew apart all the systemic assumptions that we were all making,' Buckingham recalls of their campaign. 'They went straight to what the film was and what the audience was and built the campaign around that.'[7]

More recently, Entertainment took the silent black-and-white film *The Artist* and made it a hit, generating nearly £10 million in UK cinema ticket sales. Its awards haul included seven BAFTAs and five Oscars, including Best Picture.

In the 2000s, UK distribution had three tiers. It was no longer a case of the majors on the one hand and of lots of tiny independents on the other. Now, perhaps, the most dynamic part of the business was the middle tier, occupied by companies like Optimum/StudioCanal, Redbus/Lionsgate, Icon (the UK distribution arm of Australian star Mel Gibson and producer Bruce Davey's Icon Productions), Momentum and Entertainment. They were competing with the studios while also handling art-house and, in some cases, foreign-language fare too.

Entertainment was an anomaly. It was the one genuine independent in the UK that could compete on equal terms with the majors. 'We were the leading independent distributor and our competitors were the studios. They were not independents,' Trevor Green says of this period.[8]

In the 1990s and 2000s, various small UK distributors were taken over by big international companies looking for a foothold in the British market. The process started in earnest in early 1997, when Canada's leading film company Alliance formed what was presented as a 'joint venture' with UK independent distributor Electric Pictures, which had released such films as *Orlando*, *Delicatessen* and *Blood Simple* into the UK market.

The official press release the two companies issued jointly to announce their partnership hinted at the very different ambitions. 'The combination of Alliance's financial support, and access to films, will immediately reposition Electric as a major independent distributor in the UK,' Liz Wrenn, the managing director of Electric commented. 'This in turn will enable us to market more UK pictures to a much wider audience of cinemagoers.'

Alliance's Victor Loewy, meanwhile, pointed out that the Canadian company was 'looking for a platform for the launch of our films in the UK'.

'Electric is one of the UK's best-regarded arthouse distribs, but has always been severely undercapitalized,' trade paper *Variety* noted of the new joint venture, which was partially driven by the two companies' desire to compete for one of the Lottery franchises that would be awarded later in that year.

Predictably, what began as a joint venture soon turned into a takeover. Wrenn was eventually to depart the company and the industry would quickly forget that Momentum, as it became known, had had its origins as a small indie art-house distributor.

The influx of new players helped galvanise the UK distribution market. There was a sense that attitudes toward distribution were changing. In the past, bright young entrepreneurial talents looking for careers in the film industry had gravitated toward production. Distribution had been regarded as a functional but far from glamorous or exciting part of the industry. Now, though, the sector was more dynamic and competitive than it had ever been.

There was a paradox here. To the outside eye, it was obvious that the market simply couldn't sustain this number of players. Cinema admissions were rising, reaching 173.5 million in 2009, but US blockbusters were still accounting for the majority of tickets sold. In 2008, in statistics revealed in a parliamentary report, there were 3,610 screens (96 more than in 2007) in 726 cinemas in the UK. In 2008, 61 per cent of screens were controlled by three companies: Odeon, Cineworld and Vue. The two largest of these were owned by private equity firms, Terra Firma (Odeon) and the Blackstone Group (Cineworld).

Exhibitor revenues, made up of box-office receipts, concessions and advertising, were just over £1 billion in 2008 (3 per cent higher than 2007).

Inevitably, there were casualties as some smaller distributors over-extended themselves in a bid to compete with the bigger companies on the treacherous middle ground. Tartan Film, which had been founded in 1984 by the flamboyant Hamish McAlpine together with producer Don Boyd and distributor Alan Kean, had long been one of the UK's most irreverent and adventurous distributors. The company embraced the DVD era with relish, setting up its own Asia Extreme label and releasing vast numbers of the most edgy and provocative art-house movies. It had also taken over many of the old Gala catalogue titles from directors like Ingmar Bergman and François Truffaut.

McAlpine moved into production, making a series of tawdry, low-budget movies about serial killers (*The Hillside Strangler*, *Ed Gein*, *Ted Bundy* and the like). The Tartan footprint wasn't so different to that of Optimum but it was an older, more established company. McAlpine was extremely well connected. Part of the McAlpine building dynasty, he was born on the third floor of the Dorchester Hotel (apparently because his mother didn't like hospital food enough to give birth to him on the wards). He was a colourful and impulsive figure, always ready to provoke the censors and to release films that other distributors shied away from. McAlpine, nothing if not contradictory, was also an experienced and very skilful distributor of 'conventional' art-house films and went to painstaking lengths to build up Tartan's library holdings. The Swedes, for example, always acknowledged that Tartan's 'Ingmar Bergman Collection' was more thorough, and included more titles, than anything that could be found in Sweden.

In the summer of 2008, Tartan fell into administration. The sympathetic view was that the company had simply been very unlucky. One or two of its higher-profile, more expensive films had underperformed in a way that simply couldn't have been anticipated. To its detractors, the company had overstretched itself in a reckless fashion. It had set up a US offshoot. It had acquired big, star-driven US films, for example *Wonderland* (2004), with Val Kilmer, that had done only patchy business. Its boldest and most costly decision was backing Michael Haneke's ill-advised 2007 American remake of his own 1997 art-house hit *Funny Games*.

Tartan's demise served as a cautionary tale about what could easily happen to companies in the UK's new three-tier distribution environment. Smaller independent outfits that tried to elbow their way into the middle ground were taking huge risks. They were competing against rival distributors like StudioCanal, Lionsgate and Momentum which were owned by big international parent companies and therefore had very deep pockets.

The independents were heavily reliant on a DVD market that was already beginning to change. It was clear that after a century of releasing films in British cinemas on 35mm prints, delivery systems were about to change in a fundamental way.

In 2005, the UK Film Council launched its pioneering but not altogether successful Digital Screen Network. This was a £12 million scheme through which an initial 240 screens in 210 cinemas were equipped with digital projectors. Arts Alliance Digital Cinema (AADC) had won the contract to provide these projectors.

UKFC investment in the digital screen network (giving new projectors to cinema operators) was carefully justified on grounds of cultural diversity – in return for the new equipment the cinemas would show more specialised films. The extent to which this happened is debatable – but the DSN was a world-leading initiative at the time and catapulted the UK to the forefront of digital cinema installations. By 2014, UK cinemas were effectively 100 per cent digitised.

Some expressed a utopian feeling that distribution was about to open up in an unprecedented way that would at last allow the British market to escape its dependence on Hollywood.

Eric Fellner, co-chairman of Working Title and deputy chair of the British Film Institute, expressed this sentiment in his comments to a parliamentary committee, whose report was published in January 2010. Fellner commented that the barrier to entry was the network of physical distribution and the ability to get films into cinemas and do deals with television companies:

Once digital distribution becomes available [...] where we can
go and make a film and we can stick it out there, if we can find a
couple of hundred grand or whatever to publicise [it] [...] the
final barrier to entry to the industry will disappear [...] That
is not more than five or ten years away; I do not know if they
fully believe that but a lot of people in the industry believe that.[9]

The hitch was that the Hollywood majors adapted to the new digital
era every bit as quickly as the independents. To the resentment of UK
independents, many of the new digital projectors provided through
the Digital Screen Network went to the multiplexes.

Similar complaints were sometimes made about the UK Film
Council's Print and Advertising Fund, which was put in place in 2003
to support distributors giving broad releases of 'specialised' films. The
fund supported some films, for example runaway box-office success
and Oscar winner *March of the Penguins*, that, in hindsight, didn't seem
in any special need of public subsidy. A more generous view is that the
fund helped certain 'specialised' (foreign-language, documentary or
art-house) titles achieve a visibility, and box-office success, that would
have been unthinkable otherwise.

'What we were about was the business of confidence,' suggested
Buckingham, who oversaw the fund as head of distribution and exhibition at UKFC. With the fund's backing, so-called specialised films
were being released on 70 or 80 prints, and were therefore having far
more impact in the market.[10]

As the decade ended, distributors were being forced to subsidise
cinemas' conversion to digital through the Virtual Print Fee (VPF).
The bad feeling over the VPF opened up fault lines between distributors and exhibitors. The story behind it is long and involved but, as
the haggling continued, it became apparent that digital distribution
wasn't opening up the marketplace in the way that had originally
been anticipated. The ease of digital delivery enabled the exhibitors
to book films in a far more flexible fashion than before – but also to
take them off screens quickly. Smaller companies, with less leverage
in the marketplace, found themselves in a weak position when trying
to negotiate decent runs for their movies.

At the same time, digital enabled the majors to release their films on even more screens than before. The 'blitzkrieg' strategy for Marvel superhero movies and Harry Potter adventures was now very different to what it had been when Percy Livingstone was guiding *The Sound of Music*'s occupancy of a West End cinema for over a year.

One result of the crowded marketplace was that some of the bigger UK independent distributors were driven toward production. They had output deals and had anyway been 'pre-buying' big-budget US movies on the basis of their casts and directors. The next logical step was to become involved in production themselves. They knew what kind of films they wanted. By helping to make them, they gave themselves a measure of creative control over those films – and stole a march on their rivals in the process.

With its vast 4,000-film library, StudioCanal had plenty of titles ripe for remakes by Optimum, which announced its intention to move into production in 2008. One of the UK company's first in-house productions was an updated, 1960s-set reworking of Graham Greene's *Brighton Rock*, directed by Rowan Joffé. Meanwhile, Lionsgate UK, which had already supported such films as Gurinder Chadha's *Bend It Like Beckham*, David Cronenberg's *Spider*, Ben Elton's *Maybe Baby*, and *The Bank Job*, also signalled its desire to develop and produce British films.

One constant was that some British films that seemingly emerged from nowhere continued to break through and to find huge international success. That was certainly the case with a project called *Dancer*, developed by broadcaster BBC Films and produced by WT2 (the low-budget arm of the UK's most successful production company Working Title) alongside Tiger Aspect. Its first-time feature director, Stephen Daldry, was well known for his stage work but that didn't mean the budget was big. *Dancer* was made for £2.9 million – and much of that money came from the Arts Council and BBC Films.

Dancer, as it was originally titled, was selected for the Quinzaine ('The Director's Fortnight') in Cannes. This was a festival sidebar generally reserved for art-house films. Set in 1984 at the height of the miners' strike, *Dancer* was a coming of age story about Billy, a young boy (played by newcomer Jamie Bell) dismayed to discover that his boxing club is now sharing premises with a dance class. Billy becomes intrigued by the world of ballet. His teacher (played by redoubtable British actress Julie Walters) quickly spots his talent. His father (Gary Lewis), who has recently lost his wife and who is heavily involved in the strike action, is appalled to see young Billy taking part in what he perceives as such an effeminate activity.

Prior to its first screenings in Cannes, the main interest in the film from the British press was in the casting of Julie Walters. Expectations weren't especially high. However, in the unlikely setting of the Directors' Fortnight, it very quickly became apparent that the film was a huge crowd pleaser. In his review for trade magazine *Screen International*, Allan Hunter picked up on the effect it was having on festivalgoers:

> Imagine hitting a lottery jackpot and meeting the love of your life on the very same day. That's the kind of euphoric emotional rush that *Billy Elliot* delivers. Investing the cheer-the-underdog formula of a *Flashdance* with the flinty social realism of a kitchen sink drama, it has a feel good factor that registers off the scale. If the tear-stained cheeks and cheering crowd at the first Quinzaine screening are anything to go by then it can count on formidable word of mouth. Domestic and international prospects are bullish for a British film that even the most curmudgeonly will want to clutch to their bosom.[11]

Hunter's words proved prophetic. The film eventually changed its title to *Billy Elliot* to avoid confusion with Lars Von Trier's *Dancer in the Dark*, released at around the same time. With the distribution and marketing expertise of UIP, the joint venture between Paramount, Universal and MGM/UA, behind it, *Billy Elliot* generated a blockbuster £17 million in cinema ticket sales in the UK alone and $110 million worldwide.

This wasn't just a kids' movie. As its 15 certificate and Lee Hall's expletive-filled screenplay underlined, *Billy Elliot* was a film with an edge. It touched on poverty, unemployment and industrial strife in uncompromising fashion but its underlying feeling was upbeat and optimistic.

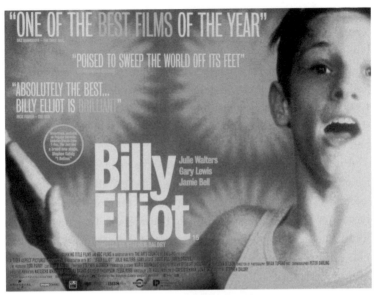

18. Go Billy! The advertising for *Billy Elliot* incorporated some rave reviews to help position the release as a hot property that everyone was talking about. In 2001, Jamie Bell, then aged 14, won the Leading Actor BAFTA award for his performance, which has led to him starring in many other successful films.

Poster – source: BFI Stills © UIP/Universal/Working Title Films; photograph – source: Getty Images/Dave Hogan. The iconic BAFTA mask was designed in 1955 by the New York-born sculptor Mitzi Cunliffe (1918–2006).

Billy Elliot was a perfect example of Alan Parker's formula: distribution pull, production push. It was a lowish-budget British movie that, in other hands, might have been given a limited release. UIP, however, had the resources as well as the passion and commitment to treat it as a blockbuster. It was sustained with a 'Go Billy!' set of advertisements rolled out when it became a hit – at a time when social media didn't exist.

Like *The Full Monty*, the film became lodged in public consciousness and went on to spawn a live musical with music by Elton John. This itself was a huge success both on stage and then on DVD. Completing the circle, in September 2014, an 'event release' of the 'live' production in UK cinemas briefly topped the box-office charts.

Many of the biggest films of the decade had a British flavour: the *Lord of the Rings* trilogy (not Brit productions but still British story material and cast); *Charlie and the Chocolate Factory* (a great decade for Johnny Depp all round); and the hugely successful 2006 reboot of James Bond, *Casino Royale* with Daniel Craig. However, *Billy Elliot* as much as the juggernauts of Harry Potter, Bond et al. proved that British-made films had the potential to reach huge audiences both at home and abroad.

This would be underlined a few years later, when a period film about a stuttering British monarch would again turn into a huge international hit at a time when British distributors were struggling to cope with market conditions that sometimes seemed to be taking the ground away from beneath their feet.

CHAPTER 11

The King's Speech

With the benefit of hindsight, it always seems obvious just why a film works at the box office. Paul Brett, whose company Prescience helped to finance *The King's Speech* (2010), claims that, after seeing a preview of the film, he approached the director, Tom Hooper, and the crew, telling them they had made a 'masterpiece' and that their film would do huge box office around the world. They listened politely but with scepticism. This was a project that both the BBC and Channel 4 had turned down amid doubts about yet more 'heritage' cinema. Nobody thought they had a blockbuster on their hands.

The film tells the story of stuttering Prince Albert (Colin Firth), later to become George VI. Poor Bertie just can't get over his stammer. When his father dies, his brother David takes the throne as King Edward VIII but is forced to abdicate after he decides to marry divorcee Wallis Simpson. Bertie therefore becomes king and he has to make some very important speeches. Largely thanks to Australian vocal therapist Lionel Logue (Geoffrey Rush), he is able to conquer his impediment. At the beginning of World War II, he makes a rousing radio address to the nation. There is little sign of his stutter. Brett recalls:

> The entire production crew thought I was mad. They thought I had lost it. I was just absolutely convinced [of its likely success]. It wasn't just that it [the film] was about overcoming adversity and nor that it was 'royal' but that it was about family. The last time I looked, most cinemagoers had or have a family.[1]

19. Finding a voice: Three months before its UK cinema release, distributor Momentum arranged a screening of *The King's Speech* at the BFI London Film Festival to help stoke positive word of mouth. This cast photograph of (left to right) Geoffrey Rush, Helena Bonham Carter and Colin Firth was taken by Dave Hogan during the film's portrait session at the festival.

Photograph by Dave Hogan – source: Getty Images

The King's Speech wasn't easy to finance. UK distributor Momentum was among the first to support it as part of the first-look deal it struck with its UK-Australian outfit, See-Saw (which produced the film alongside Bedlam Productions), in early 2008. The UK Film Council (which, ironically, was abolished at around the time the film turned into a great success) supported it but British broadcasters turned it down. The Weinstein Company came aboard early as its North American distributor and also committed to releasing it in several other territories.

The film was shown for the first time at the Toronto Festival in the autumn of 2010. It won the audience award, an important early portent. Its next screenings were at the London Film Festival where the response was close to rhapsodic.

Like Brett, Momentum president Xavier Marchand, who oversaw the release of *The King's Speech* in the UK, had been struck immediately by the film. 'We always knew we had a special film,' Marchand recalls. 'I vividly remember the first cut we saw in the editing room.'[2] Generally, first cuts are rough and incomplete affairs that you watch simply to see how a film might be improved. There will be 'temp' music and visual effects and the sound mix won't have been polished. In this case, *The King's Speech* 'worked' right from the outset. Marchand found himself not thinking about the technical hitches but 'just going with the movie'.

Momentum held early test screenings. These weren't just about finding out whether audiences liked the film. The UK distributor was keen to discover whether viewers felt the film to be historically accurate and how easily they understood the subplot about the abdication.

Around the same time, the US distributors, the Weinstein Company, held their own screenings in New York. Again, there was huge enthusiasm as well as hints about what tiny tweaks might make the film play even better. The film was hitting cinemas in a period in which social media was becoming an important new marketing tool for distributors seeking to engage and attract cinemagoers. Most films had official Facebook pages as well as trailers playing widely on YouTube and other social-media sites.

The King's Speech was given a platform release in the US on four screens just before Christmas. Momentum launched it in the UK at the beginning of January 2011. That is considered one of the best dates for 'awards movies' likely to be in the running for Golden Globes, critics' awards, BAFTAs and Oscars.

The core audience for *The King's Speech* was older cinemagoers in the '40 or 50 or 60 plus' range. Conventional marketing wisdom had it that this audience was 'slow off the mark' and tended to come to films a few weeks after their release date. Momentum's marketing team used to joke that their challenge was to convince this audience that 'when we do the opening weekend, this movie has already opened three or four weeks ago'.[3]

This older audience tends not to react to 'pure advertising' but does read newspapers and magazines and listens to radio. That was why, during the weeks leading up to the release of *The King's Speech*, Colin Firth and his co-stars began to appear almost everywhere in the British media. The gambit worked and the older audience turned out en masse for the opening weekend. There were even more of them trooping up to the cinemas during the second weekend – and weekday business was also very brisk. Word of mouth built and then the awards started coming. The British heritage film about the prince with the stutter that no broadcasters wanted to touch grossed around $415 million worldwide (and an astonishing £46 million at the UK box office alone). 'It became one of those movies that the person who goes to one movie every two years went to see,' Marchand recalls of the 'cultural phenomenon' that *The King's Speech* turned into. It was still playing strongly in British cinemas in mid-February when its Oscar haul (which included a Best Picture award) gave it a fresh boost.

The DVD release of the film was given an extra marketing hook by the royal wedding of Prince William and Kate Middleton in April 2011. *The King's Speech* DVDs became a top seller at Sainsbury's supermarkets in the run-up to the wedding.

Tom Hooper's film was a major success for UK distribution at the start of a new decade. That British cinema was on a roll was underlined when its box-office figures were trumped by those achieved by Bond movie *Skyfall* a year later, the first film release in the UK ever to reach £100 million at the box office.

Peter Taylor, managing director of Sony Pictures Releasing UK, points out that the Bond film benefited from some happy coincidences in timing. 'All of our stars aligned,' Taylor suggested.

It was the 50th anniversary of James Bond on screen. It happened to be the Diamond Jubilee and we [in the UK] were hosting the Olympics. There was a general feeling of positivity about Britain and Britishness. We realised very early on that *Skyfall* was the perfect film to indulge that and to celebrate it.[4]

The potency of the Bond brand was underlined by the stunt in Danny Boyle's opening ceremony for the Olympics in which a worldwide audience thought they were seeing Daniel Craig's James Bond and Her Majesty the Queen parachuting down into the Olympic Stadium in Stratford. This followed on from a pre-filmed sequence, partly shot in

Buckingham Palace, with Daniel Craig and the Queen and her corgis, that attracted millions of views on YouTube. That was in July. Most of the Diamond Jubilee celebrations had been held in the summer too. *Skyfall* opened in October but still seemed to benefit from the goodwill that these events engendered.

'Possibly, and I would include Harry Potter in this, James Bond is the greatest literary and film icon of all time,' Taylor noted of the impact of 007 on British cultural life. He points to the influence of Bond on everything from 'film-making style, architecture through [production designer] Ken Adam, music through John Barry, eating, drinking habits, travel, fashion – it is actually a film franchise that has moved into most facets of everyday life. *Skyfall* gave us the opportunity to celebrate that.'[5]

When it came to the marketing of *Skyfall*, it helped that much of the film was set in London, which accentuated the British feel yet further. 'None of the other Bonds had spent so much time having set-pieces in London. When we read it initially, we knew where we were going in 2012, that set the tone for everything we wanted to do.'

Fan-driven social media (especially Facebook and Twitter) enabled the distributors to be precise in targeting younger cinemagoers who might be interested in Bond. Taylor cautions, though, that the legwork still needs to be done. 'You do still have to get behind a movie. Once a film picks up its momentum on any social media, it does inevitably run with itself. To start that, you do still have to invest in it. We do put large amounts of money behind our digital campaigns.'[6]

With each new Bond film, the marketing is refined and improved. In the summer of 2015, Sony managed to make the release of a trailer for *Spectre* (the film released in the autumn of the year) into a global event. The trailer was posted online amid much fanfare. Newspapers and magazines carried it on their websites. Some fans watched the trailer on handheld mobile devices. Others were able to watch it in IMAX ahead of new Sony releases. The trailer was treated by jour-nalists and bloggers as if it was a film in its own right. It was analysed in depth as Bond experts tried to tease out what it told us about how 007 was evolving. Meanwhile the first trailer for *Star Wars: The Force Awakens* (2015) was viewed online 58 million times in a week.

With blockbusters like these, distributors could seemingly reach huge audiences and build awareness on a massive scale simply by putting a trailer on the web.

Skyfall launched in the UK in blitz-like fashion. It opened in over 550 cinemas nationwide – and on around 2,000 screens. Long gone were the days when the Bond movies would show first in West End cinemas and then enjoy leisurely roll-outs across the rest of the UK, perhaps screening first in seaside cinemas during the summer holidays. Now, as Taylor puts it, 'the demand is so immediate and so excessive that you have to be in a position to make sure that on that opening weekend, anyone who wants to go and see *Spectre* [the 2015 Bond film] can go and see it.'

Skyfall was released in at least a handful of venues on 35mm prints. It is likely to be the last Bond movie to be seen on old-fashioned cel-luloid. By 2015, there were no plans to release *Spectre* on anything other than a digital format. Physical film survived primarily because some very big-name directors (Quentin Tarantino, Christopher Nolan and Paul Thomas Anderson among them) championed it and wanted to see their films shown on 35mm. Even so, by 2015, there were very few cinemas that still had old-style film projectors.

It used to be a commonplace generalisation that movies depended on the teen audience. That was clearly changing as many UK dis-tributors recognised in their determined pursuit of the 'grey pound' audience that flocked in huge numbers to films like *The King's Speech* or *The Best Exotic Marigold Hotel.*

By 2015, the cinemagoers who had been won back to British cinemas at the beginning of the multiplex era in the mid-1980s were well into middle age. Their tastes were changing. Where once they had watched 'Brat Pack' movies, now they were ready to watch Judi Dench or Maggie Smith movies.

However, the spate of hits couldn't conceal the problems facing the sector in the new digital era.

One of the most persistent was piracy. This had been a concern of distributors as early as the silent era and was mentioned in the original mission statement of the Kinematograph Renters' Society in 1915, but now the problem was acute.

According to Oscar-winning producer Jeremy Thomas, piracy had become so entrenched that the industry seemed grudgingly to accept it. 'The exhibitors need to make money and the distributors need to make money and over all of that is this horrendous piracy,' Thomas suggested in an interview in the summer of 2015. 'It's a leaky pipe. The water, film, comes down this pipe. All through that pipe are little holes.'[7]

Others counter that his viewpoint is overstated and note that, in the UK, the Federation Against Copyright Theft and FDA itself continue to devise programmes to combat piracy.

In the video era of the 1980s and 1990s, the piracy might have involved someone making a few thousand illicit duplicates of a new film or perhaps someone using a camcorder to record a film in a cinema and then knocking off copies. In the digital era, Thomas argued, most films are 'more pirated than not'. Continuing his pipe metaphor, he suggested that by the time the water came out of the pipe at the other end, there had been so many leaks that only half or less of that water reached its destination:

It has already been taken for free by people who drill holes in the pipe. Why should what I create be free? It is not made for free. It is very, very expensive and I can't get the correct returns I should be making because half the people are consuming it for nothing. But there is no noise about it.

With online piracy rife, Thomas argued that the film industry was going through 'a Wild-West period' in which 'you can't get value because value is being stolen from all of us.'

Others talked of the way that piracy 'ate' into an entire industry. Commercials tried to stigmatise piracy by making the public appreciate that the victims weren't just the big stars with their hefty salaries but every single person involved in the film-making process, from the caterers to the electricians and location scouts, the backroom staff at distribution companies and even the youngsters tearing tickets at local cinemas. This wasn't a victimless crime. People's livelihoods were at risk. A whole industry was being undermined. Ultimately, if fewer films were made, or budgets were constrained, the biggest losers would be audiences themselves.

The British were effective in snuffing out piracy in the cinemas. At screenings of new movies, ushers were equipped with 'night-vision' glasses (many funded by FDA) so they could spot if cinemagoers were trying to record films with hidden cameras or with their phones. Online piracy was a different matter. If a website screening a pirated movie was taken down immediately, it was sometimes possible to contain the problem. However, if the site remained 'live' for as long as a day, it would already be far too late to do anything about the stolen movie. By then, that movie would long since have gone 'viral'.

What no viewer could experience while watching pirated copies of movies on file-sharing websites was the sheer majesty of the cinema-going experience at its best. As film-studio executives kept trying to remind the public, they were still making movies to be seen on 60-foot screens with large audiences in attendance.

Just as in the 1950s, when the industry reacted to the threat of TV by making widescreen blockbusters, a new premium has been put on the scale of films. The gold standard for blockbusters in 2015 wasn't CinemaScope, as it might have been 60 years before, but 3D IMAX. Speaking in the summer of 2015, Sony's Peter Taylor gave a very practical example of a film that just wouldn't work properly on a small screen. Robert Zemeckis, one of the pioneers of a new style of 3D film-making, was then completing a film called *The Walk*. This was a dramatisation of the true story told in the earlier Oscar-winning documentary *Man on Wire*. It was about the French acrobat Philippe Petit's astonishing, gravity-defying walk on a tightrope between the Twin Towers of the World Trade Center in the summer of 1974. Taylor suggested:

> Robert Zemeckis has made *The Walk* in the most extraordinarily technically engaging and thrilling way [...] The best way, and I would argue the only way, to see *The Walk* is in 3D on a cinema screen. When he [Petit] finally makes that walk and you go with him, I don't think you are going to get the effect of that on a mobile phone or a laptop. You need to be sitting there, fully immersed in the experience.[8]

Partially in reaction to the threat of piracy and to the growth in TV box-set culture, the US studios began to head to the high ground. Their strategy was to make huge-budget 'event' movies – films that could be given 'saturation' releases.

Away from the superhero pictures and $200 million blockbusters, even studio executives would privately acknowledge that the old releasing patterns didn't always make sense any more. The issue of 'windows' and their flexibility became ever more fiercely debated. By the summer of 2015, more than half of UK homes owned a tablet computer.

Various British distributors experimented with multiplatform releasing. In the independent sphere, Dogwoof had broken new ground as early as 2005 by releasing James Erskine's low-budget thriller *EMR* digitally in cinemas, on the internet and on DVD at the same time. Fellow distributor Revolver pursued a similar strategy in 2008 with its tiny-budget horror film, *Mum & Dad*. Neither of these were films likely to enjoy long runs in mainstream cinemas. They were niche movies at best. Nonetheless, the exhibition sector immediately cried foul. The standard window between the cinema release and the appearance of a film on DVD forced on distributors was 17 weeks. Anything shorter was looked at askance by the cinema owners.

In a letter leaked to trade paper *Screen International*'s Screendaily website, the CEA commented that while *Mum & Dad* was 'clearly only of at best minor importance' its multiplatform release was still an unacceptable breach of a 'point of principle'.[9] The CEA called for its members, which included most of the UK's cinema owners, to boycott the film. Such a call was hardly necessary. Very few would have shown it anyway. (The film went out on 15 screens.) However, to independent producers and distributors, it couldn't help but seem that the exhibitors were being unnecessarily dogmatic.

'Cinema is not the music industry, where existing business models are widely seen as broken,' the CEA proclaimed on its website. 'UK cinema admissions have remained strong over the last 25 years.' And furthermore:

> Many cinemas have invested huge amounts of their own money in improving the cinema-going experience, most recently

through digitisation and now installation of new technologies such as immersive sound. Without a clear window between a film's theatrical release and its release on other platforms, that investment is at risk.[10]

The attitude was understandable but paid little attention either to the needs of independent distributors or to the part those distributors themselves had played in 'improving the cinema-going experience' through the virtual print fee. Nor did it differentiate between different types of movies.

Exhibitors' claims that their investment in new technology was at risk were held to be 'nonsense' by FDA, which pointed out that there is not a shred of evidence for that claim – and importantly in the US, where greater film by film flexibility over windows does apply (sometimes three months), 'the cinema box office has not been diminished one iota.'[11]

In the opinion of the distributors, there was a world of difference between micro-budget films like *Mum & Dad* and Marvel superhero blockbusters. It seemed strange to treat them as if they were the same, all having to observe the same rules. The exhibitors countered that they had shown some flexibility – 17 weeks was a far shorter time span than the 27-week theatrical 'window' that had been in place as recently as the late 1990s. This wasn't much consolation to distributors who had released, say, a romcom before Christmas but weren't allowed to put it out on DVD in time for Valentine's Day. Nor did it take audiences' desires into much consideration.

The UK remained badly under-screened for art-house and independent movies, and the two main exhibitors in the arena – Curzon and Picturehouse – both had their own distribution operations. It was a natural assumption that when it came to booking new films, if they were faced with the choice between one of their own in-house acquisitions and a film from another distributor, they would favour the former.

If cinemas wouldn't take the films or would give them only the briefest exposure, it was only to be expected that distributors would look for other ways to reach audiences, whether on DVD or through video on demand (VOD).

The UK indies were intrigued by new ways of releasing already being explored in the US. In the late summer of 2012, Radius–TWC, the Weinstein Company's multiplatform label, actually released comedy *Bachelorette* on video on demand (VOD) a month before its theatrical release on 7 September. The film did reasonable business, claiming the number-one spot on the iTunes movie chart and earning more than $4 million on VOD by the time it reached theatres. (It had grossed around $418,000 theatrically from around fifty sites in the US by 23 September.) A similar strategy was used with Roadside Attractions/Lionsgate's thriller *Arbitrage*, which hit number two on the iTunes movie chart and earned $2.1 million theatrically from 197 sites in its first weekend. This was turning conventional wisdom on its head – ancillary was now driving theatrical rather than vice versa.

Bachelorette and *Arbitrage* were on a bigger scale than films tested previously for multiplatform releasing but they still weren't big mainstream movies. The former starred Kirsten Dunst; it had played the Sundance Festival and was produced by the *Saturday Night Live* and *Anchorman* comedian Will Ferrell. The latter was a thriller starring Richard Gere that had shown widely on the festival circuit and had been well reviewed.

'Watch Before It Hits the Big Screen' was the proposition from US distributor Magnolia through its On Demand service, which allowed viewers to access selected movies a month before they reached the cinemas. The selection was limited but it did include such art-house films as Danish maverick director Lars Von Trier's *succès de scandale*, *Nymphomaniac* (2013) and Swedish director Roy Andersson's absurdist comedy-drama *A Pigeon Sat on a Branch Reflecting on Existence*, as well as various romantic comedies and thrillers.

There was only one occasion on which a major US studio released a film online at the same time as its theatrical release – but this happened by default.

The hacking scandal of late 2014, in which Sony Pictures Entertainment's computer systems were targeted by cybercriminals (presumed to be from North Korea), had unlikely consequences for Seth Rogen's comedy *The Interview*. The film was a broad adult farce about a US TV show host who, together with his producer, becomes part of a CIA plot to kill the North Korean 'supreme' leader.

Faced with the threat of terrorist attacks, US cinemas refused to show *The Interview*, which had a reported budget of over $40 million. In the end, the film was given a small theatrical release primarily because it had become a freedom-of-speech issue that it should be shown in cinemas. The film was also made available online and very quickly became Sony's highest-grossing internet release, raking in $15 million in the first four days it was available.

The Interview eventually did better business in the US through digital downloads than at the cinema box office. The release strategy was forced on Sony by the extraordinary circumstances in which the company found itself after the hacking. The success of *The Interview* online suggested that multiplatform/simultaneous releasing could work for studios as well as for independents. In exceptional circumstances, a Hollywood studio had changed the traditional windowing system – through which films work their way slowly from cinemas to DVD, VOD and TV – and had been rewarded with very strong online results. However, the downside was that this particular example had been an exercise in damage limitation. The VOD numbers for *The Interview* may have been impressive but they were matched by the huge rates of piracy the film suffered. The film became available online at lunchtime on Christmas Eve – and had been downloaded illegally 900,000 times by lunchtime on Christmas Day.

The film's overall results still fell short of what might have been expected from a conventional theatrical release. There certainly wasn't any sense that the studios were rushing to release other mainstream movies in the same way. Their approach to 'windows' determined how films were handled in Britain too. After all, the Hollywood majors still dominated distribution in the UK. In 2014, the top ten distributors – the six American-based studios Fox, Warner Bros., Universal, Disney, Sony and Paramount, plus Entertainment One, StudioCanal, Lionsgate and Entertainment – accounted for 93.5 per cent of the market.

A key change in the UK as in the US is that the majority of households are connected to the internet and have fast enough broadband to be able to stream movies. In the spring of 2015, analysts were predicting that the subscription video-streaming market in the UK would be worth more than £1 billion by 2019. Around 70 per cent of British consumers were said to have streamed at least one video in the last 12 months. This is a seismic change. In theory, it is now possible for a film released online in the UK to be made available instantly to around three quarters of the population.

One British company not constrained by the strict 'windowing' policy imposed by the exhibitors was the Curzon group. Curzon's big advantage lay in owning its own cinemas. This meant that when Curzon released its films on VOD at exactly the same moment they appeared in cinemas, it didn't need to worry about the wrath of the cinema owners.

The company's CEO, Philip Knatchbull, made it clear that he didn't distinguish between Curzon customers watching new movies in cinemas or in their own homes. 'There is no difference to me between what a comfortable home cinema experience is through Curzon On Demand or a shared emotional experience in a public cinema,' Knatchbull declared at a BSAC (British Screen Advisory Council) Film Conference in 2012. 'Increasingly, you will see that the films we release will be released day and date on Curzon home cinema platform and on Curzon public cinema platform.'[12]

In an era in which films could be watched on smartphones, smart TVs and tablets, it was inevitable that many others would call for releasing patterns to be overhauled.

The UK film market was becoming more dynamic but also far more fragmented. Zygi Kamasa, CEO of Lionsgate UK, provoked fierce debate with his suggestion, reported by trade paper *Screen International* in late 2014, that there should be a sliding scale for ticket prices:

In most other industries, retail price is related to the cost of production, but not in the film business. A blockbuster can cost $250m and a UK independent film can cost $4m but it's £10 or more to see both. I think we should see UK films priced at £4 and US films at £10. A trip to the cinema isn't cheap anymore. I have spoken to some UK exhibitors and they are open to more flexibility because they realise they have to do something.[13]

Kamasa's suggestion didn't acknowledge the simple fact that the value of a film in the marketplace is never determined by how much it cost to make. *The King's Speech* was evidence of that. It cost a reported $15 million to make – a decent budget by European standards but minuscule in comparison to the cost of US studio movies – and went on to take roughly $415 million at the box office worldwide.

If Kamasa's formula had been adopted, it would have risked tainting low-budget British movies as a brand. Cinemagoers could hardly be blamed for feeling that such films were in some way substandard if the cinemas valued them at half the price of bigger-budget Hollywood movies. The Lionsgate UK CEO was in danger of undermining his own position when, a few months after his intervention on ticket prices, he announced, in early May 2015, that Lionsgate was committed to putting 'independent British films at the forefront of cinema worldwide' and that it would be backing up to 25 British films over the next four years. There was no mention in the announcement that Lionsgate planned to advocate reduced ticket prices for these films.

Kamasa's remarks drew attention to the cost of cinemagoing. Digital technology made films more easily available than ever before. Tens of thousands of titles were available to watch online, many for free or at very low price points, but London West End cinemas were charging £20 or more for adult tickets. (That compares to an average ticket price of 10d or 4p in the 1930s and of 7p in 1946!)[14] As Kamasa's remarks implied, cinema's status as the least expensive mainstream leisure activity in the UK was clearly under threat.

There was an increasing polarisation. Films were cheaper than ever before to watch at home – and far more expensive to watch in cinemas. What alarmed the UK's independent distributors was the erosion of revenues from DVD. Video on demand was the next Klondike. There was confidence that, eventually, VOD revenues would compensate for the loss in earnings from physical discs. The problem was the length of time it was taking for those earnings to materialise.

For many years, a low-level hum had been heard from distributors grumbling about the imminent disappearance of the DVD market. It was widely acknowledged that DVD was in its death throes – but the form was taking a very long time to die.

Calamitous events on the British high street meant that it had become far harder for shoppers to find anywhere to buy their favourite movies on disc. Retailers Zavvi, Woolworths, Our Price, Borders and Tower Records all disappeared over the first decade or so of the new millennium. HMV, one of the most venerable entertainment retailers in the UK with a history that stretched back to 1921, entered administration in 2013 and seemed on the verge of collapse.

Even so, DVDs continued to sell in very big numbers. In its end-of-2014 figures, trade body the British Video Association reported that, during the year, 22 million people in the UK bought a video to own on DVD, Blu-ray or as a digital download. A further 7.5 million people rented a video. HMV came out of administration. There were still at least some high-street stores where 'fifty-pound man' could buy his DVDs – and they were easy to order online too.

Meanwhile, Netflix, Amazon Instant Video, BT Vision and Sky Now, the major players in the UK subscription video-on-demand market, continued to expand. This provided new opportunities for independent distributors to sell the pay-TV rights to their films. Previously, BSkyB (as it was then known) had a near monopoly on pay TV and didn't buy many independent movies.

During 2014, there were 232 VOD services available in the UK (126 of them national). According to the European Audiovisual Observatory, digital ad spending in the UK was expected to reach $13.27 billion by 2017. The UK had a 34 per cent share of overall digital ad spending across Western Europe, almost twice as much as any other country.

All this suggested that there were huge new opportunities for UK distributors.

What was as apparent in 2015 as 100 years before, when the Kinematograph Renters' Society was founded, was the utterly haphazard and cyclical nature of the film-distribution business in the UK. Depending on your vantage point, it was the best of times or it was the worst of times.

The British Film Institute's statistical yearbook for 2014 trumpeted the fact that the UK film industry had doubled its contribution to GDP over the past two decades 'in real terms', generating £2.9 billion in 2012 and exporting £1.3 billion of services in the same year, leading to a healthy trade surplus of £789 million.[15] Yet, at the same time, as the Film Distributors' Association Yearbook pointed out, 'with 157.5 million cinema tickets sold, a dip of 4.9 per cent below 2013, 2014 was the UK's softest year for cinemagoing since 2008.'[16]

It was as clear as it had been a century before that distribution was a product-driven business that defied any glib generalisations. One year could seem disappointing but then box office might soar the next, thanks to new Bond movies or *Star Wars* films being released (as happened in 2015).

One distributor might seem to be king of the hill at the moment its latest film broke records for ticket sales but then, a few weeks later, the parade would move on and another company would be dominating in the marketplace. As Sony MD Peter Taylor points out:

It [the marketplace] is very tough but however many suppliers there are, on any given week, that market influence switches from one [company] to the other, regardless of owner. In the week that Bond opens, Sony Pictures rules the world. No one can touch it. With Entertainment Film Distributors, a very successful British local distributor, on the week that they open *The Inbetweeners*, no one cares about Warner Bros. or Sony Pictures. It's transient. Market influence here is always transient because it is product-driven. Everything is driven by that one or two films a week – and anyone can have access and even stumble on that film. You might not even think you have it.[17]

Depending on your point of view, the UK distribution sector is in rude health – or is in a state of crisis. Everyone knows that a run of failures is all it needs to spark the talk of doomsday but that a hit or two will have the reverse effect.

In late 2015, FDA published an analysis of the economic value of film distribution in the UK. The research showed that in 2013, the most recent year for which comprehensive data were then available, the UK's film-distribution sector had an annual turnover of £1.2 billion, sustained 3,100 full-time equivalents of direct employment, generated £132 million in export revenue for the UK economy and spent an estimated £330 million on marketing and publicity of new film releases, more than half of which was invested in a wide range of UK media outlets.

Meanwhile, in the late autumn of 2015, underlining the appetite that British cinemagoers still had to watch films on the cinema screen and the ingenuity with which distributors released them, Sony's British release of *Spectre* (the 24th 'official' Bond movie) turned into the biggest opening of all time in UK box-office history. In its first seven days of release it racked up an estimated £41.7 million ($63.8 million) from 647 cinemas and on 2,500 screens.

Over the century of the existence of Film Distributors' Association, everything has changed – and nothing has changed. The technology is in a constant state of flux. Their logistical problems are daunting and the market conditions seem stacked against them. A gaping chasm remains between the big suppliers and the smaller players and yet all the distributors are doing exactly what they have been for the last 100 years: getting movies into cinemas in the best way they can and trying to build businesses around delivering dreams in the process.

You ain't seen nothing yet!

Inventing and recounting stories being a fundamental part of human nature, great stories peopled with great characters have long been magnets for human hearts and minds. General demand for the film industry's 'raw material' of stories and experiences seems insatiable.

Of course, entertainment consumption is heavily *product*-led. Before anyone buys a ticket for a particular film, they must feel confident that they'll be amused, thrilled, moved or provoked – asked *What if…?* While a hot movie, whatever its subject matter or provenance, remains the ultimate 'must have' content, any distributor will ruefully tell you that you can't even give away tickets to a film in which there's no public interest.

Ever focused on the marketplace and consumer behaviour, distributors *position* a film, developing and communicating the reasons to see it – distinctively and persuasively – and see it *now*! If the film industry is to draw larger audiences to a broader range of titles, then in an increasingly diverse, fragmented and competitive environment, distributors possess the vital skills, passion and commitment to attract them.

The second century of film distribution dawns on a fully digital era. Practically every movie shown in a UK cinema is projected from a digital file instead of a celluloid reel. Distributors themselves have funded most of the conversion costs, ever mindful of the industry's future. Yet the transformative effects of an all-digital world are only just beginning to be felt.

Like other businesses, the film business still starts and ends with customers making choices. Films tend to reach their audiences by professional design, not merely by accident or chance. Hence, the correlation between the well-being of the distribution sector, which brings films and audiences together, and that of the wider film industry and film culture.

In 2015, UK distributors are investing around £350 million to launch 700 feature films for cinema audiences. In many cases, an initial theatrical release adds a glossy layer of kudos that helps to propel subsequent viewings in other on-demand 'platforms', although digital release patterns are in rapid flux right across the board. Reflecting the on-going shifts, the lexicographer Collins named 'binge-watch' its Word of the Year 2015.

Given abundant consumer choice, predicting theatrical box-office results well in advance is not only a tough and risk-laden business; it's well-nigh impossible. Just because one romantic comedy or sci-fi adventure performs well does not automatically mean that the next comparable release will do so too. For most titles outside, say, the year's top 40, generating a profit for reinvestment can be arduous indeed.

The lavish supply of new titles into cinemas is not universally beneficial. Not necessarily for distributors, charged with sustaining as well as launching their titles week by week. Not for journalists, confronted with more than a dozen films to report on and review each week (I believe film is chronically under-served in terms of the space and time it usually receives in UK media, especially when compared to other leisure pursuits). And not necessarily for the public, either, as many films vanish before the full potential audience has had a chance to catch them.

Cinema remains the film industry's vibrant 'shop window', where film-makers aspire to have their works showcased. I'm sure that the cinema's uniquely wonderful, larger-than-life brand of escapist entertainment will continue to thrive – provided that cinemagoing retains a general public appreciation that its monetary and emotional values compare favourably with those of the very many competing attractions in and out of the home.

At FDA we are privileged to bring UK film distributors together to consider generic issues affecting the sector and its future development (see www.launchingfilms.com), and to provide a single robust yet careful voice where appropriate. *Copyright* remains the basis on which the revenues that enable future investment in our film industry are generated. More broadly, our economic prosperity seems increasingly likely to depend on sectors where the capital is 'intellectual' – digital rather than physical goods and services.

Film is the most potent driving force of the creative industries, a sector in which the UK excels. We have earned an enviable global track record in the creation *and* delivery of content. If, as we all hope, the years ahead are the most dynamic yet for filmgoing, you can be sure that distribution people – pragmatic, full of ideas and as resolutely forward-looking as ever – will play a pivotal role.

If 'content is king', effective distribution will remain the kingmaker!

MARK BATEY
Chief Executive,
Film Distributors' Association

Film
DistributOrs'
AssociatiOn 2015
Celebrating the UK centenary of
organised feature film releasing
1915 – 2015

NOTES

INTRODUCTION

1 Will Clarke, interviewed by author, London, January 2015.
2 Lord Puttnam, interviewed by author, London, autumn 2014.
3 Paul Brett, interviewed by author, London, February 2015.
4 Ibid.
5 Philip and David Livingstone, interviewed by author, January 2015.
6 Ibid.
7 Ibid.
8 Obituary of Kenneth Rive. *Daily Telegraph*, 15 January 2003.
9 Trevor Green, joint MD of Entertainment, interviewed by author, London, autumn 2014.
10 Xavier Marchand, interviewed by author, London, February 2015.
11 Ibid.
12 Puttnam, interview.
13 Stan Fishman, interviewed by author, May 2015.
14 Ibid.
15 Ibid.
16 Ibid.
17 James Higgins, interviewed by author, summer 2014.
18 Puttnam, interview.
19 Ibid.
20 Fishman, interview.
21 Trevor Green, interview.
22 Martin Myers, interviewed by author, December 2014.
23 Ibid.
24 Ibid.
25 Ibid.
26 Ibid.
27 John Hogarth, BECTU History Project – Interview No. 328, 8 June 1994.

28 Geraldine Moloney, interviewed by author, autumn 2014.

29 Fishman, interview.

30 Myers, interview.

CHAPTER 1: THE TRAMP

1 *Cinema Year Book*, 1915.

2 Ibid.

3 *Bioscope*, 16 December 1915.

4 Ibid.

5 Rachael Low, *The History of the British Film 1918–1929* (London, 1971), p. 77.

6 *Cinema Year Book*, 1915.

7 Ibid.

8 Ibid.

9 Ibid.

10 Ibid.

11 Ibid.

12 Ibid.

13 James Higgins, interviewed by author, autumn 2014.

14 *Kinematograph Year Book*, 1914.

15 David Robinson, *Chaplin: His Life and Art* (London, 1985), Chapter 5 (Kindle version).

16 Ibid.

17 Ibid.

18 Low, *1918–1929*, p. 77.

19 Taken from minutes of General Meetings of Kinematograph Renters' Society, contained in Film Distributors' Association archives, December 1915.

20 KRS Constitution.

21 Low, p. 117.

22 A. Roland Thornton, quoted in the Kinematograph Renters' Society fiftieth anniversary brochure, 1965, contained in Film Distributors' Association archives.

23 *Bioscope*, 3 October 1918.

24 Taken from minutes of General Meetings of Kinematograph Renters' Society, contained in Film Distributors' Association archives.

25 Ibid.

26 Ibid.

27 *Kinematograph and Lantern Weekly*, 1912, courtesy of Ivan Sharpe.

28 E. G. Turner, 'From 1896 to 1926', *Kinematograph Weekly*, 17 & 24 June, 1 & 15 July 1926, cited in http://www.victorian-cinema.net/egturner.

29 Ibid.

30 Ibid.

31 *Bioscope*, 3 October 1918.

CHAPTER 2: BLACKMAIL

1   Rachael Low, *The History of the British Film 1918–1929* (London, 1971), p. 76.

2   Ibid.

3   *Kinematograph Year Book*, 1927, p. 16.

4   Kerry Segrave, *American Films Abroad: Hollywood's Domination of the World's Movie Screens from the 1890s to the Present* (Jefferson, NC, and London, 1997), p. 45.

5   Ibid, p. 19.

6   Ibid, p. 45.

7   *The Bioscope.*

8   Notes on Checking Exhibitors' Returns on Sharing Term Contracts, FDA archives.

9   Ibid.

10 Letter from Ideal Films, 1923, FDA archives.

11 The Trade Papers Committee report 1923, FDA archives.

12 *Kinematograph Year Book*, 1928.

13 'Publicity matter prices: should exhibitors pay for renters' propaganda', *Cinema News and Property Gazette*, 2 October 1924.

14 Letter from Lewis Levin, Fox Film, to the KRS, 1 November 1923, FDA archives.

15 FDA archives, 1930.

16 Cited in Low, *1918–1929*, p. 75.

17 Ibid.

18 Alan Wood, *Mr Rank: A Study of J. Arthur Rank and British Films* (London, 1952).

19 Sarah Street, 'The memoir of Harry Rowson' in David Berry and Simon Horrocks (eds), *David Lloyd George: The Movie Mystery* (Cardiff, 1998).

20 Ibid.

21 Simon Rowson, *A Statistical Survey of the Cinema Industry in Great Britain in 1934* (London, 1936).

22 Charles Drazin, *Korda: Britain's Only Movie Mogul* (London, 2002), p. 87.

23 *Kinematograph Year Book*, 1927.

24 François Truffaut, *Hitchcock: A Definitive Study*, paperback edition (London, 1986), p. 64.

25 *Dundee Evening Telegraph*, 9 August 1929.

26 *Western Mail*, 11 September 1930.
27 Ibid.

CHAPTER 3: THE PRIVATE LIFE OF HENRY VIII

1 Percy Livingstone, BECTU History Project – Interview No. 268, 20 October 1992.
2 Ibid.
3 S. G. Rayment, *Kinematograph Year Book*, 1931.
4 Ibid.
5 Ibid.
6 Rachael Low, *Film Making in 1930s Britain* (London, 1985), p. 3.
7 Kinematograph Renters' Society fiftieth anniversary brochure, 1965, contained in Film Distributors' Association archives.
8 *Kinematograph Year Book*, 1931, p. 120.
9 Robert Edmond Jones, 'The crisis of colour', *New York Times*, 19 May 1935.
10 Mark Glancy, *Hollywood and the Americanization of Britain: From the 1920s to the Present* (London, 2014), p. 152.
11 Livingstone, interview.
12 Sam Eckman in KRS fiftieth anniversary brochure.
13 'Story of the year', *Kinematograph Year Book* 1931, p. 11.
14 Eckman, in KRS fiftieth anniversary brochure.
15 Low, *Film Making in 1930s Britain*, p. 3.
16 *Kinematograph Year Book*, 1935.
17 Jeffrey Richards, *The Age of the Dream Palace* (London, 1984), p. 38.
18 *Kinematograph Year Book*, 1935.
19 *Kinematograph Year Book*, 1937.
20 John Hogarth, BECTU History Project – Interview No. 328, 8 June 1994.
21 Livingstone, interview.
22 Hogarth, interview.
23 Livingstone, interview.
24 Ibid.
25 Ibid.
26 Michael Powell, *A Life in Movies* (London, 2000), p. 215.
27 Richard Norton (Lord Grantley), *Silver Spoon, Being Extracts from the Random Reminiscences of Lord Grantley* (London, 1954), p. 161.
28 *Picturegoer*, 9 September 1933.
29 *New York Times* review of *The Private Life of Henry VIII*, 13 October 1933.
30 John Fisher, *George Formby* (London, 1975).

CHAPTER 4: THE THIRD MAN

1   Taken from minutes of General Meetings of Kinematograph Renters' Society, contained in Film Distributors' Association archives, 1944.

2   Notes Of Discussion with Sir Joseph Ball at the Ritz Hotel, 31 August 1939, FDA archives.

3   Cabinet papers, 1916–1960. Meeting of the War Cabinet, September 1939.

4   Ibid.

5   Taken from minutes of General Meetings of Kinematograph Renters' Society, contained in Film Distributors' Association archives, 1939–40.

6   FDA archives.

7   *Kinematograph Year Book*, 1940.

8   Charles Drazin, *Korda: Britain's Only Movie Mogul* (London, 2002), p. 221.

9   Michael Powell, *A Life in Movies* (London, 2000).

10 Cabinet papers, 1916–1960.

11 Angus Calder, *The People's War: Britain, 1939–1945* (London, 1992), p. 177.

12 Cabinet papers, 1916–1960.

13 Ibid.

14 Memo from the ACT, to the President of the Board of Trade on the Third Cinematographic Act.

15 Adolph Zukor, *Kinematograph Weekly*, 2 January 1947.

16 Sam Goldwyn, *Kinematograph Weekly*, 8 July 1948.

17 *Kinematograph Weekly*, 9 January 1947.

18 *Kinematograph Weekly*, 13 June 1946.

19 Cited in Linda Wood, *British Films 1927–1939* (London, 1986).

20 Correspondence in FDA archives, war years.

21 Ibid.

22 Ibid.

23 Ibid.

24 David Lean, 'Brief encounter', *Penguin Film Review* #4, 1947.

25 *Kinematograph Weekly*, 13 February 1947.

26 Drazin, *Korda*.

27 *Billboard*, 10 December 1949.

28 Karol Kulik, *Alexander Korda: The Man Who Could Work Miracles* (London, 1990), p. 287.

29 Ibid.

30 *Kinematograph Weekly*, 1 January 1948.

CHAPTER 5: TROUBLE IN STORE

1 Mark Aldridge, *The Birth of British Television* (Basingstoke, 2011).

2 Dallas Bower, 'Television and the cinema', *Wireless World*, 1934.

3 Dallas Bower, *Plan for Cinema* (London, 1936), p. 57.

4 Ibid, p. 59.

5 Asa Briggs, *The History of Broadcasting in the United Kingdom; Vol. 4: Sound and Vision* (Oxford, 1979), p. 15.

6 Television Film Production Ltd memo, rough notes for press conference, 21 October, 1948.

7 Briggs, *Sound and Vision*, p. 252.

8 *Kinematograph Weekly*, 1948.

9 Charles Barr, 'Broadcasting And Cinema 2: Screens Within Screens', in Charles Barr (ed.), *All Our Yesterdays: 90 Years of British Cinema* (London, 1986), p. 206.

10 'Round Table On British Films', *Sight and Sound*, May 1950.

11 Roger Manvell, 'Television's challenge to the cinema', in Roger Manvell (ed.), *The Cinema 1950* (London, 1951), pp. 170–86.

12 Ibid.

13 Percy Livingstone, BECTU History Project – Interview No. 268, 20 October 1992.

14 *Financial Times* annual review of British industry, 1954.

15 Hannah Andrews, *Television and British Cinema* (Basingstoke, 2014), p. 41.

16 Sue Harper and Vincent Porter, *British Cinema of the 1950s: The Decline of Deference* (London, 2007), p. 110.

17 James Higgins, interview with author, autumn 2014.

18 Ibid.

19 Report of the Joint Committee of the CEA and KRS, 9 February 1951, FDA archives.

20 *Kinematograph Weekly*, 24 June 1948, p. 21.

21 Ibid.

22 Michael Relph in *The Producer*, May 1987.

23 Harper and Porter, *British Cinema of the 1950s*, p. 244.

24 Ibid.

25 John Hogarth, BECTU History Project – Interview No. 328, 8 June 1994.

26 Ibid.

27 FDA archives.

28 Ibid.

29 See *Terra Media* website, http://www.terramedia.co.uk/reference/law/entertainments_tax.htm.

30 Steve Chibnall and Brian McFarlane, *The British 'B' Film* (London, 2009), p. 47.

31 FDA archives. (All material relating to posters comes from Poster Viewing Committee meeting minutes in FDA archives.)

CHAPTER 6: DR NO

1 Quoted in Brian McFarlane, *An Autobiography of British Cinema* (London, 1997), p. 615.
2 Ibid, p. 614.
3 Ibid, p. 615.
4 Albert Finney, *Guardian* interview, 1982.
5 John Hogarth, BECTU History Project – Interview No. 328, 8 June 1994.
6 Cited in Alexander Walker, *Hollywood England* (London, 2005), p. 468.
7 John Spraos, *Decline of the Cinema: An Economist's Report* (London, 1962), p. 94.
8 Ibid, p. 95.
9 Ibid.
10 Ibid, p. 116.
11 Ibid.
12 *Kinematograph Weekly*, 1960.
13 Hogarth, interview.
14 Byrne v. Kinematograph Renters' Society ruling, 1958.
15 Ian Grundy, 'An illustrated UK bingo history', http://playingbingo. co.uk/land-bingo/history/02-history-illustrated.php.
16 Charles Barr (ed.), *All Our Yesterdays: 90 Years of British Cinema* (London, 1986), pp. 216–17.
17 Tony Richardson, *Long Distance Runner* (London, 1993).
18 Charles Drazin, *A Bond for Bond: Film Finances and Dr No* (London, 2011), p. 23.
19 Ibid, p. 58.
20 Ibid.
21 John Brosnan, *James Bond in the Cinema* (London, 1972), p. 33.
22 Albert Broccoli, *When the Snow Melts* (London, 1998), p. 178.
23 Richardson, *Long Distance Runner*, p. 135.
24 Walker, *Hollywood England*, p. 131.
25 Ibid, p. 244.
26 Ian Cameron, *Spectator*, 7 February 1964.
27 Ibid.
28 *Spectator*, 4 November 1966.
29 Walker, *Hollywood England*, p. 344.
30 Mike Leigh quoted in Geoffrey Macnab, *Screen Epiphanies* (London, 2009), p. 67.

CHAPTER 7: STAR WARS

1   *Screen International* #1, 6 September 1975.
2   Ibid.
3   Ibid.
4   Alexander Walker, *National Heroes* (London, 1985), p. 35.
5   Lindsay Anderson, *Cinema TV Today*, 19 October 1974.
6   Walker, *National Heroes*, p. 114.
7   Jeremy Thomas, interviewed by author, May 2015.
8   Val Guest, interviewed by author, September 1997.
9   *The Bitch, the Stud and the Prawn*, http://www.bbc.co.uk/blogs/adamcurtis/
    entries/2c5a4a2a-745a-31cd-8d16-370a4cf98af5
10 Review of *The Bitch*, *Felix* (the newspaper of Imperial College, London],
    10 August 1979.
11 David Puttnam, interviewed by author, autumn 2014.
12 Thomas, interview
13 'The monster that ate Hollywood', http://www.pbs.org/wgbh/pages/
    frontline/shows/hollywood/business/jaws.html.
14 George Lucas, quoted in Geoffrey Macnab, *Key Moments in Cinema*
    (London, 2001), p. 85.
15 Walker, *National Heroes*, p.135.
16 Robin Hardy, interviewed by author, September 2013.
17 Jack Valenti, testimony at 1982 House hearing on Home Recording
    of Copyrighted Works.
18 *Billboard*, 17 November 1979.
19 Ibid.
20 Paul Edwards, 'VHS and home video – the story of its rise and fall',
    Deathbyfilms.com, 2 December 2013.

CHAPTER 8: CHARIOTS OF FIRE

1   Stanley Durwood, quoted in *New York Times*, 16 July 1999.
2   James Higgins, interviewed by author, summer 2014.
3   Geraldine Moloney, interviewed by author, autumn 2014.
4   Jeremy Thomas, interviewed by author, spring 2015.
5   Peter Buckingham, interviewed by author, summer 2015.
6   Moloney, interview.
7   FDA archives.
8   Jake Eberts and Terry Illott, *My Indecision Is Final* (London, 1992),
    p. 33.
9   David Puttnam, interviewed by author, autumn 2014.
10 Ibid.

11 The British Film and Television Industries – Communications Committee, http://www.publications.parliament.uk/pa/ld200910/ldselect/ldcomuni/37/3705.htm.

12 Puttnam, interview.

13 Aljean Harmetz, 'Sometimes a movie makes a studio proud', *New York Times*, 6 February 1982.

14 Puttnam, interview.

15 Adrian Hodges, *Stills*, July/August 1983.

16 Alexander Walker, *Icons in the Fire: The Decline and Fall of Almost Everybody in the British Film Industry* (London, 2005).

17 Ibid.

18 Ibid.

19 Sue Porter, interviewed by author, summer 2015.

20 FDA archives.

21 Ibid.

CHAPTER 9: TRAINSPOTTING

1 'Cannes dailies', *Moving Pictures*, 13 May 1996.

2 Ibid.

3 Ibid.

4 Robert Murphy (ed.), *British Cinema of the 1990s* (London, 1999).

5 David Puttnam, *New Statesman*, 14 October 2010.

6 Quoted in 'Life and death of UK Film Council', *Sight and Sound*, October 2010.

7 Ibid.

8 Stewart Till, Select Committee on Culture, Media and Sport Minutes of Evidence, http://www.publications.parliament.uk/pa/cm200203/cmselect/cmcumeds/667/3061012.htm.

9 'A Bigger Picture', report for the Film Policy Review Group, Department Of Culture, Media and Sport, 1998.

10 Chris Smith, interview with the author, 2012.

11 John Woodward, interview with author for *Moving Pictures*, 2000.

12 Ibid.

13 Ibid.

14 'Building a sustainable UK film industry'. Speech by Sir Alan Parker, chairman of the Film Council, November 2002.

15 Bernard Weinraub, '*The Full Monty* is by far the biggest film success at Fox Searchlight Pictures', *New York Times*, 15 September 1997.

16 Simon Beaufoy, *Metro*, 18 February 2014.

17 *Guardian*, 17 July 2003.

CHAPTER 10: BILLY ELLIOT

1   Will Clarke, interviewed by author, December 2014. (Subsequent quotes from Clarke also come from this interview.)
2   *Guardian*, 1 March 2004.
3   Simon Franks, quoted in Angus Finney, *The International Film Business* (London, 2010), pp. 195–206.
4   Trevor Green, interviewed by author, autumn 2014.
5   BBC website, 4 April 2004, http://news.bbc.co.uk/1/hi/business/3597923.stm.
6   Green, interview.
7   Peter Buckingham, interviewed by author, summer 2015.
8   Green, interview.
9   Eric Fellner, Parliamentary Committee, 2010, http://www.publications.parliament.uk/pa/ld200910/ldselect/ldcomuni/37/3706.htm.
10 Buckingham, interview.
11 *Billy Elliot* review, *Screen International*, 24 May 2000.

CHAPTER 11: THE KING'S SPEECH

1   Paul Brett, interviewed by author, February 2015.
2   Xavier Marchand, interviewed by author, London, February 2015.
3   Ibid.
4   Peter Taylor, interviewed by author, spring 2015.
5   Ibid.
6   Jeremy Thomas, interviewed by author, summer 2015.
7   Ibid.
8   Taylor, interview.
9   *Screen International*, 30 September 2008.
10 http://www.cinemauk.org.uk/key-issues/release-windows.
11 FDA spokesperson in correspondence with author, 2015.
12 Philip Knatchbull at BSAC Conference, London, 2012.
13 Zygi Kamasa, quoted in 'Brit films should be cheaper at cinemas, says Lionsgate UK CEO', ScreenDaily.com, 18 November 2014.
14 Average admission statistics come from John Davis, 'Efficiency and economy in films', in *Financial Times Annual Review of British Film Industry* (London 1954).
15 British Film Institute Statistical Yearbook, 2014.
16 FDA Yearbook, 2014.
17 Taylor, interview.

SELECT BIBLIOGRAPHY

Barr, Charles (ed.), *All Our Yesterdays: 90 Years of British Cinema* (London: BFI, 1996).

Calder, Angus, *The Myth of the Blitz* (London: Cape, 1991).

—— *The People's War: Britain, 1939–1945* (London: Pimlico, 1992).

Chibnall, Steve and Brian McFarlane, *The British 'B' Film* (London: BFI, 2009).

Drazin, Charles, *Korda: Britain's Only Movie Mogul* (London: Sidgwick & Jackson, 2002).

—— *A Bond for Bond: Film Finances and Dr No* (London: Film Finances, 2011).

Finney, Angus, *The International Film Business: A Market Guide* (London: Routledge, 2010).

Fisher, John, *George Formby* (London: Woburn-Futura, 1975).

Harper, Sue and Vincent Porter, *British Cinema of the 1950s: The Decline of Deference* (Oxford: Oxford University Press, 2003).

Kulik, Karol, *Alexander Korda: The Man Who Could Work Miracles* (London: W. H. Allen, 1975).

Low, Rachael, *The History of the British Film 1918–1929* (London: Allen & Unwin, 1971).

—— *Film Making in 1930s Britain* (London: HarperCollins, 1985).

—— *The History of the British Film 1896–1906* (London: Routledge, 2011 edition).

—— *The History of the British Film 1906–1914* (London: Routledge, 2011 edition).

McFarlane, Brian, *An Autobiography of British Cinema* (London: Methuen, 1997).

Macnab, Geoffrey, *J. Arthur Rank and the British Film Industry* (London: Routledge, 1993).

—— *Searching for Stars* (London: Continuum, 2000).

—— *Screen Epiphanies* (London: BFI/Macmillan, 2009).

Manvell, Roger (ed.), *The Cinema 1950* (London: Pelican, 1951).

———— *The Cinema 1951* (London: Pelican, 1951).

Morgan, Guy, *Red Roses Every Night: An Account of London Cinemas Under Fire* (London: Quality Press, 1948).

Murphy, Robert, *Sixties British Cinema* (London: BFI, 1992).

———— *British Cinema of the 1990s* (London: BFI, 1999).

Norton, Richard (Lord Grantley), *Silver Spoon, Being Extracts from the Random Reminiscences of Lord Grantley* (London: Hutchinson, 1954).

Powell, Michael, *A Life in Movies* (London: Faber, 2000 edition).

Richards, Jeffrey, *The Age of the Dream Palace: Cinema and Society in 1930s Britain* (London: Routledge, 1989).

Russell Taylor, John, *Hitch: The Life and Times of Alfred Hitchcock* (London: Faber, 1978).

Spoto, Donald, *The Dark Side of Genius: The Life of Alfred Hitchcock* (Boston: Da Capo, 1994).

Truffaut, François, *Hitchcock: A Definitive Study* (London: Simon & Schuster, 1986).

Walker, Alexander, *National Heroes: British Cinema in the Seventies and Eighties* (London: Harrap, 1985).

———— *Hollywood, England: The British Film Industry in the Sixties* (London: Orion, 2005).

———— *Icons in the Fire: The Decline and Fall of Almost Everybody in the British Film Industry* (London: Orion, 2005).

Wapshott, Nicholas, *The Man Between: A Biography of Carol Reed* (London: Chatto & Windus, 1990).

INDEX